This Land is Our Land

Also by Suketu Mehta

Maximum City: Bombay Lost and Found

SUKETU MEHTA

This Land is Our Land

An Immigrant's Manifesto

JONATHAN CAPE
LONDON

1 3 5 7 9 10 8 6 4 2

Jonathan Cape, an imprint of Vintage,
20 Vauxhall Bridge Road,
London SW1V 2SA

Jonathan Cape is part of the Penguin Random House group of companies
whose addresses can be found at global.penguinrandomhouse.com.

Penguin
Random House
UK

THIS LAND IS YOUR LAND
Words and Music by Woody Guthrie
WGP/TRO-© Copyright 1956, 1958, 1970, 1972 (copyrights renewed)
Woody Guthrie Publications, Inc. & Ludlow Music, Inc., New York, NY
administered by Ludlow Music, Inc.
International Copyright Secured. Made in U.S.A.
All Rights Reserved Including Public Performance For Profit
Used by Permission

First published by Jonathan Cape in 2019

penguin.co.uk/vintage

A CIP catalogue record for this book is available from the British Library

ISBN 9781787331426

Typeset in 10.2/14.25 pt Sabon LT Pro
by Integra Software Services Pvt. Ltd, Pondicherry

Printed and bound in Great Britain by Clays Ltd, Elcograf S.p.A.

Penguin Random House is committed to a sustainable future
for our business, our readers and our planet. This book is
made from Forest Stewardship Council® certified paper.

For Ramesh and Usha Mehta

There is no happiness for him who does not travel, Rohita! Thus we have heard. Living in the society of men, the best man becomes a sinner ... Therefore, wander!

The feet of the wanderer are like the flower, his soul is growing and reaping the fruit, and all his sins are destroyed by his fatigues in wandering. Therefore, wander!

The fortune of he who is sitting, sits; it rises when he rises; it sleeps when he sleeps; it moves when he moves. Therefore, wander!

—Indra, protector of travellers, in the Aitareya Brāhmana

Contents

PART IV: WHY THEY SHOULD BE WELCOMED

PREFACE

This is a book about people leaving their homes and moving across the planet: why they move, why they're feared, and why they should be welcomed. Although much of it deals with American immigration, the issue has never been more global. From Finland to France, from Sweden to Slovakia, there's a populist resistance to immigration, built on fear and prejudice, which this book hopes to dispel.

In the book, I use the term 'rich countries' to refer to the US, Canada, Europe, Australia, New Zealand and Japan. I realise that there are countries which don't comfortably fit in these categories; they may have been 'poor' early in the twentieth century, like China and India, but are less so now. But rather than get into the semantics of which countries are 'developing' or 'developed', I've chosen to use 'rich' and 'poor' countries as shorthand, and I trust my readers to know the difference.

The complexities of global migration are personal for me. The reason my family immigrated to America is not because Americans colonised India; it's because Britain did so, and my grandfather was compelled to leave his village for Kenya. It set off a chain of migration that led to my moving to New York in 1977. Other members of my family moved to the UK, Australia and Dubai – and are still moving.

Migration today is a global issue, and needs global solutions. Colonialism, inequality, war and climate change affect us all, rich or poor, wherever we may dwell. Whether you believe in open borders, closed borders, or something in between, I hope that this book will generate empathy and understanding for those who have to cross them. The heart should have no borders.

PART I
The Migrants Are Coming

I

A Planet on the Move

One day in the 1980s, my maternal grandfather was sitting in a park in suburban London. An elderly British man came up to him and wagged a finger in his face. 'Why are you here?' the man demanded. 'Why are you in my country?'

'Because we are the creditors,' responded my grandfather, who was born in India, worked all his life in colonial Kenya, and was now retired in London. 'You took all our wealth, our diamonds. Now we have come to collect.' We are here, my grandfather was saying, because you were there.

These days, a great many people in the rich countries complain loudly about migration from the poor ones. But as the migrants see it, the game was rigged: First, the rich countries colonized us and stole our treasure and prevented us from building our industries. After plundering us for centuries, they left, having drawn up maps in ways that ensured permanent strife between our communities. Then they brought us to their countries as 'guest workers' – as if they knew what the word 'guest' meant in our cultures – but discouraged us from bringing our families.

Having built up their economies with our raw materials and our labour, they asked us to go back and were surprised when we did not. They stole our minerals and corrupted our governments so that their corporations could continue stealing our resources; they fouled the air above us and the waters around us, making our farms barren, our oceans lifeless; and they were aghast when the poorest among us arrived at their borders, not to steal but to work, to clean their shit, and to fuck their men.

Still, they needed us. They needed us to fix their computers and heal their sick and teach their kids, so they took our best and brightest, those who had been educated at the greatest expense of the struggling states they came from, and seduced us again to work for them. Now, again they ask us not to come, desperate and starving though they have rendered us, because the richest among them need a scapegoat. This is how the game is rigged today.

My family has moved all over the earth, from India to Kenya to England to the United States and back again – and is still moving. One of my grandfathers left rural Gujarat for Calcutta in the salad days of the twentieth century; my other grandfather, living half a day's bullock-cart ride away, left soon after for Nairobi. In Calcutta, my paternal grandfather joined his older brother in the jewellery business; in Nairobi, my maternal grandfather began his career, at sixteen, sweeping the floors of his uncle's accounting office. Thus began my family's journey from the village to the city. It was, I now realize, less than a hundred years ago.

I am now among the quarter of a billion people living in a country other than the one they were born in. I'm one of the lucky ones; in surveys, nearly three-quarters of a billion people *want* to live in a country other than the one they were born in, and will do so as soon as they see a chance. Why do we move? Why do we keep moving?

On 1 October 1977, my parents, my two sisters and I boarded a Lufthansa plane in the dead of night in Bombay. We were dressed in new, heavy, uncomfortable clothes and had been seen off by our entire extended family, who had come to the airport with garlands and lamps; our foreheads were anointed with vermilion. We were going to America.

To get the cheapest tickets, our travel agent had arranged a circuitous journey in which we disembarked in Frankfurt, where we were to take an internal flight to Cologne, and then onward to New York. In Frankfurt, the German border officer scrutinized the Indian passports belonging to my father, my sisters and me, and stamped them. Then he held up my mother's passport with distaste. 'You are not allowed to enter Germany,' he said.

It was a British passport, given to citizens of Indian origin who had been born in Kenya before independence, like my mother. But the British did not want them. Nine years earlier, Parliament had passed the Commonwealth Immigrants Act, summarily depriving hundreds of thousands of British passport holders in East Africa of their right to live in the country that had conferred their nationality. The passport was literally not worth the paper it was printed on.

The German officer decided that because of her uncertain status, my mother might somehow desert her husband and three small children to make a break for it and live in Germany by herself. So we had to leave directly from Frankfurt. Seven hours and many airsickness bags later, we stepped out into the international arrivals lounge at John F. Kennedy International Airport. A graceful orange-and-black-and-yellow Alexander Calder mobile twirled above us against the backdrop of a huge American flag, and multicoloured helium balloons dotted the ceiling, souvenirs of past greetings. As each arrival was welcomed to the new land by their relatives, the balloons rose to the ceiling to make way for the newer ones. They provided hope to the newcomers: look, in a few years, with luck and hard work, you, too, can rise here. All the way to the ceiling.

It was 2 October – Mahatma Gandhi's birthday. We made our way in a convoy of cars carrying our eighteen bags and steamer trunks to a studio apartment in Jackson Heights where *The Six Million Dollar Man* was playing on the television. On the first night, the building super cut off the electricity because there were too many people in one room. I stepped out and looked at the rusting elevated train tracks above Roosevelt Avenue and wondered: where was the Statue of Liberty?

*

At McClancy, the brutal all-boys' Catholic high school where my parents enrolled me in Queens, my chief tormentor was a boy named Tschinkel. He had blond hair, piercing blue eyes and a sadistic smile. He coined a name for me: Mouse. As I walked through the hallways, this word followed me: 'Mouse! Mouse!' A small brown rodent, scurrying furtively this way and that. I was fourteen years old.

One Spanish class, Tschinkel put his leg out to trip me as I was walking in; I kicked hard at it as the entire class whooped. 'Mouse! Mouse!'

As I left the class and walked to the stairwell, I felt a hand shoving me forward. I flew straight down the small flight of stairs and landed on my feet, clutching my books; I could as easily have not, and broken my neck. When I complained to the principal, I was told that such things happen. It was within the normal order of the McClancy day.

Four decades later, another German-American bully from Queens became the most powerful man on the planet. The 2016 election particularly struck home for me. Trump is typical of the fathers of the boys I went to high school with. He grew up in Jamaica Estates, then a gated white island in the middle of the most diverse county in the United States. That explains everything about him, his fear and hatred of people different from him.

According to Trump, Haitians 'all have AIDS'. If Nigerians were allowed into the United States, they would never 'go back to their huts'. Mexicans? 'They're bringing drugs; they're bringing crime; they're rapists.' About immigrants in general: 'Everything's coming across the border: the illegals, the cars, and the whole thing. It's like a big mess. Blah. It's like vomit.' All this was shocking to many people, but familiar to me, because I'd heard it from the McClancy boys – and some of the teachers.

When my family moved to the almost all-white suburb of Ridgewood, New Jersey, from Jackson Heights to find better schools for my sisters, I found that the hatred wasn't confined to McClancy. One morning we awoke to find that someone had painted across our car 'SMEGSMA'. I can only guess that the semi-literate vandal had intended to write, but couldn't spell, 'smegma', the biological term for the crud that gathers under an uncircumcised penis's fore-skin. My parents and sisters and I gathered around the car, trying to divine the point of the vandal's imprecation and whether it was in some way connected to our ethnicity.

I have been in America for forty-two years. For thirty of those years I have been an American citizen. Every year, my confidence in my position in the country grew. When I went abroad – a summer in London, nine months in Paris, even when I went back to India for a couple of years – I would return to America with relief, because there I could be American. I couldn't be English in Eng-land, or French in France; even when I went back to India, I wasn't wholly 'Indian'; I was an 'NRI', a 'non-resident Indian'. And so, each time I saw the Long Island beachfront from the window as my plane approached JFK, I felt a gladness. America was my home. There I belonged, because everyone else belonged.

Or so I felt until the first Tuesday of November 2016. The morning after, knots of people were weeping on the streets all over Lower Manhattan. My undergraduate students at New York Uni-versity asked me, 'What are we supposed to do now?' I had no answer because I didn't know, myself, what I would do now. The white racists who had been hiding under rocks since the 1960s slithered out after Trump's victory and joined his battle. Is this their last roar before America becomes a majority-minority nation? Or will they succeed in their aim of stopping or greatly reducing immi-gration, of forcing immigrants to leave America?

Immigrants have endured tough, and sometimes cruel, policies for decades. But each month of Trump's presidency has escalated the attack. He got elected by stoking fear of migrants. Then he stoked fear of everyone else: the press, non-whites, women, Dem-ocrats, the NFL. And the people who voted for him out of fear of migrants rode the wave of fear all the way with him, and now

Americans are at each other's throats. Trump will try to hold on to power and win re-election by continuing to stoke it: build that wall, shoot anyone who tries to climb over it. The evidence, so far, shows that his tactic works. Because it's not Trump alone. Ninety per cent of Republicans, as of summer 2018, support this man. A third of the country, more or less.

My home is in the other two-thirds.

This book is being written in sorrow and rage – as well as hope. I am angry: about the staggering global hypocrisy of the rich nations, having robbed the poor ones of their future, now arguing against a reverse movement of peoples – not to invade and conquer and steal, but to work. Angry at the ecological devastation that has been visited upon the planet by the West, and which now demands that the poor nations stop emitting carbon dioxide. Angry at the depiction of people like my family and the other families that have continued in my family's path, because they had no other choice, as freeloaders, drug dealers and rapists. I'm tired of apologizing for moving. These walls, these borders, between the peoples of the Earth: they are of recent vintage, and they are flimsy.

People are not plants. Migration is a constant of human history. But with the advent of the Industrial Revolution, we started travelling greater distances in shorter times on trains, steamships, cars and jet planes. And in recent years, as the legacies of colonialism, inequality, war and climate change have made it close to impossible for people in the poor countries to live a decent life, we've become a planet on the move. Between 1960 and 2017, the overall number of migrants tripled. Today, 3.4 per cent of the world population, or one out of every twenty-nine humans, lives in a country different from the one they were born in. If all the migrants were a nation by themselves, we would constitute the fourth-largest country in the world, equal to the size of Indonesia. By mid-century, migration will account for 72 per cent of the population growth in the USA, and up to 78 per cent in Australia and the UK. This is changing elections, culture, cities – everything. Mass migration is *the* defining human phenomenon of the twenty-first century.

Never before has there been so much human movement. And never before has there been so much organized resistance to human movement. All over the world, countries are building high walls and fences against this movement: in Hungary, in Israel, in India and, if Trump has his way, in the United States. They're moving their armies and navies to their borders to intercept – and in some cases shoot at – desperate caravans and boats of migrant men, women and children.

It's not just white fear that's putting up the walls. In South Africa it's fear of Zimbabweans; in India it's fear of Bangladeshis. Another effect of mass migration is the withdrawal of countries from multilateral institutions and treaties, like the European Union and the North American Free Trade Agreement, and into narrow nationalism, a pinched vision of the country's role in the world that has the effect of impoverishing it, economically and culturally.

Pretty much anyone who was not Asian could get on a boat to America, until the Immigration Act of 1924, which set racial limits based on the ethnic composition of the United States in 1890. Today, among the rich countries, the United States ranks nineteenth in terms of how many immigrants per capita it takes in annually. For every thousand residents, New Zealand welcomes 11.7 immigrants per year. Germany takes in 12.6. The United States suffers 3.6; only five Organization for Economic Cooperation and Development countries are less welcoming. America long ago stopped lifting its lamp beside the golden door.

Increasingly, Europe is the same story. The population of African cities is slated to triple, from half a billion today to one and a half billion by 2050. By then, the working-age population of sub-Saharan Africa is projected to increase by 800 million. Many of them will head north, to Europe: the number of immigrants in the larger European countries is set to increase threefold in this period. But in many of them, politics today is defined by a competition to see which party can prevent immigration most effectively, not by which one has the best strategy for dealing with the inevitable and integrating the new arrivals most successfully.

Meanwhile, the world grows ever more horrific for human beings caught in conflicts, internal or international. In 2012, there were 930,000 newly registered asylum seekers driven out from their countries. Three years later, there were 2.3 million. Not since the end of World War II have there been more refugees and displaced people all around the world.

The rich countries have always claimed the freedom to move around the planet, not just to sightsee or seek employment, but to invade, to conquer. At airports around the world, the holders of Indian and African passports line up miserably in queues hours long while their fellow passengers holding American and European passports, gilded passports, swan through immigration.

In Abu Dhabi I noticed that the brown people, usually working in menial or service jobs, were called 'migrants', while the white people, employed as executives or professionals, got to call themselves 'expats', a much more glamorous term than 'migrant', implying wealth, long afternoons at the club, fat housing allowances. Above all, it implies that your movement has been *voluntary*, unforced by historical or economic circumstances.

Today's migrants are rarely so fortunate. Half are women, a recent phenomenon, and they are raped and molested and harassed all over the world in vastly greater numbers than native-born women. Eight out of ten undocumented Central American women who migrate to the United States are raped en route, according to an investigation by the cable channel Fusion. Before they set off, they equip themselves with contraceptives. When you move countries, your greatest – sometimes only – asset is your body, which also becomes your greatest vulnerability. Sex becomes currency, to be exchanged for protection from the smugglers, the *coyotes*, or the police. The arrangement is called *cuerpomátic* – after the Central

American credit-card processor Credomatic – because it involves using your body, *cuerpo*, as currency.

The bodies of children are also at stake. It used to be that parents went abroad and sent back money for their children. But now the parents watch the children grow up, get attacked on the way to school, get recruited into gangs; and say to the children, 'Go – go north, because you won't be able to live here. There is no life here.'

Migration is like the weather: people will move from areas of high pressure to those of low pressure. Like the weather, this movement is equally hard to fight. Well over half of all undocumented immigrants come into America not through the borders but by flying in and overstaying their visas. A wall will do nothing to stop them. And so they will keep coming, on foot or in boats, on planes or on bicycles, whether you want them or not – because they are the creditors – whether you realize it or not.

In 2015, a group of immigrants, mostly Syrian refugees, found themselves stopped at the Norwegian border with Russia. They had obtained Russian visas in Damascus or Beirut, flown to Moscow, and taken a train to Murmansk, which is 130 miles from the Norwegian border. The Russians would not allow people to walk across the border; the Norwegians would not allow people to drive across the border.

So the refugees bicycled across the border. Five hundred a week. Thousands of migrants, pedalling on rickety bikes, across the magic line to Europe. The bureaucrats had not thought of banning bicycles.

Ever since the invention of passports, the right to a home, to a nation, has existed in conflict with the right to move freely, to leave home and to find another home. Article 13 of the Universal Declaration of Human Rights states, 'Everyone has the right to freedom of movement and residence within the borders of each State. Everyone has the right to leave any country, including his own, and to return to his country.' It says nothing about what happens when someone leaves his country, or whether or not he has a right to reside in another country. Article 14, though, gives everyone the right to political asylum in another country, and Article 15 gives everyone the right to a nationality and the right to change that nationality. These contradictions are what the world is grappling with today.

During the Great Depression, an Okie named Woody Guthrie began travelling around the country, listening and gathering stories and songs. In 1944, he recorded a song that, after the Weavers popularized it, has become America's alternative national anthem. Most Americans are familiar with the opening and closing lines of 'This Land Is Your Land'. But what is less known is that in other variants there are three extra verses, which make it a protest anthem and a prophetic one at that. One of the verses was handwritten by Guthrie in 1940:

> Was a big high wall there that tried to stop me
> A sign was painted said: Private Property
> But on the back side it didn't say nothing–
> This land was made for you and me

There are also two other verses in a longer version of the song:

> In the shadow of the steeple I saw my people,
> By the relief office I seen my people;
> As they stood there hungry, I stood there asking
> Is this land made for you and me?
>
> Nobody living can ever stop me,
> As I go walking that freedom highway;
> Nobody living can ever make me turn back
> This land was made for you and me.

With those last three verses, the Guthrie song becomes not just the American anthem, but a universal migrants' anthem, wherever in the world they come from, and wherever they are going. This land is their land; this land is our land.

2

The Fence: Amargo y Dulce

For years, if you didn't have papers or lacked the authorization to leave the United States without the right to come back, the only place along the 2,000-mile US–Mexican border where you could meet your family face-to-face was at the end of the line: a small patch of land adjoining the Pacific Ocean between San Diego and Tijuana. It was inaugurated by First Lady Pat Nixon in 1971 as a 'friendship park' between the two nations and originally did not have a fence. Families on both sides could meet and have picnics together without hindrance. 'May there never be a wall between these two great nations,' Nixon said. 'Only friendship.'

In 1994, as part of Operation Gatekeeper, the Clinton administration decided that 'only friendship' was no longer the case; it would erect a barrier – a fence – between these two great nations. Families could meet across the barrier of twelve-foot-high steel bollards and pass food back and forth. In 2009, the Obama administration shut down the American side of Friendship Park and put up a second fence behind the first one. After protests, Friendship Park reopened in 2012, but with a thick double mesh; if a child wanted to touch her mother, for instance, she could stick her little finger inside the fence, and her mother could do the same on the opposite side, and the tips could touch: the dance of the fingers, the 'pinkie kiss'. '*Amargo y dulce*' is how the migrants describe the experience. Bittersweet.

Every once in a while, in its magnanimity, the government opened a door adjoining Friendship Park, and people could actually hug their family members – for no more than three minutes. This wasn't done often; the door was opened only six times after

2013. On one of those occasions, in November 2017, a couple showed up on opposite sides of the border wearing wedding clothes, got married under the watchful eye of the Border Patrol, and then went back, separated again. The groom on the American side, as the newspapers later found out, was awaiting sentencing for a drug conviction. Ten months earlier, a customs search of his Volkswagen Jetta at the nearby port of San Ysidro had uncovered forty-three pounds of heroin, forty-seven pounds of methamphetamine and forty-three pounds of cocaine. The newspapers called it the 'cartel wedding', and the Border Patrol had egg all over its face. It had, unwittingly, provided armed security for the drug dealer.

The next month, a Border Patrol officer named Rodney Scott took over the San Diego sector and shut the Door of Hope for good. The Border Angels, a local non-profit organization, had been working on a seventh opening of the gate, so that parents whose children were disabled, but were on the other side, could hug them for a few minutes. Scott declared that this gate would no longer open for human beings. 'It's a maintenance gate ... to be used for maintenance purposes only.'

Scott also came out with a list of new restrictions on families visiting Friendship Park: they could meet from only 10 a.m. to 2 p.m. on Saturdays and Sundays for ten to thirty minutes at a time. And only ten people at a time would be allowed in, down from twenty-five previously. And they couldn't take any photos or videos or even record their family members' voices on a tape recorder. The government's explanation? 'The US Border Patrol is committed to ensuring the safety and security of those who visit Friendship Circle.' How taking a photo of a family member, with armed guards watching, compromises anyone's safety or security was not in the explanation.

The fence is a heavily rusted mesh structure, ugly, industrial, foreboding. It snakes down the hillsides and all the way into the sea. People on horseback trot on to the American beach from the dude ranches that line the road to the park. On the Mexican side, there is liveliness, food, crowds. '*Música, música, música,*' offer the strolling men dressed in cowboy hats, carrying accordions or guitars, to serenade the reunions.

The Border Patrol doesn't check the papers of most people entering the park. It's not an official policy to tolerate those they suspect of being illegal aliens at Friendship Park; but of the thousands of visitors in 2017, only one or two were arrested for being undocumented.

Two little girls on either side of the fence run off from their families for a bit, and the older one bends down to touch the younger one's finger. She is so young that even her index finger fits through the mesh. The girl on the Mexican side is eating from a bag of fried food; she tries to push some through to the girl on the American side, but the yellow lump of food is too big to go through the hole, and it falls to the ground.

The girl's mother, who has been talking to a man on the other side, turns to look for her daughter; her eyes are red from crying.

Another family shows up from Colorado Springs. Their mother has come from Ciudad Juárez. The little ones are lifted up to peer at their *abuela*. They all try to touch fingers.

Alfredo Varela walks into the enclosure. He is from Irvine, California, he tells me, and hasn't seen his brother for twenty years. He came over at thirteen with his mother, who later returned to Mexico and can't come back. He is a facilities technician and is on 'something like DACA', which allows him to stay in the country but not cross this fence to hug his only brother.

Alfredo, who grew up in Tijuana, is a keen amateur photographer; he likes to take photos of sunsets on the ocean. He points to the sea and says, 'We used to ride our bikes on that beach' – back and forth beyond the two countries, when he was a kid. Nobody bothered them. They would carry their passports with them in case anyone asked. His brother was more adventurous and would go farther out into San Diego; Alfredo stayed on the beach.

His brother finally arrives, and Alfredo walks towards the barrier. He is standing a little apart from the fence, smiling. Then he leans in. He takes off his sunglasses and his cap, showing his closely cropped head, his face. There is laughter from the other side. He leans forward and puts his hand up to the metal. So does his brother.

Alfredo comes back the next day, on the Sunday, to speak to his brother some more before he goes back to Guadalajara, a two-and-a-half-hour flight away. 'I did the math and realized it was actually twenty-five years since I'd seen him,' he tells me, wonderingly. He's been putting pressure on his brother to get a passport so that he can get a tourist visa to come and visit him.

In a way, Alfredo is glad they could only talk through the mesh, because it felt less than satisfactory to his brother: 'He feels like he's visiting me in jail.' Now his brother will feel motivated to visit him, even though it's a risk. It costs $160 to even apply for a tourist visa, which is a lot of money in Mexico, and the application could well be rejected.

There was an unexpected family bonus on this trip for Alfredo. He was looking through Facebook to see if he knew anyone in San Diego and happened to come across his uncle, his father's brother, whom he hadn't seen since he'd been in the United States because the uncle is undocumented and won't risk taking the highway out of the city, where there are multiple Border Patrol checkpoints. So Alfredo met his uncle, met his nephews, in their house. It made him feel good, meeting the only other family he has in this country, and they made plans to meet again soon.

Alfredo has a work authorization, which he has to renew every two years but doesn't allow him to go out of the country. If there's an emergency, like a funeral or the impending death of a close relative, he could apply for a waiver. But he misses his family at Christmas time. 'All I want for Christmas is to give my mother a hug,' he says.

A lesbian couple, a schoolteacher and her partner who are moving from southern California to Seattle, have come to the park with their two puppies, pugs named Guinness and Modelo, after the beers. One of them hasn't had his rabies shot, so they can't take him to Mexico. So they've come to show their 'children' to the schoolteacher's mother across the fence. The puppies put their legs up at the fence; the mother tries to touch them.

A man and a woman walk out of the meeting point. The woman is sobbing, and the man has his arm around her. They turn out to be a brother and sister who are Dreamers. They came here aged eleven and twelve. They've just met their parents for the first time in ten years. 'I could smell them,' he says with happiness.

For two days straight, I have been speaking to children, parents, siblings, and best friends, moments after they've seen their loved ones after years and years. Most of them end up weeping. I've never seen so many people break down in such a short amount of time; it is the Park of Tears. If you've ever stopped speaking to someone in your family, go to this park and watch the families separated by a government trying to talk to one another through the wire mesh, trying to force their fingers into the little holes to touch their mother's or their grandmother's finger. Friendship Park is at once a monument to bureaucratic stupidity and the absurd rules that lawyers make, as well as to the power of love and family to surpass them. It is the cruellest and the most hopeful place I have ever seen.

I drive out with Rae Ocampo, a genial young Filipino Border Patrol officer, for a tour of the entire fourteen-mile border fence that starts in the mountains and winds down to Friendship Park, just before it ends in the sea. The residents of the slums abutting the wall in Mexico have thrown heaps of garbage over the fence into the United States. Ocampo spends most of his days driving up and down the fence line, peering into Tijuana. He has never been there. 'I might run into someone I've arrested. It's not safe.'

Ocampo shows me a whole series of patches on the bottom of the outer fence, covering openings that the *coyotes* have made with wire cutters. It is these openings that Trump had viewed on a visit here, as he demanded his big, beautiful wall. Eight prototypes for that wall are now set up, some solid concrete, some nine-foot pillars. They are monstrous and inhuman, meant to be not just insurmountable but intimidating – deliberately brutalist. A signal to America's southern neighbours: keep out.

It remains to be seen if a wall, no matter how high, will deter desperate migrants who have no other option but to cross. The Border Patrol regularly finds tunnels emerging in the warehouses near the border, though they are too expensive to dig solely for human cargo and are mostly used for drug smuggling. As the number of people crossing illegally drops, the amount of drugs coming across increases. In 2017, 782 pounds of fentanyl, enough for 200 million lethal doses, was intercepted at the San Diego border – up six times from the previous year. No wall is going to stop these drugs from coming, because the cartels are increasingly smuggling their shipments through the official border crossings; they're hidden inside trucks or even disguised to look like parts of the trucks themselves.

We drive past a spanking new private airport in Tijuana, which is connected to the other side of the border by a land bridge. From America, you can pay sixteen dollars to cross the bridge and take a flight from the airport to anywhere in Mexico and many Latin American destinations. The flights cost considerably less than you would pay at San Diego International, a twenty-minute drive north. When you return, you will be greeted with welcoming smiles by US customs officers, who are paid by the owners of the airport. So there is one system of entry into the United States for the rich coming from the airport and another for the not-so-rich pedestrians who often have to line up for hours for the free crossings nearby. Just like you can pay for a business-class air fare, you can now pay for business-class immigration counters.

I am standing in Friendship Park when Rodney Scott, the San Diego sector chief, comes by. He points out a white pillar beyond the fence. It indicates the actual demarcation of the border, but it is on the Mexican side, surrounded by families, food vendors, and mariachi bands. He wants to move the fence to the boundary.

There are around 20,000 Border Patrol agents now, compared with nine thousand in 2000, and the agency's budget has quadrupled. (Its parent agency, Customs and Border Protection, is the largest law enforcement agency in the country, with over 60,000 employees.) The Border Patrol's territory is divided into twenty sectors. Each is a fiefdom in which the sector chief has absolute authority.

Scott is a white man in his forties, speaks with a Midwestern accent, and has the air of a viceroy. He has decided that there is to be no hugging. He alone decides. The families do not decide; they have no voice. He decides that the Friendship Garden shouldn't have painted tyres buried in the ground to mark the perimeter. He doesn't like the look – it's too Mexican – and so it has to go.

I have a simple question for him: Why won't he let families hug? Why won't he let Alfredo give his mother and his brother a hug for Christmas?

'I understand that the people want to hug through the border fence. It's really not the purpose, though. We won't be doing that,' he says with finality. He says he's had evidence that, in areas close to the border, 'sensitive information for the United States was being passed through the fence on thumb drives'.

There will be no hugging through the fence now or in the future, Scott says, because the people who want to do so are usually criminals. 'There are 320 ports of entry in the country where you can cross the border pretty easily. The only reason that people couldn't – not the only reason, but the majority of people – they can't cross the border to actually physically meet their relatives, there's some kind of crime they've committed that put them into that situation. The normal American and/or the normal Mexican can actually get a border-crosser card, or actually just cross very easily.'

I bring up the case of people who have work authorizations that don't allow them to leave the country, like Alfredo, or the Dreamers.

The Dreamers are here illegally, Scott says. He compares them to queue jumpers at public events. 'Pick any amusement park that you want, or any movie, or even Black Friday, the day after Thanksgiving, where people line up for hours or days in advance to get into the event, right? So, in any one of those events, if you're standing in line and a family cuts in front of you in that line to get in, you're gonna be a little bit angry about it ... Now, you complain, and security walks up and grabs the parents and says, "You can't do this, but it's not your kids' fault that you cut in line, so we're gonna let the kids go in." Ahead of your family, ahead of all the people that've been waiting in this line – that's for years in some cases, but in my analogy, overnight. Is that fair? So that's why it's so complicated. It's not a simple "Oh yeah, it's not the kids' fault".'

When the fence was open, people were passing 'stored-value cards', among other things, to their relatives, according to Scott. 'That's actually currency smuggling.' He now wants the relatives to move even farther apart. He's planning a bollard-style fence, which would allow people to see their families better than the current mesh does but would move them four feet apart. 'So you still won't be able to pass things through it, you still won't be able to hug through it, or shake hands, but you'd be able to actually see the person that you are talking to.' Not even a pinkie could kiss under Scott's plans for his fence.

Scott is a devout Christian and thinks of his profession in Christian terms. 'I believe that my job is my calling. I ended up here for a reason somehow.'

'What happens when you have to separate a child from its mother?' I ask, bringing up the Trump administration's recently announced policy of forcibly separating migrant children from their parents. 'How do you reconcile that with your biblical principles of giving hospitality to a stranger?'

'I don't see the conflict that some others see,' Scott responds. 'I go back to the original sin, to the Garden of Eden. There were consequences: they got deported out of the Garden of Eden, and God created a border around it.'

He elaborates: 'My understanding of biblical principles is there's always consequences for your actions, and you're not exempt from them. If you want to take another biblical story, of the last days on the cross, a sinner was forgiven, but no one took him off the cross. He still had to pay the price for his transgressions ... We carry out our job very compassionately every day, but we didn't create borders. They've been around since the beginning of time, we didn't create the concept of deportation, so I think it was created in Genesis 3:23.'

It wasn't Obama, as his critics allege – it was God who was the deporter in chief. And the first illegal aliens were Adam and Eve.

Scott talks about a debate he'd had with a pastor about asylum. 'He was pushing "We should be sympathetic" and, you know, "Your Christian beliefs, you're supposed to help these people, be compassionate". And I pointed out that they are lying. Like, these people are literally coming with a script from a smuggler and intentionally trying to game the system, if you will, by lying.'

Scott also has problems with the way that asylum is granted and who it's granted to. 'Look at the asylum process right now. There's so many false claims and so much fraud in the asylum. People like Christians trying to flee Syria or the Middle East literally get stuck in this years-and-years-long process, and they're looked at very, very sceptically, because there's so much fraud. So people that need the help ... people that really have a legitimate reason ... they've applied, they've gone through the legal processes, they're having to wait years now.' He doesn't mention Muslims fleeing the Middle East, who make up the vast majority of asylum applicants from the region.

According to Scott, the undocumented can be persuaded to 'self-deport'. 'I honestly believe that if you tell the majority of illegal aliens "We really don't want you here", they would go home. I really do believe in this self-deporting philosophy, that the reason this problem continues is because our country kind of has this message like, "Hey, we want strong border security, but as soon as you're past the guys in green, you're good. I want you to cut my lawn, I want you to clean the hotel, you know ... I'll give you a job, I am gonna hide you from immigration." We have this split personality.'

In San Diego in summer 2018, in spite of Scott's efforts, there were 48 per cent more attempted crossings than in the same period the previous year, and a spike of over 77 per cent that spring. Adam and Eve are trying every day to sneak into the Garden of Eden.

A few months after our meeting, Scott was in the news for ordering the Border Patrol to fire tear gas and pepper spray on a group of migrants who were trying to rush the fence. They were part of the 'migrant caravan' from Honduras, which Trump had been demonizing daily for weeks, calling them 'stone-cold criminals' as they made their way north from Mexico. He had hoped that the issue would rally his base to come out to vote for Republicans in the mid-term elections. Scott claimed that the migrants were throwing rocks at the Border Patrol officers. The airwaves and newspapers were filled with images of men and women fleeing from the gas, clutching their screaming children, some of whom were still in nappies. What makes life so hellish in places like Honduras that a mother would risk putting herself and her kids through this kind of ordeal?

After meeting Scott, I go to the other side of the fence, in Tijuana, to visit Marie Galvan, the social director of Instituto Madre Asunta, a Catholic Church-run women's shelter. She tells me what drives the forty to sixty women and children who show up at her shelter daily. 'Violence, threats of violence, from narcos, other armed groups.' When they flee, generally by bus, they are followed. When they get off at junctions to change buses, the armed men are waiting for them, wanting them to pay, with money or their bodies. She's been at the shelter for twenty-four years. Before, the children didn't know why they were migrating. Now they do: 'Because someone in the family was killed.' She sees this realization in the drawings they make in her art classes: people shot, but also whole families playing together. 'They're not migrating for economic reasons or for family reunification. Right now, it's the war of drugs; right now it's the violence. *La guerra.*'

In 1980, the United States passed the Refugee Act, raising the number of refugees allowed in annually to 50,000. That year, 3.5 per cent of all asylum petitions filed came from refugees fleeing the Northern Triangle countries of Honduras, Guatemala and El Salvador. As the US-exported gang violence took hold, the percentage increased, to 11.3 per cent in 2000, 26.4 per cent in 2006 and 33.8 per cent in 2015. The outflow became an exodus.

Galvan introduces me to Saira, a pretty 23-year-old Honduran mother. She comes into the reception room of the shelter trailed by a smiling fourteen-month-old boy dressed in a green shirt. She's trying to rejoin her husband and five-year-old son, who are waiting for them in Texas. 'I am here to save his life,' she says of her cherubic little boy.

'They killed my husband's friend. They were together, and my husband saw everything. They killed him with a piece of glass; they cut his neck, and my husband saw the people who did it.'

Her husband worked at a *maquiladora* in San Pedro Sula in Honduras, but he was laid off when the factory downsized. He found work as an assistant to a construction worker, along with the friend he saw getting killed.

Saira doesn't know why the gang killed her husband's friend, but she can guess. 'When the *maras* [the gangs] see single boys like that, young men, on the street, they want them to join their *maras*, to make them bigger.' Her husband had found the construction job through a pastor, and so the whole family started going to church, and bringing the friend, who was not married, along with them. 'And they did not like it. They did not like that instead of joining the *mara*, he was going to church.'

After his friend was buried, the gang started looking for her husband, and he fled to the United States. Two days later, the gang showed up at Saira's house. 'I was alone. They told me to inform my husband that he needed to show up to communicate with them. If not, my son was going to pay the price of my husband being absent.' Tell your husband, the gang members said, that in a few years their boy had to join the gang, or they would murder him.

When her husband fled, their plan was that he would establish himself in Texas, apply for asylum, and then call for her. But after the gang came knocking on her door, she got on a bus and began her journey without telling her husband. It took her three months to get here – a very hard journey. From Honduras she crossed over into the southern Mexican state of Chiapas and applied for travel papers for herself and the baby. She met another Honduran woman also on the run. The *maras* had visited the woman's family back in Honduras and told them that they knew she was in Chiapas. 'They told them that the gang members weren't just in one post; they are everywhere.' Hearing this, Saira panicked and fled Chiapas without waiting for her papers.

She was hungry throughout, but a bigger priority was to feed her baby. When she got to Tijuana, she walked into a store to buy food and walked out without her phone. Someone had stolen it. She had no way of communicating with her husband or five-year-old son, to tell them that she and the baby were coming. She has now applied for asylum and has been waiting ten days for her turn to be interviewed. Saira hopes that by the following week, her number might be called.

Saira grew up with a single mother, who now lives in a faraway town. In San Pedro Sula, only her brother and his wife are left.

'Are they in danger?'

The gang didn't know about them because they didn't live in the same house as Saira. 'But I imagine that now that I am not there, because there's no one home, they might be asking for us.' She told her brother to tell people that she wasn't related to them, that she'd left and rented out the house. If she's denied asylum, she can't go back to San Pedro Sula.

'When you get to America, what would you like to do?' I ask her. 'What kind of future do you see for yourself and for your son?'

'That my kids are okay, a place where they can go to school in peace. To have tranquillity when I sleep. Not this not knowing if I'm going to get assaulted at home, or someone is going to be killed.'

Saira never aspired to go to the United States. 'From a very young age, I've suffered and have been here and there with my mother, struggling to make a living.' Finally, she had a house and possessions; she felt she had 'accomplished' things: 'A family, and my own home, where no one mistreated me. I do not wish, I never dreamed of being there [the United States] and doing the big things like having money.'

I ask her if she's heard of the family separation policy. Her little boy, who's happily playing with my phone and a plastic spoon, might be snatched away from her and thrown into a detention centre thousands of miles away.

She has. The other day, another migrant woman was speaking to her in the asylum queue and asked her how she could take her chances in crossing, knowing that her child might be forcibly ripped from her arms by the Americans.

'I told her that the love that I feel as a mother is like that: knowing that he might be far away, but that he's alive, that one day I might see him again.' Because this could be the alternative: 'Placing him in a box below the earth and knowing that you'll never see him again ... ' Saira can't continue, and great big tears form in her eyes.

It is our most elemental drive: to survive; and, having survived, to propagate; and, having propagated, to do anything and everything to make sure that our progeny lives better than we have. It is this, more than anything else, that is the animating force of global migration. If you, living in New York or London, can understand why you want your child to go to Yale or Cambridge and will sacrifice a house or a car so that they can do so, you can understand why a Honduran mother might sacrifice her honour or her life to make sure that her child can live with dignity in the north. She wants what you want: a better life for her kids – or even, more simply, just the continuation of life. And that's not possible where she lives. Because the rich nations have taken what is necessary for a better life away from her, and hoarded it for their kids.

As attorney general, Jeff Sessions sought to eliminate domestic violence and gang warfare as reasons for a 'well-founded fear' for asylum. So if your government puts a gun to your head because of your political belief, you can apply for asylum; but if a non-state actor like MS-13, the criminal gang that is the de facto government in much of Central America, does the same, you can't.

Oxford University's Alexander Betts describes much of today's human mobility as 'survival migration'. He points out that the criteria established for refugees, which are from the postwar era, are outdated. Today, environmental degradation, starvation and gang warfare are as much threats to life as the Nazis were in the twentieth century, but these threats are not recognized in the official definitions of 'persecution'. This new kind of survival migration, says Betts, is of 'people who have left their country of origin because of an existential threat for which they have no domestic remedy'.

'Come here legally,' demand the haters on Fox News. But 80 per cent of people who have applied legally for asylum in America from El Salvador, Honduras and Guatemala in recent years have had their applications denied, so the odds are against people like Saira. By comparison, 90 per cent of asylum seekers from the former Soviet Union were welcomed in.

On the Tijuana side of Friendship Park, a photographer named Maria Teresa tells me how she found the gap: she was watching a girl standing close to the fence, weekend after weekend, talking to her boyfriend on the other side; and then one day, a ring appeared on her finger. How did it get there? Maria Teresa wondered. Then she found out how, and she points it out to me now: there's a semi-hidden place where a section of the mesh ends, next to a supporting pole, big enough for part of a whole palm to slip through, four fingers all the way up to the knuckle.

Maria Teresa introduces me to Luis, a 34-year-old man from Sinaloa, who's come to introduce his parents and his two little kids from an earlier marriage to his wife Cynthia, a robotics student at the University of California San Diego and a Dreamer, who is pregnant with their son. They've been together for a year and got married five months ago. Luis is from one of the most violent areas of Mexico, and he'd crossed over in 2000, 'to live in peace and to work'. Gradually, he built up his own construction business in LA, until two months ago, when he went to get his driving licence. The next day, Immigration and Customs Enforcement (ICE) arrested him and summarily deported him, over his protestations that his application for a green card was already in process.

Cynthia had crossed when she was eight. Three years ago, she was sexually assaulted in the United States and has started the process of getting a 'U' visa, which is given to victims of violent crimes who can help put the perpetrators behind bars. But that will take three years at least, with no guarantee that it will be successful. She can't cross over to Mexico, and so she'll have her baby without Luis present, even though the boy's going to have the same first name.

This is the second time Luis has made the twenty-four-hour drive up from Sinaloa to meet his new bride. For the first time, Cynthia's meeting the whole family in person. Luis's little girl reaches up to touch the long pink nail that her new stepmother pokes through the mesh.

Luis and Cynthia speak on the phone every day. But it doesn't substitute for this face-to-face meeting, this kissing of pinkies.

'You know, there's a gap where you can touch more,' I tell Luis, with my newfound knowledge. They follow me to the gap. Luis thrusts his hand through the gap, where it meets his bride's hand.

'Oh yes!' Luis exclaims in English, his whole face bathed in delight. 'It's nice!'

They stay like that for a while, holding hands. Then Cynthia starts crying. And Luis raises his arms, mimes pulling apart the ugly iron fence between him and his wife with his bare hands.

3

Ordinary Heroes

Before you ask other people to respect the borders of the West, ask yourself if the West has ever respected anybody else's border. How often has Britannia taken to the waves in search of borders to breach, territories to conquer? How often has it signed treaties with native rulers, only to flout them and kill or imprison those rulers or their descendants, when it suited Britain?

How often has the United States gone over the southern border or into the Caribbean or south-east Asia? How often does it keep doing so, going over the borders of Iraq or Afghanistan? The United States did not act lawfully with other nations, including the Native American nations on its soil, through most of the nineteenth and twentieth centuries. How can it now expect the human victims of that enormous illegality to obey the laws of the United States and stay home or wait thirty years for a visa to rejoin their families?

I am not calling for open borders. I am calling for open hearts.

The migrants are no more likely to be rapists or terrorists than anyone else. They are ordinary people just like those who haven't had to move. But the ordeals they've had to face in their journey, and the sacrifices they make for family – both for their children in the new country and the parents and siblings they support in the old – have made them into ordinary, everyday heroes. The false stories of the populists, their fearmongering, their bigotry, can be fought only by telling a true story better, so that it isn't lost in a fog of numbers and arguments and counterarguments.

Wherever there are immigrants, there are stories; because of their dislocation, they have a need for recollection. When I arrived with my family in Jackson Heights, Queens, in 1977, the area was filled with phone centres where people would go to call their families in other countries. They had booths or cubicles where men and women stood or sat on a chair, and spoke into a phone, and, often, wept. They were talking to their wives, sons, fathers, whom, if they were undocumented, they would not see for ten or twenty years while they were working to send them money. There were always promises: I'm coming back soon; we'll bring you over as soon as I've made enough money to pay the *coyote*; Americans are good people, and the government will soon give me a green card because I work so hard, and then I can come back to see you.

The first thing that a new migrant sends to his family back home isn't money; it's a story. Of the arduous journey, the snow on the streets, the rude immigration agent or the kindly social worker; the lights of the Eiffel Tower or the cold reception from the cousins with whom he's staying. The frequency and nature of this storytelling have changed over the ages as technology has evolved. My friend Abdelkader Benali, a Dutch Moroccan writer, tells me about the *kissa*. Before calling cards made international calls cheap, Moroccan migrants would mail a cassette tape back to the family, in which the migrant would record his *kissa*, his tale of the new land. The whole family would gather to listen to side A, which would be about work, the weather, money, politics. Then there would be a general throat clearing and the room would empty out and only the wife would be left. She would turn over the tape and listen to side B, which would be filled with declarations of love and longing, and a little bit of lust.

Yes, migrants do lie; sometimes they lie to their own people, because they have to justify the migration. A central African French teacher in the New Jersey schools named Jean-Gratien tells me about Rwandan immigrants in northern Europe. The state gives them money to buy things such as furniture. But they buy the cheapest furniture and save up the money for a round-trip ticket home, and for props for a story they want to tell back home. They wait for the summer holidays, and buy an expensive suit for themselves and the most impressive shoes – boots made of crocodile leather, say. The airports of Europe, in the summer, are filled with these returning African migrants, garbed in extravagant shoes.

When they get home, they rent an expensive car for two weeks. The first morning home, the people of the family, of the village, gather around the migrant to hear stories of the new land. The migrant, with his fancy clothes, new shoes and big car, tells them what a big man he's become in Rotterdam, in Paris, in Berlin. 'I am selling a story,' Jean-Gratien says. 'I elaborate, I make up things.' His mother cannot refuse small loans while he's there, because after all, he's a big man in America. Then the migrants go back to the cold countries, and the only time they're in a car is when they're making deliveries.

These stories recruit new migrants. They're not the whole truth, and they're not all lies. 'Did you hear about the two boys from Niger who stowed away in the bottom of an aeroplane?' asks Jean-Gratien. 'They were dead when the plane landed. They found a letter they'd written, about their idea of life in Europe.' The two boys had been killed by the story – the story of success in the rich countries.

A friend tells me about going to the roof of a building in Dubai and being surprised to see a miniature mosque, a replica of the Kaaba. The construction company will hire only Muslim labourers. They work on top of a tall building, but they need to pray five times a day. There's no time for them to come down to the ground and prostrate themselves, or to go to a proper mosque. So the company has set up this portable one. Every Muslim has to ritually wash before prayer, so another worker takes a water hose and hoses down the workers five times a day.

The workers live a brutal existence. They make $150 a month; but they are required to spend $80 a month at the 'company store', which cheats them as they buy essentials. So why do they keep coming? Part of it is economic, but part of it is also the strength of the story – often fraudulent – that each immigrant takes back to his village when he comes with a suitcase full of trinkets: electronic toys, a stereo, cheap jewellery. These knick-knacks embellish the story: that life is better elsewhere, that the migrant is making progress.

A man I met once in Delhi told me about his cousins in Kentucky. Every summer in his childhood, the cousins would visit his family in Delhi, and the family would drop everything to host their American relatives, taking them here and there, preparing costly feasts, sleeping in the living room so that the visitors could rest undisturbed in the bedrooms. What the cousins regularly sent over were photos of themselves in front of their 'bungalow', which means 'villa' in the Indian context, not a one-floor cottage as it does in America. Photos of themselves with their arms around their large new television, or lying on the bonnet of their large new car. I knew what the man from Delhi was talking about, because my family sent exactly these same kinds of photos to our relatives in India, partly to reassure them that we were doing well in the new world, and partly to stoke their envy.

When the man from Delhi grew up, he got a chance to visit his cousins in Kentucky for the first time. He expected them to be living like millionaires. When he finally got to their fabled home, he started screaming obscenities at his cousins. He saw their 'bungalow', the shabbiest on the block, and their ordinary car, and saw that they lived at a much lower standard than did his own family in Delhi, who had been made to feel impoverished every time his cousins visited. All his childhood he had felt deprived, because of this lie. He howled out his abuse at the Kentucky liars.

I give a ride to Colette and Géralde, two Cameroonian women I'd met at an African immigrants group, at 167th Street and Grand

Concourse in the Bronx. It looks like a rough neighbourhood – this was in 2008 – but when they show up, they say it's safe because 'there are a lot of Africans here. Everybody's African.' Neither of them is in the country legally.

As I walk with the two young women to my car, a black man yells out to them, 'Can I be your bodyguard?'

Colette is a plump, jolly, exuberant woman with a large gash on her breastbone. 'My brother scratched me when I was a kid,' she explains. And then she had a couple of injections to prevent infection, which widened the scar, as injections in developing countries often do. 'I don't want to hide it.' It is prominent, like a large burn mark.

Géralde, wearing a red polka-dot top, a jean jacket and tight white shorts, is twenty-eight and shyer. She is four months younger than Colette; they see each other every day and talk for at least an hour. When Colette's mobile phone battery dies, Géralde says it's because of all the time she spends talking to her friend. She calls her variously 'my twin' and 'my sister'. In my car, they both sit in the back, hoping I won't mind, 'because she's my sister and I have to sit with her'.

Colette works at the weekends as a home healthcare aide. 'I take care of an old lady.' Her husband drives a yellow cab. They would like to move elsewhere – the Poconos or upstate. Where the schools are good, where there are no gangs. 'Our children are our future. We want to do it for them.'

Will they move where there are other Africans?

'There are Africans everywhere.'

'What keeps you in New York?' I ask.

'Even if you don't have documentation,' Colette explains, 'you can find a small job in New York.' The city is the last refuge of the paperless.

Géralde is beginning her nursing degree at Hostos Community College; she pays for her credits in cash, $140 a credit. She has just taken a biology final, which she found easy because she had already studied the subject in her high school in Cameroon, where the educational standards are higher than in the United States. Her mother owns a school there. She has a boyfriend here, a Nigerian, who is doing a PhD in computer science at the City University of New York graduate centre. He is a citizen, but he hasn't forgotten his traditions. 'He knows about voodoo.' She's now working as a nanny for a white family on the Upper East Side.

Géralde has a six-year-old daughter in Cameroon. She left her when she was eight months old, with her mother, and came to America.

It must have been hard to part with her daughter at eight months, I remark.

No, she responds. 'I would just give my daughter to my mother every day. My mother told me to go to America. I miss my mother more than my daughter.' She came here because there are no jobs in Cameroon, and with the father dead, Géralde's daughter needs her mother's money more than she needs her mother.

I ask about their jobs. They say that they've encountered prejudice, but it's indirect, or innocent. Géralde was asked by her employer to do the children's laundry, in which she found her employer's underwear. 'In Africa we are taught to hide our underwear. You can do bad voodoo to someone if you get their underwear. I had to wash her underwear.'

'And fold it,' Colette adds.

But still, when Géralde first started working as a nanny, she got so attached to the little white girl she took care of that she would sometimes call her by her daughter's name before she caught herself. 'I still have a picture of her on my wall. I send her flowers, gifts.' I've found this with many of the immigrant nannies: they spend their lives caring for somebody else's child while their own are strangers to them. And little by little, the child they are paid to take care of starts occupying a bigger place in their hearts than the ones that came out of their bodies.

'How often do you speak to your daughter?' I ask.

'Every day.'

'How long for?'

'Ten dollars.' That's how much the calling card lasts – about an hour.

Géralde lives with her brother in a one-bedroom apartment. 'The Muslim Africans live six people in a room. They sleep on the floor. We could never do that. We need beds.' She pays $900 a month in rent, and makes $1,500 a month from her nanny job. She sends money every month to her daughter, whom she hasn't seen for five years. When she calls her, her daughter gives her the rundown of every single thing that has happened in the day; if she misses her call by a few days, the little girl will begin with the first day and go on until she's recounted every day.

Then Colette tells me that, contrary to her feigned indifference earlier, Géralde really misses her daughter. 'She cries every day. I tell her, "You will see her. God has a plan."' But her daughter doesn't know quite who she is on the phone. 'She's Auntie Géralde to her,' Colette says.

'What does she call you?' I ask Géralde. 'Does she call you "*maman*"?'

'She calls everybody "*maman*". I'm Géralde Maman. When she was asked who's her mother, she named my sister-in-law.'

She lifts her eyes. They are full of water. She lifts a finger to them just before it can spill over.

When I drop off Géralde, I tell her I have two children too.

'Where are they? Are they with you?'

I tell her I'm divorced, and they spend half the time with me. Later I realize that she wasn't asking if they live with their mother or me; she hadn't the remotest idea that I was divorced. She was asking if they were in India or America. It is a natural question for Géralde to ask of other immigrants.

Every immigrant has left a love behind. Every immigrant has abandoned a lover or a child or a best friend and has made false

promises of return. Back home, the grandparents prepare extravagant meals, lay out the table in the garden, light the lamps in the
evening for the children who will never come back. Back home,
the children wait for their mothers to call every Sunday.

I knew an Indian babysitter without a green card in New York
who hadn't seen her children for a decade. They had been left in
the care of her in-laws while she and her husband struggled in New
York, to send money back, in the hope of becoming legal someday
and bringing the children to join them. Every Sunday she spoke
to them. One day somebody was showing her some pictures of a
wedding in her town in India. 'Who's that?' she asked, pointing to
a teenage girl. The person showing the pictures looked at her in
surprise. 'That's your daughter.' The babysitter burst into tears.

I saw the possible and dismal future of the world when I spent a
semester teaching at New York University Abu Dhabi in spring
2017. I teach at the most internationalized institution of higher education on the planet. NYU has three fully fledged campuses, and
also some twenty-seven study-abroad portals, which can be found
on every continent. My NYU Abu Dhabi students were from all
over the planet, wandering around a campus built for three times
their number, a land without students for students without a land.

Outside my window in Arabia, I could see sand, palm trees, and
not a single Arab. It is a nation of resident foreigners, who have
built the Emirates with their labour. Abu Dhabi is easily the most
multicultural city I have ever lived in. And it taught me that white
people have no monopoly on racism. It was a country of pearl
divers until the 1960s, when the oil money started gushing in. With
the money, the Emiratis started importing labour; 88 per cent of the
people are from elsewhere, the highest percentage of migrants in the
world. The 12 per cent lucky enough to be Emirati occupy themselves with flippancies: falconry, horse racing, bidding for licence
plates with the lowest numbers (the royal family has the single-digit
ones). In the Emirates, all races and colours and nationalities are

welcome, as long as you don't get political. Make money and send it home. You don't live in Dubai or Abu Dhabi, you commute there to a job. Ten or eleven months working every day, then a month or two back in Lagos or Dhaka, laden with presents for your wife and children and parents. You will be pampered with the choicest foods, as a provider. They will recognize your ordinary heroism.

Dubai, the emirate next door, has 30,000 prostitutes. The hotels' lounges are depressing places where expat businessmen meet migrant whores. At one of them, a Chinese girl from Guangzhou, five months in the country, stands by us and smiles, waiting to be asked. What is she doing here? As with many of the Latina women travelling north through the Americas, she is offering the only commodity she has after her long journey: her body.

In the gold souk mall, in downtown Abu Dhabi, I feel happy because I could be in a mid-size town in Kerala. All around me are Malayalis buying electronic appliances for their loved ones back home. Then eating in the food court: a Kerala thali served on banana leaves for eight dirhams, about two and a half dollars. On the NYU campus, everyone speaks Hindi but the sahibs. I am one of the sahibs, but I am also brown. An African man, probably a professor, asks me if I work at the car rental desk. An Australian man who runs the scientific lab asks me if he can help me, assuming I might be wanting to break into the lab, then turns to joking about mad scientists when he realizes I am of his rank.

The taxi driver who picks me up in the NYU Abu Dhabi campus shortly after 7 a.m. is African. As soon as the cab gets to an empty road, he pulls over to the side and beseeches me, 'Pee-pee. I'll be just a second.' And he runs out, squats in the bushes by the road, and is back in ten seconds, relieved.

His name is Robert Kwasi, and he's from Ghana. He's been here for less than a year. Last year a recruiter for the taxi company came to Ghana and picked up 150 Ghanaians. 'The government there is bad, so we can't get jobs,' he says.

Robert works eighteen hours a day, seven days a week. He'll be on his way to his camp after dropping me off. 'I will sleep, and wash my body,' he tells me. But often, he tries to sneak in a nap in his cab. He was doing that three days ago when one of the taxi company's management vehicles took a picture of him sleeping; that cost him a 500 dirham ($136) fine. The same day, a police car caught him sleeping; that was another 500 dirhams.

It is against the company's rules for him to park and get something to eat, so he rushes into a cheap restaurant when he can, but more often subsists on biscuits and tea. 'It is bad for my body.' Even in the cab he has to eat furtively; it is against the rules to eat in the taxi. He points to a camera just above the rear-view mirror, recording both of us.

The Ghanaians were promised a basic salary of 800 dirhams ($218) a month, but when they got to Abu Dhabi, they found out that they were working on commission only. So they can't afford to get sick and miss a day of work. Accommodation is free, in a barracks forty-five minutes out in the desert, where Robert is in a room with nine others in a system of bunk beds. He is not allowed to cook, because the company wants them to pay for food at the canteen. The company comes into their rooms sometimes and destroys their cooking equipment.

If his taxi is scratched when he returns it at the end of his shift, he is fined 300, 400 or 500 dirhams – more than the cost of repairing the scratch. Robert is secondary to the taxi he drives. His body is of less value than the body of the car; if he's sick, the company won't take care of him, but if the car suffers a scratch, the company will spring into action and demand that he fix it.

I ask him how his Arab customers are. They are fine, he says. 'They just pay and they go.' Some Arabs will not take a cab driven by a black driver; others will not take cabs driven by Indians, Pakistanis or Nepalese, because they believe blacks are cleaner and speak English better.

He is working to send money back to Ghana. 'In my country I am a man of position,' he says. He didn't go to university, 'but my oldest is studying to be a doctor'.

'It's great that he's studying to be a doctor,' I say.

'Daughter,' he corrects me. 'All three of my children are girls.' Then, for the first time, his face softens at the memory of his girls, and with a gentle laugh, he says, 'I am close to them.'

Robert Kwasi is a hero. He is in a country not his own, living a life as an adjunct to a machine, forgoing all pleasure – listening to music, eating his native food – to work for his three daughters. Every human need – sleeping, shitting, fucking, eating – is against the rules of the company. He can't even talk on his mobile phone with his fellow drivers, as the ones in New York do.

Afterwards I go back to my lavish NYU campus and sit that evening by the sea at the Hyatt, paying more for drinks in one day than Robert earns in a week. Because I am American. In the age of globalization, your dignity is determined by your passport. If you're American or European, you will get your Emirati visa in the VIP section, and other nationalities will wait on you. In other countries, borders will fall magically at your advent, and visas will be provided on arrival at the airport. If you're Indian or Filipino, you will wait endlessly in line and be treated with casual rudeness, along with all the other Unimportant Persons. In the twenty-first century, your humanity is defined by your nationality. And those who have no nationality – the Palestinians, the Rohingya – are fucked. They will wander the earth, powerless.

This is the future of citizenship: a hierarchical model as in the Gulf nations, in which 88 per cent of the population works for the other 12 per cent and has no rights whatsoever. All men are not created equal. Just like the undocumented Salvadorans slaving away in the kitchens and farms of America, or the 'guest workers' in Europe who are expected to leave after their host nations stop needing them. I've always found the term 'guest worker' puzzling.

If you invite a guest into your home, you give him food and drink; you don't ask him to wash the dishes and clean the toilet. If he does do it, he is no longer a guest; he is your roommate.

A pedestrians' revolt in Doha gladdens me. I am waiting to cross the road with a crowd of around a hundred other pedestrians at an interminable traffic signal by the Corniche. The expensive mastodons of the Qataris zoom by: Land Rovers, Lexuses. The light doesn't change; it's been ten minutes. Then there's a momentary gap in the traffic, and a couple of the pedestrians, almost all migrant workers, step forward, followed by ten more, followed by twenty, and finally the whole mob rushes forward into the twelve lanes of the boulevard, whooping and dancing and laughing as the big cars screech to a halt and furiously honk and flash their lights. But there's nothing they can do short of run us over as we move forward, the ragged army, reclaiming land.

4

Two Sides of a Strait

TANGIER: WAITING FOR EL DORADO

All over the world, the ordinary heroes are on the move, whether it's in Central America, or Ghana, or other parts of sub-Saharan Africa. In summer 2018, I visited Europe's equivalent of the US–Mexican border – the straits that separate southern Spain from northern Morocco.

In 2017, Morocco rejoined the African Union after a thirty-three-year absence. It is now trying to set up Casablanca as the capital of Africa. Trade with west African countries is flourishing. And so is the human traffic across the border. You see them everywhere, the African migrants, speaking French or English rather than Arabic. Some invited by their hosts, others not. For many of them, of course, Morocco isn't a destination; it's a transit country. Sub-Saharan migration across the Mediterranean and into Spain jumped tenfold from 2016 to 2018. Morocco and Spain have negotiated a treaty that returns migrants attempting to cross over, which the two countries have held up as a diplomatic success.

There is a terrace overlooking the Mediterranean at the bottom of Tangier's old town where migrants from all over west Africa gather and look past the yachts toward the cliffs of Andalusia. Tangier is the last step of the long journey across Africa. You can see El Dorado, just 9 miles across the strait. It is here that I meet Khalil, a 26-year-old man from Conakry, the capital of Guinea. He and his wife have been in Tangier for nine months. Last week they had a baby boy, Isaca. Khalil is waiting until the baby is a month old to make the crossing.

Khalil's *pension* is just below and to the right of the terrace. As I climb up, a Moroccan man challenges us: Who am I? Why am I here? He wants to examine my bag, to extract his commission. All the other guests are African. On the wall of the landing, there's a tourist poster of the Tower of London.

Khalil takes me into his room, which has yellow walls and a bare light bulb, and shuts the door behind him. Three women are inside: his wife and two other African women, whom he introduces as his sister and his grandmother. On the floor is a plastic bottle of cooking oil, half an onion, and a pile of unwashed mugs in a pot. There's a small gas cylinder in the room, a clear fire hazard, and another one outside. They use the one in the room mostly to make tea. There are three beds, with brightly patterned polyester blankets lumped on them. It costs them €2.50 a night for the room.

Khalil's father died, and he has a little sister and a mother in Conakry and a brother in Belgium, who has a wife, who has papers and works cleaning houses. In Conakry, Khalil worked in a call centre. 'It's not easy,' they keep saying. The teachers in Conakry haven't been paid in three months, so they're on strike. But Khalil shows me pictures on his Facebook page of his life back in Conakry. There, too, people dress up, have parties, have fun, have a Facebook life.

Guinea's population lives in extreme poverty, but it is not a poor country. It has between a quarter and half of the world's bauxite reserves, and gold, and diamonds. A series of Western corporations, including Rio Tinto and a hedge fund named Och-Ziff Capital Management, have systematically exploited the country's enormous mineral wealth by 'negotiated' contracts with the country's leadership that siphon off an extortionate share of the profits.

According to a 2017 US Securities and Exchange Commission (SEC) complaint, Och-Ziff bribed Guinean officials to the tune of 'tens of millions', from 2007 to 2012. The previous year, the firm paid a $213 million criminal penalty to the US Justice Department and another $199 million fine to the SEC for corrupt practices in Africa. These were a slap on the wrist compared with the profits the company had made already. With these profits, Dan Och, the fund's chairman, bought an apartment at 220 Central Park South, the most expensive building in New York, where units sell for up to a quarter of a billion dollars. (He's kept his penthouse at 15 Central Park West, which is valued at $100 million.) Michael Cohen, an American who was the European head of Och-Ziff, bought a 900-acre estate in the English countryside. In 2018, US officials charged him with criminal fraud and bribery related to the hedge fund's African activities. (The case was later dismissed on a technicality: the statute of limitations had expired on the crime.) The money earned by Guinean locals is mainly accrued by the president and his many wives; and that money, too, follows the company profits out of the country. Every year, $150 billion leaves Africa for overseas tax havens.

It took Khalil and his wife two weeks to go from Guinea to Senegal to Mauritania to Morocco in a series of trucks. Sometimes the drivers would demand money or threaten to abandon their cargo in the desert. He travelled with sixteen people; at night the women slept in the truck and the men on the road. They had very little food, and only a small bottle of water they sipped from, not knowing how long it would last.

They arrived in Casablanca, stayed there for a week, and met an African smuggler, who convinced the two of them to give him €2,500 to cross into Spain. Then the smuggler disappeared with their money. 'His skin is black, but he's not African,' says Khalil, bitterly.

They moved north, to Tangier, and found a room with a Moroccan family. After a while, they couldn't make the rent and were kicked out. They found shelter with a Senegalese migrant who said, 'Join me in my room.' Then Khalil's wife found out that she was pregnant for the first time.

They had the baby in a Moroccan hospital, which treats blacks differently than it does Moroccans. Khalil's wife went into labour in the morning, so she went to the hospital, but was told that she had to wait until the evening to be admitted. She sat in the corridor all day, without anyone checking on her.

I am given Isaca, the five-day-old baby, to hold on my lap; there's none of the rigmarole of visitors washing their hands before touching the baby. He looks at me through rheumy eyes, fuzz from his foetal skin still on his cheeks. Such a wrinkly little thing, probably premature. He is overdressed and sneezes, but flexes with surprising strength as I hold him in my arms. It is hot, stiflingly hot; the window is jammed shut and there's a curtain over it, and the door leading to the corridor is kept closed. There are mosquitoes and bad air in the room with the baby.

The mother breastfeeds the child in full view of all of us. They need seven medicines for the baby and the mother. The Moroccan hospital delivered the baby for free but didn't give them medicines, which cost $90, money they don't have. The newborn hasn't seen a doctor.

Someone who crossed over to Spain with a baby earlier has told Khalil to buy a medicine at the pharmacy that will keep the baby quiet for the duration of the crossing, and to swaddle the baby tightly so the sea won't wet him. Khalil is intent on buying medicine that will keep the baby quiet for twenty-four hours. Fearing for the baby's life, I tell him not to do it.

They have to get a group of people together now and buy a boat, a plastic boat – the more money, the bigger the boat and the more powerful the motor. And they need to pay the captain and bribe the coastguard. If they are intercepted by the navy, they'll be picked up from the small boat and be put in the naval boat and brought back. If it's bad weather, they'll drown, like two of Khalil's friends did. None of the people in this room know how to swim. In 2016, for every forty-seven migrants who crossed the Mediterranean, one person died. Lately, the fatalities have been rising even higher: one out of every eighteen won't make it to shore. On the 9-mile ride, through dangerous currents, the migrants sing spiritual songs, praising and appealing to whatever gods they worship.

The coastguard will give them a sign and the navigational GPS signals, which they have to follow. The ideal time to cross over is Ramadan, which is coming up. Everyone is hungry, and the police spend much of the day sleeping. On the twenty-seventh day of Ramadan, the heavens open up and the Prophet ascends on his horse to heaven.

They know it's dangerous, they know they might die making the crossing; but when you've come this far, when you've crossed deserts and mountains, this is the final bit. Because you can see Spain, you can see your destination. Khalil wants to go to Europe. No matter the difficulties, he won't turn back, because, he says, 'my family needs my aid'.

In Belgium, Khalil would like to play professional football. In Conakry, he was a midfield attacker, number 9, in a second-division team. Khalil is not playing football here. He doesn't have the right shoes – he's wearing fake Crocs, and he doesn't have an outfit. He once tried to play football in a field, but Moroccans drove them off. So he can't play, he can't exercise, and at night the baby cries.

A friend and I have brought the family baby clothes, two boxes of them, and some others in a bag. Our gifts sit on the bed beside the mother, unopened. They will probably sell them. On the crossing, they will travel with just a knapsack each. Tangier is littered with discarded objects, shed by the migrants just before they cross.

Khalil calls the older woman his 'grandmother', but she's not the mother of either of his parents. She is in the same family as his mother and is planning to cross with them. It's unusual to find a woman her age – she could be in her sixties or seventies; it's hard to tell, because life has been hard on her – making the crossing. She blesses us for bringing the baby clothes.

Hawa, the younger woman, also turns out not to be Khalil's sister, but a cousin. She is twenty-nine years old. She has large lips, and wears a scarf over her head and a winter jacket. She speaks a little English; her husband studies English in Conakry. There, she 'sold things. On a little table.' She had to leave school after the tenth grade when she got pregnant. She couldn't get her diploma.

Hawa has four children, two boys and two girls, aged eight, six, four and one. Her husband can't find work, and the children are in the care of her mother. The one-year-old had his birthday yesterday. She called him. She shows me a picture on Facebook of her baby boy, dressed in a birthday outfit. I remember my eldest son's first birthday and what a production we made out of it by inviting 200 people to a restaurant in Lower Manhattan, how I went shopping for a dress for him, how Gautama, dressed like a medieval Italian prince, watched the American puppeteer who'd studied *kathputli* in Rajasthan for years as he manipulated the marionettes, all for the benefit of our little prince. It was, after all, his first birthday. Gautama didn't care. We did.

Hawa is on the verge of tears. 'I miss my children. It is hard. It is hard.'

What would it have been like, three weeks ago, on the day she got into the car, four people in the back, two in the front, to begin the long trek to Europe? How would she have said goodbye to the youngest one, knowing it might be years or decades before she saw him again?

'I want my children to learn. I want them to go to school. I want them to get a diploma.'

A man comes in with food for all of them, and he gives the change to Hawa; she must be paying for them now because she's the newest. She'll get to Europe somehow, she says.

Where will she stay?

'Anywhere.'

She says she wants to work.

What kind of work will she do?

'Work.' She doesn't say 'I'm going to Europe because the government will give me money'. She will do any kind of work. And then she will send for her children – she doesn't know when. 'I can't go back.'

She details the choice of passage. She could go on a lifeboat, the kind propelled by 'a small stick', she says, making rowing motions with her arms, which costs €500, or on a motorboat, which costs between €2,000 and €2,500.

I sense that there is some tension between her and the rest of the family. They say they will cross when the baby is strong, maybe in a month, two months.

'Not two months. Definitely not!' Hawa bursts out. 'Two or three weeks.'

'Three weeks,' says Khalil, tentatively.

As I walk back to my apartment, I pass two big yachts, one of them a five-masted sailing ship, all lit up and resting at harbour. I can see them from my balcony, coming and going at will. Tangier is a port city par excellence, from where Ibn Battuta sailed out to discover the world. The French, Spanish, Portuguese, British and finally the Americans took claim on this port, with its medina crawling up the hillsides. It's where Paul Bowles, William Burroughs and the Beat writers came to discover themselves. They could come here, as expats, and live here for as long or as little as they liked, and go back, or die here, as they chose.

TARIFA: AN AFRICAN MAKES A HOME IN EUROPE

Flashing my American passport, I get on a fast, comfortable ferry from Tangier, at the tip of Africa, and disembark on the continent of Europe an hour later. Tarifa is known, thanks to the wind whipping around the southernmost tip of Europe, as the finest kitesurfing destination on the continent. You can see the kite surfers zooming across the water, the golden flowers of Europe, for whom the sea isn't a graveyard but a vacationland on which to play daredevil. On shore, topless white women sun themselves on white-sand beaches. After every full moon – prime crossing time of the month – debris from the migrants' boats washes up on the same beaches, objects discarded when the boat takes on water or life-jackets hurriedly thrown off after the migrants make it to land.

Many of the young Spanish girls walk around Tarifa sporting the same braided, African-style hair. The source is in the back of a lively shop selling clothes and tourist souvenirs. Her name is Favoui, and she's from Nigeria. She wears a white bandanna around the multicoloured braids that adorn her head and has an easy smile.

I ask her how old she is.

'Well, now I'm forty-one,' she says laughing. 'I don't want to say it!'

There are giraffe masks on the wall of the shop, and Indian and African garments for sale, mostly for tourists. Two young Spanish women, voluptuous, come in for their hair-braiding appointment. They are white, and their hair is black and blue. Favoui attends to them, and an hour later they walk out looking, or at least feeling, like Amber Rose or Kim Kardashian.

Favoui is from Delta State in Nigeria. She comes from a polyg-amous home. Her father was in the air force, and she had a lot of brothers. She lived well as a child, but then her parents separated and Favoui lived with her mother.

As a young woman, Favoui would see the people from her vil-lage who'd gone to Europe drive back to the village in their big cars. Living in her shack, made of tarpaulin and mud, she would see the houses that the migrants built for their parents, made of wood and brick. So, she thought, 'I have to go to Europe'.

This desire begins early, she tells me. In Nigeria, children of four-teen or fifteen leave the village to go to Europe. They hear their friends talk about life there, and they pick up and go; sometimes, they don't even tell their parents they're going. The smugglers tell the young men, they can go to Europe and pay when they get there. They make them sign oaths, cut their wrists, and do a blood ritual. They tell them their soul will be stolen if they don't pay.

Delta is the richest oil-producing state in Nigeria, but the local people don't see much of the money or the oil. Favoui recalls growing up without lights. Sometimes there would be no electricity for days. 'Three days, no light. Four days, no light.' But closer to the end of the month, just before the bill was due, the company would switch on the electricity for two or three hours and make their customers pay. After they did, the power cuts would begin again.

So anyone who could afford it had a generator and either bought fuel or stole it from the pipelines transporting the wealth of their state out of it. 'You have to have this thing that makes you to have light.' But the generators were extremely dangerous 'because people buy the most cheapest one, and they don't even know how to use it, and a lot of houses get burnt. Children, parents, get burnt.'

It happened in her village often. Favoui remembers a family who had left their generator on in the kitchen at night while they slept, because it was really hot in the summer and they needed the fan. But the generator leaked carbon monoxide, and the family fell asleep. 'They were breathing and breathing and breathing, and the next morning, they were all dead.'

The Nigerian Delta is where, four years before Favoui left, the Nigerian government executed Ken Saro-Wiwa and eight other activists who had led a non-violent campaign against the Shell oil company. The giant Anglo-Dutch conglomerate has been drilling in the area since 1958 and has extracted over $30 billion in oil. Very little of it goes to the people living in the states across which Shell's pipelines run, where much of the area has been reduced to a vast wasteland of oil spills, bereft of virtually all fish or wildlife. In 2017, Amnesty International uncovered documents pointing to Shell's complicity in the Nigerian military's murder, rape and torture of citizens who were opposed to the multinational's plunder of its oil wealth.

In 1999, Favoui left her village to set out for Europe. She travelled with a group of migrants in a 4x4 through several countries and ended up in the Sahara, going from village to village. The Tuaregs, men with scarves around their faces, hid them in a series of houses. 'If you were lucky, they came back for you.' There were bandits everywhere. Occasionally, their convoy would be intercepted by the police, who would tell the smugglers, 'If you don't want us to arrest everybody, we need some ladies tonight.' So the smugglers would go inside and pick out some of the women from the convoy to be given to the police, as bribe or sacrifice.

She was in Morocco for over a year. Her first son was born in Rabat. One night the police came to the hotel where she and other migrants were staying in Tangier. She had overstayed her six-month visa and was now illegal. The police burst in and 'everybody started running'. They ran up to the roof and a couple of them jumped over the narrow alleyway to the adjoining roof. But one of them didn't make it; he fell into the alleyway and died.

Favoui was held in a detention centre in Morocco for four days along with her baby. Some of the prison wardens felt pity for her and brought milk for the baby. Since her son had been born in Morocco and was a Moroccan citizen, she wasn't arrested and deported and could move around Tangier relatively freely. Other female migrants would sometimes borrow her baby to walk to the market. 'Every day is a story, every day is a life.'

Another of the migrant women had just had a baby Favoui would play with. After Favoui crossed, the woman followed. She met Favoui in Tarifa and silently held out her arms, empty. It had been a dark night when she'd crossed. The smugglers made the migrants wade out to the boat waiting at sea. She put her legs in the sea, holding her baby. A wave came.

Favoui thought she would cross through the Spanish enclaves of Ceuta and Melilla, which are on the Moroccan mainland. In the beginning, it was easy, and they didn't have to brave the sea. 'It's only the barbed wire. We wait when the army is sleeping in their cots, and everybody starts running over the wire.' But then another wall of barbed wire sprang up around the enclaves, and a third. And now it's like *The Hunger Games*: men run towards the triple fence on dark nights and attempt to climb it. On the other end they find Spanish policemen waiting for them with clubs. Only the strongest make it across all three fences, and through the wall of policemen; if they make it past them, they're in Europe and can claim asylum.

When Ceuta and Melilla became tougher to cross into, the migrants started going with the fishermen, through Las Palmas into Tarifa.

The night Favoui crossed, she was with her eleven-month-old son and three months pregnant with her second son. She was in a group of migrants, taken by the smugglers over the Rif mountains and then to the sea at one or two in the morning, guided only by the light of the moon. They got to the boat, which had an African pilot. Some of the pilots have experience steering a boat; others don't but claim they do. In return, they don't have to pay the smugglers for their passage. Favoui had no idea if her captain had any experience or not. Plus, a boat meant for seven often carries forty or fifty people. In the open ocean, it could start sinking.

On the boat, she was one of two women, along with a bunch of men: Senegalese, Moroccans, Algerians. The boat went into the strait and started taking on water. 'Everybody was shouting *"Ha'Allah … ha'Allah hakku barrum navahal quai"*.' When she heard that, she started crying. 'Oh my God! Have mercy on me! Forgive me my sins! Save my baby!' The water kept coming, and people started throwing their possessions overboard, and taking their clothes off, to make the boat lighter. It was very early in the morning now, and the captain tried to steer the boat toward the Spanish coast, avoiding inhabited places. If they got to the beach, they would have to start running.

But before they got to the coast, they found themselves surrounded by Spanish police boats and a helicopter. They had come to rescue them because they saw the boat drowning. '*Niño?*' they asked. 'Baby?'

So Favoui raised her hand. She was pregnant, vomiting. They took her to the mainland, to a shelter, gave her food and a medical check-up, and then took her to the closest city, Algeciras. There, after being briefly detained, she stayed for a couple of years and asked for and got political asylum, which was much easier to obtain than it is now. Then she moved to Tarifa and made a living selling trinkets and souvenirs on the streets of the tourist town. She also attended school and learned Spanish.

The local community helped her a lot, and she made friends. She got odd jobs cleaning houses, taking care of the parks, and working in restaurants in the evenings. It was difficult doing all this with two little children at home. So she had to pay for someone to babysit them, for €300 a month. Another €900 went for rent, and at the end of the month she was left with nothing.

Then she discovered that Spanish girls actually liked their hair African-style, and she offered her services. People around town got to know her; the summer visitors got to know her. Along with hair braiding, she started making necklaces and buying gaily decorated African scarves and selling them.

Seven years after Favoui crossed, her husband joined her, and he now manages a campground in Tarifa. Their two boys are now eighteen and sixteen. The elder one is studying sports medicine in college and the younger son wants to study dentistry. After her husband came, she gave birth to a daughter, who will soon be eight.

She knows many people who go back home to visit. But Favoui has never been back, even after she acquired legal status in Spain. When she heard of her father's death, she was very depressed and cried a lot. 'Because he never see his grandchildren, because of my wrong decision.' Afterwards, she said to herself, 'I'm going back with everybody,' but she never had enough money.

Through it all, through the selling of things on the sidewalk, through the raising of three children, Favoui sent money back to her family in Nigeria. Since she opened this shop last year, her expenses have gone up, and it's become harder to send money.

So she'll send €100 now and then to her mother, when she can, or €50. With the money she remitted, her mother could build a proper house and take care of Favoui's siblings. Favoui is paying the bill for her brother's university education. According to World Bank estimates, the twenty-five million emigrants from sub-Saharan Africa remitted $37 billion in 2017; Nigerians alone sent back $22 billion.

Meanwhile, Favoui is establishing a bit of Africa in Tarifa. Beautiful paintings hang on the wall of her shop, made by a Senegalese friend who lives in the town. She tries to help him out by showcasing his work, which her customers can buy. 'Because we are trying to make the shop the Africa Home.'

You can tell from the way her customers interact with her that she is adored by the Spaniards in the town. She feels lucky and happy. 'When I came, the first people I met, they were really so hospitable with me.' That convinced her to stay in Tarifa. She has felt racism; she knows it when she sees it, she knows it exists here too. But she feels that the town has taken her in. 'They help me a lot because I have no brother, no sister, for seven years no husband, nobody. So they are all my family, just like I have my family here.' When she has an evening off, she'll go to a Jehovah's Witness meeting in Algeciras.

In spite of the glow on her face, Favoui's body has finally caught up with her years of toil. She has arthritis. 'I can tell in the body, because when I get home, all the body pays, because now I'm a little bit sick here since I've been working in the streets for twelve years. I have this problem of the bones. I have to take the injections every three weeks. Because before, I never take care of myself. When it was in the cold season, I sell the scarves on the street. So I have to wear my jacket and sit there, because it is when I sell. When it is summer, I am always there ... So I try to be more positive, but sometimes I feel more down because I think of all my journey and I ask myself, "How can I be sick now?" There are some times I cannot even open my hands.'

She works seven days a week; the store is open from noon to 9.30 p.m. But just last week her older son said, 'Mama, you never take time off to be with us.'

'That touched me,' Favoui recalls. 'So now I try to spend Friday with them.' But it's Friday today, and she's still working – she's selling stuff in the store, she's braiding hair.

The popular image of Spain is that of a country where people take two-hour lunches and then a siesta for another hour or two, and stay out eating and drinking until past midnight. We don't think of Favoui, working until she develops arthritis so that the pleasure seekers can seek their pleasure. She needs Spain because her region of Nigeria has been robbed of its future; but what is equally true is that Spain needs Favoui, and her industriousness, to ensure its future.

'Have you ever taken a vacation?' I ask.

She laughs.

PART II
Why They're Coming

5

Colonialism

When migrants move, it's not out of idle fancy, or because they hate their homelands, or to plunder the countries they come to, or even (most often) to strike it rich. They move – as my grandfather knew – because the accumulated burdens of history have rendered their homelands less and less habitable. They are here because you were there.

Consider the subcontinent. For 5,000 years we had been one people, ruled undivided from the borders of Persia to China by emperors from Ashoka to Akbar. Within this territory, boundaries formed, expanded, dissolved, merged. Periodically, parts of us broke off into independent kingdoms or suzerainties and then came back together. We were a nation of many different countries.

Then the British came and ruled us for 200 years by pitting us against each other so that we couldn't be pitted against them, and now for seventy years we have been split into three nations, between which it is nearly impossible to travel. And the governments of all three nations emphasize how 'we' are so different from the others. One Friday evening during the fiftieth anniversary year of Partition, in 1997, I went to Wagah, the only land border crossing between India and Pakistan, to see the flag ceremony, which attracts people from both sides. I had heard it was a big draw, and I wanted to know why.

Well before sundown, the crowds started assembling. They were people from the surrounding villages as well as tourists from farther off, people dressed for a holiday, bringing along their children and picnic baskets. All around the border post, café chairs abounded under umbrellas sporting, in between the Pepsi logos, the patriotic slogan '*Mera Bharat Mahaan*' – 'My India Is Great'. Very loud Hindi film music was blaring from the Indian loudspeakers, for which the lyrics might have been patriotic, but it was being played at the wrong speeds, so it was difficult to know. This was answered from the Pakistani side with the following robust refrain:

> Pakistan is ours
> We are all Pakistani
> Pakistan! Pakistan! Pakistan!

The barracks of the Indian Border Security Force (BSF) were decorated with its logo, 'Duty unto Death'. This was next to a rack of rifles and a full-length mirror adorned on top with a bright red query: 'Am I looking smart?' The BSF soldiers spent much time in front of it attempting to answer the mirror's question. They resembled nothing so much as roosters, with a red-and-white comb adorning their turbans and white socks that went halfway over their polished black shoes. There was much good-natured shoving back and forth between the crowd of spectators, who moved forward inch by inch, and the soldiers, who tried vainly to hold their ground.

Then the drill sergeants on both sides called out, and the parade began. One of the BSF soldiers and, on the other side, one of the Pakistani Rangers, dressed in black *salwar-kameezes*, strode right up to the gate so rapidly that it seemed they must collide violently. But at the last minute, they stopped an inch from each other, thrust their jaws and chest out, hooked their thumbs in their belt loops, abruptly turned at right angles to each other, and goose-stepped away. Successive pairs of soldiers repeated this performance, a kind of strutting bravado, a jointly choreographed imitation of war.

Finally, twin trumpeters played 'Retreat', both flags were lowered slowly down a pair of crossed ropes – when they intersected on their downward path, both groups of spectators applauded vigorously – and the soldiers let the crowds rush to the fence. Hundreds of us ran up to the gate; there was tremendous excitement, and when I was at the gate, I could see why: if I stood up and looked, I could see, separated by an eight-foot gap, *Pakistanis*! I saw them all: Pathans in their knotted turbans, madrassa students with their skullcaps, the women in their *salwar-kameezes*; Baluchis, Sindhis, Punjabis. So we looked at them, we Indian Gujaratis, Kannadigas, Punjabis, Bengalis, and were amazed to see that they looked just like us.

But we were forbidden by the soldiers to touch each other, or talk to each other. We could not even wave at each other. Those who tried to wave had their hands slapped down by the soldiers – national secrets might be given away by hand signals. But we could take pictures. The only people in the gap between the two gates, the eight-foot-wide no-man's-land, were two Japanese tourists with video cameras, turning their lenses on both sides indiscriminately. So we smiled at each other and took pictures with our little compact cameras. The massed ranks of Indians and Pakistanis, men and women and babies, on this Friday evening in May, when the sun was finally beginning to show mercy on the thirsty earth of Punjab, looked and gaped at each other and made contact by smiling.

Afterward, some of us who got special permission from the soldiers were allowed to walk to the Pillar, an obelisk set in the ground a few yards away from the gate, where Indians and Pakistanis can come close without a fence separating them, but still not touch or talk. Years later, at Friendship Park, I thought back to this moment, this other sanctuary spot. It had felt, oddly, more humane, more permeable.

The soldiers stood around with their backs to each other, mostly, and then someone on the Pakistani side talked to one of the Rangers, and he shyly came up to a friendly Indian soldier. The Indian checked to see if his superiors were watching, turned around, and then the two enemy soldiers were both standing together grinning for the Pakistani tourist's camera. 'Is this India? Is this Pakistan?' the tourists wanted to know again and again, asking the soldiers to point out precisely where the boundary is, what country this farmland belongs to, what country the obelisk belongs to, what country those trees and this piece of ground belong to.

In August 1947, the British left the subcontinent, leaving behind two countries: the secular state of India; and Pakistan, which defined itself as a Muslim state and was composed of Punjab, Sindh, the North-West Frontier Province, Baluchistan and the eastern part of Bengal. After the exchange of populations was over, 11 per cent of India was still Muslim, but most Hindus and Sikhs had left Pakistan.

Even at the peak of the empire, the British ruled the vast subcontinent with a relatively small force. They could stay in power because they deliberately followed a policy of 'divide and rule', sowing discord among the various religious groups of the subcontinent and showing special favour to the Muslim League to weaken the nationalist movement and extend their rule in India as much as possible. The partition of the entire subcontinent was foreshadowed by the 1905 partition of Bengal into the Muslim-majority East Bengal and the Hindu-majority West Bengal. This policy was further pursued in the setting up of separate electorates for minority groups. Thus, the 1932 Communal Award set up separate electorates and constituencies for, among others, Muslims, Sikhs, Christians, tribals, untouchables, women, organized labour, businessmen, landlords and academics.

Partition was an idea that was hatched in England among a group of elite Indian Muslims who wanted a separate homeland for the subcontinent's Muslims, whose rights, they believed, would not be protected in a majority-Hindu India. The ultimate effect of these intellectual propositions advanced at sparkling London dinner parties was that the common people back home saw the human beings they most loved – their small children, their mothers – slaughtered before their eyes. They were atrocities of the worst sort; people were killed in the worst way: roasted alive in their homes, clubbed to death with hockey sticks, hacked with swords, and left to rot in the heat; women were raped in the worst way, with their daughters and their fathers forced to watch.

Patrick Spens, the chief justice of the Federal Court of India and the chairman of the 1947 Arbitral Tribunal, was interviewed in London in 1963 about Partition. He was asked, 'What were the causes of the bloodshed which followed the transfer of power?' Lord Spens replied, 'The main cause was the haste with which we parted with India. The connections of centuries were severed within days without any proper thought ... The Labour government here wanted to get rid of India as quickly as possible.'

In 1947, the British, having successfully ruled India for over 200 years, were desperate to leave. They sent down a barrister named Sir Cyril Radcliffe and gave him five weeks to draw two lines down a map, separating a population of 400 million along religious lines. He knew nothing about the region; he had never been there and couldn't wait to get out. In the weeks before and after independence, people near the border didn't know on which side they'd be; whether they'd be living in Muslim-, Hindu- or Sikh-majority areas. So they fell upon each other, to drive the minorities out, in India and in Pakistan. Fourteen and a half million people had to leave everything and move across Radcliffe's lines in a matter of weeks – the greatest mass migration in history.

The actual handover was done in haste, and the bloodshed that followed represented a gigantic failure of control by the British-led army and police forces. It was also a disastrous lack of foresight on the part of Lord Mountbatten, the last viceroy, and his superiors in London. Two million people died in the ensuing violence. And Radcliffe's lines might come back to imperil the entire planet. Two of the three countries that the British created through their map making are nuclear powers. They have gone to war three times since independence and are at constant risk of a fourth and final war.

The two countries also spend an inordinate amount of their GDP (2.5 per cent for India and 3.5 per cent for Pakistan, versus 1.8 per cent for the UK) on buying arms to fight each other instead of feeding their people. The legacy of that botched map making haunts the two billion people of the region today: the various communal outbreaks in the subcontinent are directly traceable to that colossal and premature sundering those seventy years ago. Much of the hunger and civil strife that persists in south Asia today has its origins in Partition. Here, as in so many places where Western colonialism changed the maps, there continues to be massive migration within and outside the region.

In 2015, Shashi Tharoor, the former UN undersecretary general for communications and public information, gave a compelling Oxford Union speech that made the case for (symbolic) reparations owed by Britain to India. 'India's share of the world economy when Britain arrived on its shores [at the beginning of the eighteenth century] was 23 per cent. By the time the British left [in 1947], it was down to below 4 per cent. Why?' he asked. 'Simply because India had been governed for the benefit of Britain. Britain's rise for 200 years was financed by its depredations in India.' Meanwhile, just over the Himalayas, the British sent in gunboats to open up China for its traders during the Opium Wars. China was flooded with foreign goods, and its share of world GDP gradually sank from a high of 33 per cent in 1820 to a low of 5 per cent in 1978.

No museums in the UK are devoted to Britain's colonial past. The British would rather celebrate their achievements in the two world wars. If the empire resurfaces at all in British TV or movies, it's cloaked in sepia-hazed nostalgia. Let's look at its real colours.

In 1770, the British East India Company – the world's first multinational corporation – increased the taxes it forcibly collected on crops, and ten million people, a third of Bengal, starved to death. Another twenty-nine million Indians under British rule died of famines in the nineteenth century, partly because India was forced to export ten million tons of food a year. It's a global period that the American writer Mike Davis calls 'the late Victorian holocaust'. Then, in 1942, the British, fearing a Japanese invasion of eastern India, stopped the importation of rice from Burma. They also destroyed existing stocks of rice under a policy called 'denial of rice'. Australian ships carrying grain were diverted to the Balkans, to prepare for a future invasion of Greece. The next year, more than two million people starved; many others were lost to the diseases that followed. Altogether, between three million and five million people died in that British-made famine.

My father, who was a boy growing up in Calcutta at that time, remembers the mothers with babies sucking at their withered teats in the street below our house; the soundscape in Calcutta was a continuous chant, 'Mother, some rice gruel?' The British had reduced them to begging, not for rice, but for the leftover water from boiling the rice.

A revisionist view of the British Empire is making the rounds these days. According to the Stanford historian Niall Ferguson, 'No organization in history has done more to promote the free movement of goods, capital and labour than the British Empire ... And no organization has done more to impose Western norms of law, order and governance around the world.' Bruce Gilley at Portland State University published a paper, in the leftist journal *Third World Quarterly*, of all places, titled 'The Case for Colonialism'.

> For the last 100 years, Western colonialism has had a bad name. It is high time to question this orthodoxy. Western colonialism was, as a general rule, both objectively beneficial and subjectively legitimate in most of the places where it was found ... Colonialism can be recovered by weak and fragile states today in three ways: by reclaiming colonial modes of governance; by recolonizing some areas; and by creating new Western colonies from scratch.

After an outcry, *Third World Quarterly* withdrew Gilley's paper, but he soon found a defender in Nigel Biggar at Oxford. Biggar called Gilley's paper a 'balanced reappraisal of the colonial past' and called for 'us British to moderate our post-imperial guilt'. Biggar also announced that he would be starting an academic project at Oxford called Ethics and Empire, to question the notion that 'imperialism is wicked; and empire is therefore unethical'. It would also develop 'a Christian ethic of empire'.

It's no wonder that even though the empire isn't the first thing that today's Brits associate with their country's past, 59 per cent of Britons surveyed in 2014 thought the British Empire is 'something to be proud of'. A third of those surveyed would like it if Britain still had an empire.

Winston Churchill loathed Nazis and Indians, and tried to kill as many of both as possible. 'I hate Indians. They are a beastly people with a beastly religion,' Churchill said. The Indians deserved the 1943 famine, he said, because they were 'breeding like rabbits'. As the Cambridge historians Christopher Bayly and Tim Harper note, 'The prime minister believed that Indians were the next worst people in the world after the Germans. Their treachery had been plain in the Quit India movement. The Germans he was prepared to bomb into the ground. The Indians he would starve to death as a result of their own folly and viciousness.'

In another region ruled by the British, Churchill had advocated using chemical weapons against rebellious Iraqis. 'I am strongly in favour of using poisoned gas against uncivilized tribes,' he declared. Along with the earlier Sykes–Picot Agreement of 1916 – a secret agreement between France and the UK to carve up south-western Asia among themselves – Churchill bears much of the responsibility for creating the modern Middle East, amalgamating people at war with each other and forcing them to live behind arbitrary borders. According to the Churchill scholar Warren Dockter, 'he is largely responsible for how Jordan and Iraq were divided up'. When he was colonial secretary, he also had a principal role in creating the most enduring border issue of the modern era. 'Churchill literally created the kingdom of Jordan, for example, and the original Palestinian mandate,' notes Dockter.

In all, 40 per cent of all the national borders in the entire world today were made by just two countries: Britain and France. The case of Africa was even worse than south Asia and the Middle East. After shipping off slaves, after plundering its resources, the colonizers left, drawing up borders that had almost no relevance to the tribal nations that the continent was composed of. Just look at a map of Africa now. It abounds in straight lines. These lines vivisected the motherlands of hundreds of tribes. The authors of a 2015 study in the *American Economic Review* identified 357 groups that were split by these colonial boundaries. 'In the majority of cases, Europeans did not consider ethnic features and local geography in the design of colonial borders,' the authors note. As a result, many of the tribes have been in constant conflict with each other in their desire to regather into a single nation; incidents of political violence were 57 per cent higher in the partitioned homelands than in the intact ones, the study found. These conflicts are fuelled with arms sold to them by the former colonizers. And by the multinational corporations that replaced the governments.

In country after country, the British committed mass atrocities, which are now minimized by revisionist historians like Ferguson and Gilley. But there is another history: the one remembered by the people who were its victims. During the Mau Mau guerrilla movement for Kenyan independence, my grandfather was dragooned into working as a cook for a concentration camp where the British held the rebels. One day he happened upon a large pit lined with black bodies. 'They threw them in, like dogs,' he remembered. The British imprisoned and tortured 150,000 Kenyans in these camps.

He also remembered the Stanley Hotel in Nairobi, which had a sign during World War II: 'No dogs or Indians allowed.' One day a Sikh officer in the British army strode in. He was in Africa to fight for the king. But he was Indian, and so the white officers demanded that he be ejected. The guards advanced upon the Sikh. He drew his pistol. 'I die, you die,' he said. The empire that he was ready to sacrifice his life for on the battlefield wouldn't allow him into its clubs because of the colour of his skin. 'I die, you die,' he said, and the colour bar was lifted for him, out of fear of what it would do for morale on the part of the Indian troops.

My grandfather related this story to me with pride. The Sikh was risking his life, but he would no longer take the everyday humiliations that my grandfather had to endure all the time that he was working as a salesman for a Scottish trading company in Kenya. Later, when he was living in London, he took pride in sending me lists of the richest Indians in the UK, some of them richer even than the Queen.

Towards the end of the Age of Empire, European countries began importing huge numbers of migrants from the former colonies to work in their factories and at low-wage jobs that their own people didn't want to do. The French recruited over 200,000 labourers from north Africa, Indochina and Madagascar during World War I to work behind the lines. But still there weren't enough, so European countries looked beyond the states they'd colonized. Britain recruited 100,000 Chinese contract labourers and France 40,000 to dig trenches and collect the bodies of dead soldiers. After three years, they were expected to go back to China. But 3,000 of them couldn't, because they had been killed. Thousands more died of flu and dysentery. It wasn't even their war.

The recruiting really stepped up in the postwar era, because so many men of working age had been killed. In 1951 there were around 157,000 immigrants (only 20,000 of them non-white) from Britain's former colonies in the country. In ten years, there were over four times as many, the vast majority of them non-white.

Not many people outside France realize that most of the north Africans living in France today are children or grandchildren of French citizens. France conquered Algeria in 1848 and made all

Algerians French citizens in 1947. It turned Morocco and Tunisia into 'protectorates'. In 1962, after an incredibly bloody war, in which it's been estimated that over a million Algerians died, France finally left, leaving the newly independent country to pick up the pieces. Over a million Algerians, white and Arab, moved to France in the years after because the Algerian economy was in tatters.

But there was a problem. Citizens though the north Africans may have been, France had badly neglected to educate them. When France left Algeria in 1962, 85 per cent of the population was illiterate. When they moved, they carried their illiteracy with them: 35 per cent of the male migrants and 45 per cent of the females had never attended school. There were no jobs for them, and they were shunted into the *banlieues* outside French cities. North Africans are now blamed for everything from shoplifting to terrorism in today's France.

The French have never really got used to the presence of Arabs among them. I once spent a summer in Tours and became friends with a genial university student from Morocco named Mustafa. He was fond of reading Derrida and liked to cook; he was the friendliest man in Tours. One day he was waiting at a bus stop next to a mother and a small boy playing with a football. The boy kicked the ball over to Mustafa, who moved the ball this way and that with his feet, and kicked it back to him. Then he watched as the mother slapped her son across the face, shouting at him, 'Don't play with a dirty Arab!' She gathered up the ball and dragged her son away, leaving Mustafa standing alone at the bus stop.

The impact of the French colonial project extended well beyond Africa. France and the rest of Europe were shocked when Toussaint-Louverture led the first successful slave rebellion in the Americas, in 1791 in Haiti. In return for accepting its former colony as a sovereign nation in 1825, France demanded, with gunboats aimed at the island, 150 million gold francs (later magnanimously reduced to 90 million, around $40 billion today). The country paid, to

American and French banks, and paid, through earthquakes and hurricanes, until 1947.

The extortionate payments wrecked Haiti's economic progress and were instrumental in reducing it to being the poorest country in the Americas. As a result, millions of Haitians have had to migrate in search of work to the Dominican Republic, where they are systematically discriminated against and, periodically, violently purged. A million Haitians have migrated to the United States, and sizeable numbers have gone to other countries such as Canada, France and Chile. In 2003, the Haitian president, Jean-Bertrand Aristide, asked France for $21 billion in reparations. The French shrugged.

What about America? 'The United States was not a colonizer,' people claim. 'Unless you count the Philippines. We were a colony ourselves.'

In 1848, Mexico was forced to cede half its territory to its northern neighbour, including most of what is now California, New Mexico, Arizona, Nevada and Utah, and parts of Colorado, Wyoming, Kansas and Oklahoma. The official name of the agreement was the Treaty of Peace, Friendship, Limits and Settlement between the United States of America and the Mexican Republic. In March 2017, Cuauhtémoc Cárdenas, a Mexican politician, teamed up with a lawyer named Guillermo Hamdan to draw up legal arguments that would nullify the treaty and charge the United States for the 168 years that it had ruled over this territory. They have a point. Just look at the names of the territory: Nevada. California. Colorado. 'Take back your country' is a slogan that could, therefore, equally be adopted by Latinos as well as whites.

As we've seen, migration from poor countries to rich ones is often the inevitable result of colonial depredation. But how exactly did the colonizers rob the colonies? First, they looted the treasuries of the native kings. Hence, the Indian Koh-i-Noor diamond in the crown jewels. Second, they imposed extortionate taxes on their subjects. Third, they forced the subjects to grow crops like cotton but prevented them from setting up industries that could turn the cotton into textiles; this was saved for the industries back in the home country. Thus, the mills in Manchester spun Indian cotton into cloth, which was then sold back to Indians at massive mark-ups, mark-ups which Indians had to pay because they were prevented from starting their own textile factories. (This is why Gandhi's spinning wheel wasn't just a powerful symbol; it was also a strikingly effective form of economic warfare against the British, because it gave every Indian a little textile factory in their own home.)

Fourth, they forced the colonial armies to fight their wars, both within and without – most famously, the Gurkhas of Nepal, some of whom continue to serve in the British Army. Until recently, they were not allowed to settle in the UK and their pensions were lower than those of their fellow British soldiers. There were also north Africans – the 'Army of Africa' – that the French had dragooned into fighting in the Crimea, the Franco-Prussian War, the two world wars, its post-WWI occupation of the German Rhineland, and its savage war in Algeria. The Dutch had their Moluccans, whom they marshalled in the Royal Dutch East Indies Army, to fight their fellow Indonesians so that the Dutch could keep ruling.

But there's very little acknowledgement of their service today in the colonizing countries. The film *Dunkirk*, for example, completely airbrushes out the role of the many Commonwealth soldiers who fought on that beach, including four companies of the Royal Indian Army Service Corps. 'Observers said they were particularly cool under fire and well-organized during the retreat,' notes the historian John Broich. 'Their appearance in the film would have provided a good reminder of how utterly central the role of the Indian Army was in the war. Their service meant the difference between victory and defeat.' Altogether, 2.5 million Indian soldiers fought for their masters in the Second World War, and 90,000 of them died in the process, without recognition or thanks.

Colonialism began with a huge migration, when millions of Europeans moved overseas to invade, settle and rule other countries.

When Columbus arrived in the Americas in 1492, there were up to 100 million people living on the continent. Within 150 years, there were only 3.5 million. They died of imported diseases or starvation, or were massacred by the colonizers.

The London School of Economics anthropologist Jason Hickel observes that what the Europeans were after was not so much gold but silver. Nearly 18,000 tons of silver were shipped to Europe between 1503 and 1660, three times the total European reserves of the metal. By the early 1800s, that total had risen to 110,000 tons. At 5 per cent interest, Hickel notes, this would amount to a debt of $165 trillion that Europe owes Latin America today.

After silver came slaves – fifteen million Africans were kidnapped or purchased from local slavers and shipped across the Atlantic. 'In the North American colonies alone,' Hickel writes, 'Europeans extracted an estimated 222,505,049 hours of forced labour from African slaves between 1619 and 1865. Valued at the US minimum wage, with a modest rate of interest, that's worth $97 trillion – more than the entire global GDP.'

The rise of Britain was inextricably linked to slavery. It shipped Africans to its American colonies, where they toiled in cotton and sugar cane fields to make money for the empire. In the sugar mills the slaves worked eighteen hours at a time. 'Slave-owning planters, and merchants who dealt in slaves and slave produce, were among the richest people in eighteenth-century Britain,' says the historian Robin Blackburn. 'Profits from these activities helped to endow All Souls College, Oxford, with a splendid library, to build a score of banks, including Barclays, and to finance the experiments of James Watt, inventor of the first really efficient steam engine.'

The Industrial Revolution in Britain would not have been possible without profits from the slave trade, argues Blackburn. Around 1770, Britain earned £450 million (in today's terms) a year from slavery; total domestic investments, including the infrastructure needed for industry, came to £500 million.

From 1761 to 1808, the British took 1,428,000 Africans away from their families and shipped them across the world. From this monstrous crime, they amassed £8 billion in today's money. Britain officially ended slavery in 1833. Its Caribbean slaves were set free, for a price: they would have to work forty-five hours a week for another four to six years for their former masters, as 'apprentices', without pay.

Even after Britain exited the Atlantic slave trade and abolished slavery in its colonies, it continued to benefit from slave labour. 'As late as 1860,' writes Blackburn, 'six million slaves toiled in the fields of the American South, Cuba and Brazil, producing vast quantities of cotton, sugar and coffee. The thousands of millions of hours of slave toil helped to underpin the global ascendancy of Victorian Britain ... Britain got off to a good start at the time of the Industrial Revolution, and Britons today still enjoy a consequent afterglow of prosperity.'

Meanwhile, in Congo, Belgium's King Leopold went looking for rubber and ivory and ended up murdering ten million people. Congolese children whose parents could not meet their quota of rubber for their Belgian masters were arrested, and their hands and feet chopped off in front of their parents. In fifty years of Belgian rule, from the 1870s to the 1920s, the population of Congo halved.

Congo's political situation since has been chaotic, and remains so today. It has suffered from a combination of chronically bad governance and wholesale looting by Western multinationals. But Portland State's Gilley is of the opinion that 'maybe the Belgians should come back.'

All told, in the colonial period, Europeans increased their share of global GDP from 20 to 60 per cent, Hickel points out. 'Europe didn't develop the colonies. The colonies developed Europe.' The Scottish comedian Frankie Boyle sums it up: 'We fear the arrival of immigrants that we have drawn here with the wealth we stole from them.'

6

The New Colonialism

Of course, the colonizers aren't responsible for every bad thing that is now happening in the former colonies; some of it is our own damn fault. Many of the issues that make people emigrate are home-grown: corruption, malfeasance and mismanagement by local rulers; and inherent societal issues that preceded colonialism, such as the treatment of women.

When the colonialists left, they set up structures of governance that worked well some of the time, not so well at other times. After the British left the subcontinent, Pakistan and Bangladesh cycled through a series of military governments and corrupt civilian politicians. The army stayed out of Indian politics but many of the democratically elected politicians failed the country miserably.

There's a backlash against secular intellectuals in India these days, and the favourite canard that's levelled at them by the Hindu nationalists is that they're imposing Western values on Indian civilization. As with the neonationalists in Poland or Hungary, there's a wholesale rejection of Western liberal democratic values as a foreign intervention – whether the agent is George Soros or Greenpeace.

So, it's complicated. The colonizers did not practise these liberal values when they ruled our countries; but they are certainly worth adhering to in principle – whether they come from within or without. Yet the sorry history of colonialism renders anything associated with them suspect, and the baby gets thrown out with the bathwater.

In any case, colonialism isn't over. It is, like Faulkner's definition of the past, not even past yet. Corporate colonialism is the new colonialism. When the colonial regimes withdrew their soldiers and viceroys, they replaced them with their businessmen. You see them in the five-star hotels in the capitals, and in the foreigners' compounds, living exactly as their imperial forebears did, except there are a few black and brown faces in the country club these days, creamed off from the population that they now rule over jointly.

I realized this when I went to Bhopal in 1995 to report on what had happened to the Indian city eleven years after the made-in-America catastrophe. A pesticide plant owned by the American-headquartered chemical company Union Carbide blew up and sent a massive poisonous gas cloud floating over the city, shortly after the company had switched off safety mechanisms to save money. The gas cloud killed more than 20,000 people and maimed another half a million, with genetic defects in the children of the survivors continuing into the present generation.

Carbide got away with murder because it was a multinational. It claimed its Indian operation was responsible, and then simply folded it up. It could not be sued in America, and the United States refused to extradite Carbide's president, Warren Anderson, who was wanted on manslaughter charges in India. He lived a long life in the Hamptons and died peacefully in Vero Beach, Florida, while his victims continued to try to survive with damaged lungs and eyes in the slums of Bhopal.

If the United States bombed India, India could take it up with the United Nations. But if an American or a British or a Dutch corporation killed 20,000 Indians, what court or international body could the victims appeal to? A multinational corporation is impervious to liability precisely because it operates in multiple nations; cut off a limb in one, and it grows another somewhere else. The head is protected by the laws of the country it's headquartered in. The Socialist International and libertarian economists dreamed of a world without borders for human beings. Instead, what we have is a border-free world for multinationals.

*

They looted us for centuries, they took whatever was worth taking, and they continued taking after we became 'independent' – of their governments, but not of their corporations. The numbers are indisputable; colonial countries enriched themselves at the expense of the subject nations, and there's a case to be made for reparations to be paid. There *is* a giant programme of reparations under way, but it's reverse reparations, by the poor of the world to the rich: to the oil companies, the chemical companies, the mining companies, which have figured out how to corrupt the governments of the developing countries and continue stealing.

The history of the multinational corporation is inextricably linked with the onset of colonialism. The world's first multinationals were chartered by European countries to administer their colonies: the East India Company, the Dutch East India Company, the Royal Africa Company. Today's multinationals are bigger than entire countries: if Walmart were a country, it would have the twenty-fifth-largest GDP in the world. A multinational company has only one allegiance: to its shareholders, who tend to be in the rich countries. So it can enter or leave a variety of countries as suits its purpose: whether it is for commodities, cheap labour or a captive market. It can take advantage of weak or corrupt governments, or lax labour or environmental laws for its factories – and then play one weak country off against another if local activists raise a fuss. Most of all, because of the global, amorphous structure of a multinational, it can move money around countries with very little oversight.

There are multiple ways in the global financial system to funnel money upward from those who have little to those who have a lot. Often, this is dark money, secret money, blood-tinged money that shrinks from sunlight and prefers to dwell in its own 'haven', where corrupt corporations and despots and oligarchs can safely park the billions they've amassed. Over a tenth of all the world's GDP is hidden from Caesar in these tax havens – some used to hide personal wealth, others to avoid corporate taxes.

The City of London effectively operates as the biggest tax haven in the world. It is a corporation, with its own constitution, a separate legal entity from the rest of London and even the UK. Even Queen Elizabeth, when she wishes to enter the City, is met at the border by the lord mayor, who engages her in a ritual of entry. The City of London has a curious voting system, with some 9,000 votes assigned to the human beings living there, and more than twice that number given to the corporations that have set up shop in the square mile.

'When the British Empire crumbled in the mid-1950s, London replaced the cozy embrace of gunboats and imperial trading preferences with a new model: tempting the world's hot money through lax regulation and lax enforcement,' writes the journalist Nicholas Shaxson. 'There was always a subtle balance, involving dependable British legal bedrock fiercely upholding UK domestic rules and laws while turning a blind eye to foreign law-breaking. It was a classic offshore-tax-haven offering that tells foreign financiers, "We won't steal your money, but we won't make a fuss if you steal other people's."'

The UK and its overseas territories host one in five of the world's tax havens, more than any other country. They hold a combined pile of £1.4 trillion that's sheltered from taxes, according to a recent study by the University of California, Berkeley, economist Gabriel Zucman. 'We have, to put it provocatively, a second British empire, which is at the very core of global financial markets today,' says Ronen Palan, a professor of international political economy at City University in London.

Developing countries lose three times as much to tax havens as the $125 billion in aid that they receive. There are some sixty tax havens in the world, most of them controlled by the West. Money being smuggled out of sub-Saharan Africa and into them is growing by 20 per cent a year. In 2011, tax havens held $4.4 trillion of the wealth of developing countries. This is wealth that should be used to grow crops, educate children and develop cities in the poor countries. Instead, it's sitting in Luxembourg and the City of London.

Max Bearak of *The Washington Post* summarized an ActionAid report about how this works and what it costs a country like India:

> In 2007, Vodafone, one of the world's biggest telecom providers, moved to buy Hutchison Essar Ltd, an Indian subsidiary of a Hong-Kong based company. But Hutchison Essar, despite only operating in India, was not based there – rather, it was registered as a business in the Cayman and British Virgin Islands, tax havens in the Caribbean, and Mauritius, another, this time in the Indian Ocean. Vodafone bought the company through a subsidiary of its own – registered in the Netherlands, also a tax haven. None of those places levy a capital gains tax, and so India was not able to claim the $2.2 billion it otherwise would've earned had tax havens not been an option for the companies. That sum is worth almost the entire annual budget for subsidized meals for school-going children in India.

In 2016, a full 40 per cent of the profits of global multinationals were promptly moved to tax havens, according to Zucman. And because multinationals have figured out ways to avoid paying tax in developing countries whose tax authorities aren't up to the complexity of the job, those countries increasingly rely on revenue sources such as sales taxes, which disproportionately hurt the poor.

Massive leaks such as the Panama Papers and Paradise Papers have shown the scale of the problem, and that it is a global problem. Of the world's GDP, 11.5 per cent ($8.7 trillion) is being held in overseas tax havens by a handful of the richest – the households owning more than $50 million in assets, including such eminences as Queen Elizabeth. If the rich countries were serious about fighting tax havens, they would agree to a world financial registry. This would benefit them, too, since we'd finally know who exactly owns all those $100 million apartments overlooking Central Park or Hyde Park.

*

Trillions of dollars a year in net resource transfers make their way from the poor to the rich countries, according to a landmark 2016 report from Global Financial Integrity, an American think-tank, and the Centre for Applied Research at the Norwegian School of Economics. Unlike previous studies, this report includes outflows of illicit or unrecorded money.

Since 1980, at least $16.3 trillion has gone from the developing to the rich countries – an amount equal to the annual GDP of the United States. The report breaks it down: $13.4 trillion in 'unrecorded capital flight' – what Indians call 'black money'; and $4.2 trillion in interest payments. In 2012 alone, poor countries lost $700 billion in 'trade misinvoicing', a practice whereby corporations falsify invoices to take money out of the country and into tax havens. An equal amount was lost through 'same-invoice faking', where a multinational fakes invoices between two of its subsidiaries in different countries, to shift profits to a lower tax jurisdiction.

'If we add theft through trade in services to the mix, it brings total net resource outflows to about $3 trillion per year,' the *Guardian* noted in a summary of the report. 'That's twenty-four times more than the aid budget. In other words, for every $1 of aid that developing countries receive, they lose $24 in net outflows.'

This has a direct bearing on the ethics of immigration. Between 1970 and 2010, Mexico lost $872 billion in illicit financial outflows, and most of the money ended up in American banks. Around this time – from 1965 to 2015 – sixteen million Mexicans immigrated to the United States. They weren't doing anything wrong; they were just following the money. *Their* money.

The philosopher Joseph Carens points out the greatest inequality of today's world: that of citizenship.

> Citizenship in Western democracies is the modern equivalent of feudal class privilege – an inherited status that greatly enhances one's life chances. To be born a citizen of a rich state in Europe

or North America is like being born into the nobility (even though many of us belong to the lesser nobility). To be born a citizen of a poor country in Asia or Africa is like being born into the peasantry in the Middle Ages (even if there are a few rich peasants and some peasants manage to gain entry to the nobility).

Or as the economist Michael Clemens, of the Center for Global Development, puts it:

> How much money can you ever hope to make in your lifetime? I can make a decent guess without knowing your education level, race, or social class. I just need to know what country you live in. If you live in the United States, by far the biggest reason you will earn vastly more than a typical person in, say, Mali or Haiti is not because they have less perseverance, intelligence, or talent. It's primarily because that person lives in Mali or Haiti. What country you live in is more important in determining your life outcomes than anything else about you. In fact, what country you live in is more important than everything else about you, combined. This inequality of opportunity is driving the current migration crisis. It means that economic opportunity and personal security are handed out mostly by lottery: a lottery of birthplace.

According to the economist Angus Maddison, in 1960, when states were just beginning to emerge from colonialism, citizens of the world's richest country were thirty-three times wealthier than people in the poorest country. By 2000, in a globalized world that was supposed to lift all boats, they were 134 times wealthier. The structure of the World Trade Organization keeps poor nations poor. It forces them to open their markets to multinationals. The WTO demands free movement of goods but not of labour.

It is also true, as the economist Branko Milanovic points out, that if you ignore national boundaries, global inequality among the world's individuals has dipped since 2000, principally because of the rise of the middle class in India and China, at the same time as inequality *within* countries has risen. 'Most people believe that inequality is rising – and indeed it has been rising for a while in a number of rich countries,' says Milanovic. 'It's harder to understand that at the same time, you can actually have global inequality going down. Technically speaking, national inequality can increase in every single country and yet global inequality can go down. And why it is going down is because very large, populous, and relatively poor countries like India and China are growing quite fast.' Global capitalism has underdeveloped some countries while allowing others to grow.

The British Labour leader Jeremy Corbyn, in a December 2017 speech at the UN's Geneva headquarters, enumerated the four biggest threats facing humanity: the concentration of wealth and power in the hands of a tiny corporate elite; climate change; 'the unprecedented numbers of people fleeing conflict, persecution, human rights abuses, social breakdown and climate disasters'; and the use of military power over diplomacy to resolve disputes.

The day following his speech would be International Anti-Corruption Day, Corbyn noted. 'Corruption isn't something that happens "over there". Our government has played a central role in enabling the corruption that undermines democracy and violates human rights. It is a global issue that requires a global response.'

The problem isn't so much the taxation; it's the reporting. In our world, we have no idea who owns what. Corbyn demanded that multinationals be required to undertake country-by-country reporting. He also noted that tax authorities in the developing world lack the expertise to figure out how the rich, with their legions of highly paid lawyers and accountants, rob them of billions of dollars of tax revenue.

Corbyn brought up the extortionate debt payments that many poor countries find themselves in thrall to. He cited Thomas Sankara, the president of Burkina Faso, a few months before he was assassinated in a French-backed coup in 1987: 'The debt cannot be repaid. First because if we don't repay lenders will not die. But if we repay ... we are going to die.' Sankara gained a reputation as 'the African Che Guevara'; he openly defied the International Monetary Fund and the World Bank. The coup plotter, Blaise Compaoré, said that he had to kill his former friend because 'he jeopardized foreign relations with former colonial power France'.

As soon as Compaoré assumed power, he quickly moved to reverse Sankara's nationalizations of companies and crawl back to the IMF. In 2014, the BBC noted that Compaoré 'had become the strongest ally to France and the US in the region'. And what did the country get for its reversal of Sankara's policies? Today, Burkina Faso is among the least developed countries in the world; in the UN Human Development Index, it ranks seventh from the bottom in a list of 189 countries. So the logical thing for the Burkinabe to do is to get up and move. The country has 19 million people; 1.5 million Burkinabe have moved to Ivory Coast, which is as poor as Bangladesh. But wages there are twice as high as in Burkina Faso, and Burkinabe in Ivory Coast send $350 million in remittances home every year. Ordinary heroes, surviving against extraordinary odds.

7

War

All around the world, civil upheaval causes people to flee, and many conflicts have been ongoing for years or decades. There are the wars that everybody knows about, such as in Afghanistan and Syria; then there are the little-known ones, such as the Moro Muslim conflict in the Philippines, which has cost a cumulative 120,000 lives, and the Ituri conflict in the Democratic Republic of Congo, which has taken over 60,000. Many of these conflicts have their origin in colonialism or botched colonial population transfer or map making.

The Rohingya crisis in Myanmar, for instance, has its origins in British recruitment of ethnic Muslim migrant labour from India to cultivate the rice paddies of Burma. Under these policies, the Muslim population tripled between 1871 and 1911. During World War II, the British promised the Rohingya a separate 'Muslim National Area' if they supported the empire. After independence, many of the Buddhist Burmese saw the Rohingya as outsiders or colonial stooges, and these tensions have boiled over in recent times – exacerbated by rumours spread through Facebook – leading to mass killings of the Rohingya, along with rapes and expulsions. Almost a million of them have fled over the border to Bangladesh.

A friend of mine was working with an international NGO in a refugee camp in Bangladesh in 2017 when she noticed something odd: there were children older than five and younger than two, but very few two- to five-year-olds. It was, she discovered, because when the Rohingya fled from the army and the militias, children of that generation couldn't run as fast as the older ones and were too heavy to be held by their parents. They fell behind, and the soldiers advanced on them with machetes.

Colonialism wasn't just a European enterprise, of course. Though there was never an 'American Empire', the history of Central American countries from their beginnings as states is a history of the United States intervening whenever it chooses to replace political leaders who do not bend to American will or serve American corporate interests. In the twentieth century, the United States supported bloodthirsty dictators such as Guatemala's Efraín Ríos Montt and Nicaragua's Anastasio Somoza with guns, troops and money. These interventions left the countries bankrupt, bereft of both social services and thriving businesses. Many attempts to grow native industries or to bring about social welfare schemes that spread the wealth from the US-supported elite to the indigenous populations were vetoed in Washington; the leaders supporting those changes were accused of being communists, and replaced at gunpoint by more malleable ones.

In 1952, Harry Truman took a dislike to Jacobo Árbenz, the president of Guatemala, who passed a land reform bill that benefited one-sixth of the population. Unfortunately, the bill cut into the profits of the United Fruit Corporation, which was based in New Orleans and owned 42 per cent of all the land in Guatemala, all the country's banana production, all the country's telephone and telegraph network, and all its railways. As a United Fruit executive explained, 'Guatemala was chosen as the site for the company's earliest development activities, because at the time we entered Central America, Guatemala's government was the region's weakest, most corrupt and most pliable.'

United Fruit complained to Truman about the reform bill. Truman authorized the CIA to launch Operation PBFORTUNE to topple Árbenz. The United Fruit Company actually lent one of its freighters to the CIA to transport its mercenaries. Details leaked and the plan was aborted. Truman's successor, Eisenhower, decided to try again with Operation PBSUCCESS. The plan was hatched by the Dulles brothers, John Foster, Eisenhower's secretary of state, and Allen, the CIA director, who sat on United Fruit's board. The CIA raised a private army to invade the country and force Árbenz to resign. The land reforms were rolled back. Essentially, the United States government illegally overthrew the democratically elected president of a country to benefit one of its (politically well-connected) corporations.

A series of coups and countercoups followed – a revolving door of American-backed dictators going in and out of the presidential palace – with every American president implicated, a situation of permanent political instability that lasts to this day. More than 200,000 Guatemalans died over the next four decades in civil strife. The history of American involvement with Guatemala parallels the history of British involvement with India. But unlike India, Guatemala became an economic basket case. So Guatemalans decided to do what anybody who is owed a debt does: they went to have a talk with the debtor. The biggest source of Guatemalan foreign income now is remittances from the 1.5 million Guatemalans in the United States.

In the 1980s, neighbouring El Salvador was in the grip of a civil war that eventually took 75,000 lives – most of them poor peasants shot by the army or death squads marshalled by the local oligarchs. And who provided money, arms and training to these death squads? That champion of liberty, the United States. This is where Ronald Reagan decided he would draw a line in the sand against communism. He flooded the small country with military and economic aid to prop up its generals, more so than any other except Israel and Egypt.

'Many Americans would prefer to forget that chapter in American history,' writes Raymond Bonner, who covered El Salvador for the *New York Times* in that period.

> Salvadorans haven't forgotten, however. In El Mozote and the surrounding villages of subsistence peasants, forensic experts are still digging up bodies – of women, children, and old men who were murdered by the Salvadoran army during an operation

in December 1981. It was one of the worst massacres in Latin American history ... Some 1,200 men, women and children were killed during the operation. Old men were tortured. Then executed. Mothers were separated from their children. Raped. Executed. Crying, frightened children were forced into the convent. Soldiers fired through the windows. More than a hundred children died; their average age was six.

The massacre was carried out by the Atlacatl Battalion, which had been created in the US Army's School of the Americas and which had just completed a three-month counterinsurgency training course in Fort Bragg, North Carolina. In El Mozote, the unit's first operation after completing the course, they applied the lessons they had learned. 'The United States was complicit' in the massacre, Todd Greentree, who was then a political officer in the US embassy, told Bonner recently.

Young men fleeing the massacres ended up in the United States and formed gangs for self-protection. Thus was MS-13 born; not in the barrios of San Salvador, but in the badlands of Los Angeles and in the prisons of California. When they were deported back to El Salvador, they formed a parallel government there, grew rich and better armed with guns sold by Americans, and then made their way back into the United States, a homicidal ping-pong game of the dispossessed.

In much of Latin America, the United States functioned, and still does, as a colonial power. As late as 2007, Chiquita Brands (which United Fruit had shape-shifted into) pleaded guilty to supporting a paramilitary and drug trafficking group, the United Self-Defence Forces of Colombia, to which it gave $1.7 million and 3,000 AK-47s to fight union organizers and extort farmers into selling only to Chiquita. The United Self-Defence Forces used the money to systematically murder thousands of peasants and union organizers. The US Justice Department refused to extradite the company's executives from Ohio to Colombia, even though the company had officially acknowledged propping up an entity that had been labelled a 'terrorist organization' by the American government.

Officer Tanaomi is, like most of his fellow Border Patrol agents, fairly right-wing. But after listening to Sanchez, Tanaomi says, 'Wow. I never heard of these things before. I mean, I studied history in high school and all that, but I never heard of these things.'

Why are Mexicans, Guatemalans, Hondurans and Salvadorans desperate to move north, to come to US cities to work as dishwashers and cleaners? Partly, it's because of their history with Spanish and then Yankee colonialism; partly, it's because of race and class conflict and systematic corruption; and these days, it's because of the drug war, whose casualty figures are, proportionally, higher than those in Syria.

The sociologist Rafael Alarcón sketched out the role of drug trafficking in Mexican–US migration for me. In the early 1980s, there was an implicit agreement between the narcos and the Mexican government: '"Okay, you have to take all the drugs to the United States. You don't sell the drugs in Mexico." Creating a market in Mexico would have been devastating.'

Most of the killings over drugs now happen because of the wars between the cartels inside Mexico. 'The thing that always amazes me is that there is no violence in the US,' Alarcón says. The cartels distribute the drugs in the United States, but do not fight each other, and the police don't kill the narcos as they do in Mexico. The violence stops at the border, even though most of the product has been shipped across it. 'The violence in Mexico is a powerful reason for people to leave.'

And it's not just that people are afraid of getting killed. It's also because they can't work, because the narcos control production. In Michoacán, the lime trade is controlled by the cartels, and the lime farmers have to pay a *derecho de piso*, a fee to the narcos, in order to work. 'They don't have to kill these people, they just threaten them,' he says.

It is a cost–benefit analysis that each migrant makes: the cost of staying versus the risk of getting deported or having your children taken from you if you cross and are caught. 'Well, now the risk of crossing is probably less important than the risk of staying if they live in a violent area,' notes Alarcón.

Unlike the situation in Europe, the biggest reason refugees come to America's borders isn't the big wars in the Middle East; it's the small wars in our backyard. The spread of small arms, propelled by the vigorous resistance of the National Rifle Association (NRA) to any controls on their worldwide dispersal, is a factor in numberless small wars around the planet. We buy their drugs and sell them the guns to terrorize their youth, who look to the first freight train north to escape their situation.

In 2014, Mexican authorities seized 15,397 firearms, ranging from machine guns to pistols, and submitted them to the US Bureau of Alcohol, Tobacco, Firearms, and Explosives (ATF) for tracing. The agency found that 11,061 of them – 71 per cent – originated in the United States. In the Caribbean, 64 per cent of the guns coming in are American; in the Bahamas, 98 per cent of the guns come from its giant continental neighbour.

All this came out in the open in 2011 when Congress discovered that the ATF had been 'letting guns walk' over the border, in what it called Operation Fast and Furious. The idea was that 2,000 AK-47s and other weapons of war would be provided by the ATF to purchasers buying guns on behalf of the cartels, who would then lead them to the druglords. Fourteen hundred of the guns disappeared without a trace.

I began understanding the passion for guns in America when I learned about their history: he who held the gun was the law. The foundational principle of America wasn't religious liberty; it was the rule of the gun, which allowed the white settlers to dominate and massacre the natives. This country could not have been settled by the force of oxbows.

Half of all the civilian guns in the world are in American hands. Guns are our national insanity. But it is an insanity that we don't keep within our borders; we export it. Every day, around a thousand migrants are intercepted crossing the border from Mexico to the United States. Every day, some 700 guns travel unhindered over the border the other way. Their value increases threefold the moment they cross over.

At the Casa del Migrante in Tijuana, I met a middle-aged man who had a hardened face and body. Ronaldo is from Amatlán, in Guatemala, and was in the United States for twenty-five years before he was deported. Back home, he lost his grandmother, whom he was closer to than his mother, and the sadness turned him into an alcoholic and a drug addict. He started doing stints in US jails.

In LA, Ronaldo found Christianity, at a church on Sunset Boulevard. He would go with the other church members to talk to young Latino men on the street, to bring the gospel to them. 'We went to the *Mara Salvatrucha* [MS-13] where they began. You know where Western and Santa Monica is? There is no gang there today. But that's the place where they began,' he says. Ronaldo can point out exactly where in Los Angeles the different Central American gangs got their start, because he knew them then. 'The 18s, they began in MacArthur Park,' at a MoneyGram on the corner of 7th Street.

What happened next, he went on, is that 'the United States started deporting people because they didn't accept them, but they didn't know their background. They just didn't want them. They say, "Nah, these people are bad, they cannot be here." Between 2000 and 2004 alone, the United States dumped 20,000 criminals into Latin America, into a system with no capacity to control or rehabilitate them.

Ronaldo tells me what happened after they were deported: 'They started to get together over there and started to do the same thing in our countries. And our countries, they weren't like that. The United States sent them over there. The gangs are bad people that have been deported from the United States.'

I asked Ronaldo where the *maras* get their guns.

'They purchase the guns in the United States.'

'How much can you buy a gun in Guatemala for?'

'One thousand quetzales. A hundred dollars.'

'It's easy to get a gun?'

'Very easy. Anybody that wants one can get one. If you want ten of them, they give you ten of them.'

In December 2006, the UN General Assembly voted on establishing a panel of experts who would study the feasibility of a small arms treaty that would staunch this murderous flow. The vote was 153 countries in favour, and 1 – guess which? – against.

'The United States has frequently been on the opposite side of its hemispheric neighbours by opposing international controls on the small-arms trade,' a 2008 report from the Center for Defense Information states.

> The United States was the lone dissenter on establishing a treaty to control the arms trade, has consistently stalled and weakened efforts to develop other international measures, and has been ineffective in stopping the cross-border trade with Mexico. US arms policies, including loopholes in existing laws and opposition to creating strong international agreements, clash with US programmatic initiatives and have allowed US arms to flow to Latin America with continued devastating consequences.

Americans sell their neighbours the weapons of mass destruction and buy the main crop their farmers have left to sell, their coca leaves and marijuana plants. Both the selling of the guns and the buying of their drugs renders these countries ungovernable. And so, if you're a parent in a barrio in one of these countries, it makes logical sense to urge your children to save their lives while they can and go north, not just to earn a dollar, but to stay alive. Because the only other choice, if they are to stay alive, is to work for the narcos.

One out of ten people born in El Salvador, Honduras and Guatemala is already living in the United States – more than three million people, most of whom have been in America for over a decade. Now their relatives are coming to join them. The annual flow of migrants from the Northern Triangle countries, which was 115,000 in 2014, has been increasing at twice the average rate of overall immigration.

Trump's wish list in 2019 called for $26 billion for immigration enforcement and detention, and another $18 billion for his wall. As Roberto Suro, the founder of the Pew Hispanic Center, points out, 'That's almost the combined gross domestic product of El Salvador and Honduras [$48 billion]. A fraction of the enforcement budget well spent on economic development would reduce migration pressure. It would be a better use of taxpayer dollars than trying to intercept people in flight at a militarized border and then criminalizing them. Aside from the utility, it is the right thing to do. American interventions, political, military and economic, helped create the conditions prompting many migrations, including this one.'

In 2016, the Obama administration got Congress to fund a $750 million aid package for Central America. It was meant to improve governance: fight corruption, improve policing, and create opportunities at home so their citizens wouldn't have to move. The next year, the murder rate in Honduras, one of the countries the aid package helped, fell by 25 per cent. Then Trump came in and slashed aid to those countries by over 35 per cent.

Just as the sale of small arms fuels domestic strife and spurs migration, the sale of heavy weapons is instrumental in creating conflict between nations. To date, 130 countries have signed the 2014 United Nations Arms Trade Treaty, the only serious effort to stem the trade in conventional arms around the world. Of those countries, ninety-nine have ratified the treaty in their national parliaments, while thirty-one countries, including the biggest arms exporter – the USA – have signed the treaty but not ratified it. The treaty has come under unrelenting opposition from the NRA, which mounted a full-throated campaign of slander, saying it constituted an end run around the Second Amendment (which the fact-checking site Snopes unequivocally branded as 'false'). But under Trump, there isn't a chance in hell that Congress will ratify it.

According to the Stockholm International Peace Research Institute, sales by the world's one hundred leading arms-producing and military services providers rose by 38 per cent from 2002 to 2016. The majority – 58 per cent – of these companies were American. The UK has sent £4.7 billion in arms to Saudi Arabia for its brutal campaign against Yemen, which it seeks to bomb into submission. Across the Atlantic, Trump and King Salman shook hands in May 2017 over a $110 billion arms deal – with an option to buy $250 billion more over the next decade. Notwithstanding Trump's characteristic hyperbole, if the full deal is executed, it would be the biggest weapons deal in history.

According to the Armed Conflict Location and Event Data Project, over 57,000 Yemenis, the majority of them civilians, have died in the war, mostly through American-supplied weapons. More than two million have been displaced, hundreds of thousands have left the country, one million people have cholera, and fourteen million human beings are facing starvation. It is the world's worst ongoing humanitarian crisis.

In June 2017, the Senate voted to clear the first part of the deal, an amuse-bouche of half a billion dollars in 'precision-guided munitions' to drop on the desperate Yemenis. That same year, Trump announced his 'Muslim Ban' on citizens of countries forbidden to enter the United States. Prominent on that list is Yemen.

War creates refugees, and it is important to follow the chain of responsibility. Millions of people have died in Muslim countries in recent decades as a direct result of our adventures abroad. We bomb them from the air and ground and from our warships. We kill indiscriminately and then lie about it; as a 2017 *New York Times* investigation of the casualties from coalition airstrikes in Iraq showed, the death rate is thirty-one times greater than officially acknowledged.

The United States has justified this by saying, We're taking the war to them before they bring it to us, like they did on September 11, 2001. But in the United States, the vast majority of terror attacks are by white supremacists, not Muslims. In Europe, the vast majority of terror attacks are by native-born Europeans, not immigrants. In the wake of a terrorist strike, 'Why do they hate us?' is a legitimate and useful question. Because unless we get the true answer, we won't be able to stop the next strike, and the one after that, and the one after that.

Who created Islamic terror? Let's follow the money. It was largely bankrolled by the most extreme faction of the religion, the Wahhabis, in Saudi Arabia. It's one of the most rigid and dogmatic forms of the religion on the planet today, and for decades it had the full backing of the Saudi ruling family. In Pakistan, if you're a poor parent, you can send your child to a Wahhabi madrassa funded by the Saudis, and your child will get a Koranic education, and you will get a few thousand rupees a month. And your child might grow up and join the Taliban.

This ideology isn't just the greatest threat to the West today; it's the greatest threat to all Muslims today. But why has the Saudi strain of the religion triumphed over all others, such as the peaceful, syncretic Islam long dominant in Indonesia? It is in part because Americans like to drive big SUVs. Big SUVs need a lot of fuel, which Americans buy from the Saudis. The Americans have propped up the Saudi royal family against all domestic and foreign opposition – even when they murder a *Washington Post* columnist like Jamal Khashoggi – because we are addicted to a regular supply of oil, which the royals guarantee. The UK is no less addicted: oil accounts for over half of the £2.4 billion worth of goods imported from Saudi Arabia.

Why are Syrians and Iraqis desperate to move out of their countries? Not for the lights of Broadway or the springtime charms of Unter den Linden. It is largely because the West – particularly, the Americans and the British – invaded Iraq, an illegal and unnecessary war, and set in motion the process that destabilized the entire region, which had already been chopped up by earlier colonialists under the Sykes–Picot Agreement of 1916. The Americans disbanded Saddam Hussein's army, and the demobilized soldiers went back to their villages, dispirited, desperate. Meanwhile, the Americans installed a Shiite-led government in Baghdad, and the ex-soldiers made common cause with the most extreme Islamists to form ISIS, which blitzed across a huge chunk of Syria and Iraq with frightening dispatch. Millions had already fled Bashar al-Assad's brutal crackdown on his citizens; now many more had to flee.

They have reaped what the West has sown. If there were any justice, the 1,600-acre Bush family ranch in Texas should be filled with tents hosting Middle Eastern refugees. You break it, you own it.

8

Climate Change

In 2009, Mohamed Nasheed, the president of the Maldives, put on a wetsuit and air tanks, ordered his ministers to do the same, and dived to the seabed for a cabinet meeting held entirely underwater. It was a preview of what is to come, very soon, for the half-million people who live on the island nation: in a few decades, all of them will have to move, or live underwater.

'You can drastically reduce your greenhouse gas emissions so that the seas do not rise so much,' the Maldivian president appealed to the industrial countries. 'Or when we show up on your shores in our boats, you can let us in. Or when we show up on your shores in our boats, you can shoot us. You pick.'

In the twenty-first century, the number one driver of migration might be climate change. According to the UN, a fifth of the world's population will be affected by floods by 2050. And so, many of them will move to dry land. According to the International Organization for Migration, at least 200 million people will be displaced by climate change by 2050. The figure could be as high as one billion, which would be one out of every ten people.

Aromar Revi, the director of the Indian Institute for Human Settlements and an author of a recent IPCC report, predicted, 'In some parts of the world, national borders will become irrelevant. You can set up a wall to try to contain 10,000 and 20,000 and one million people, but not 10 million.'

The prognosis is not good. 'Toward the end of this century, if current trends are not reversed, large parts of Bangladesh, the

Philippines, Indonesia, Pakistan, Egypt and Vietnam, among other countries, will be under water,' says Michael Gerrard, director of the Sabin Center for Climate Change at Columbia Law School. 'Some small island nations, such as Kiribati and the Marshall Islands, will be close to disappearing entirely. Swaths of Africa from Sierra Leone to Ethiopia will be turning into desert. Glaciers in the Himalayas and the Andes, on which entire regions depend for drinking water, will be melting away. Many habitable parts of the world will no longer be able to support agriculture or produce clean water.'

Migration driven by climate change has been dramatically increasing in the recent past. Since 1992, 4.2 billion people have been affected by droughts, floods and storms. Today, 1.8 billion people are suffering the effects of drought, land degradation and desertification.

People think of the Syrian civil war as a conflict between Sunnis and Shiites, or a proxy war between Saudi Arabia and Iran. But another way to look at it is the natural result of a three-year drought, the worst in the region's history, between 2007 and 2010. The wheat withered in the fields; the cattle died of thirst. A million and a half villagers swarmed into the cities, there to be recruited by militias, the only jobs many of them could get. The country exploded. When you can't make a living by your ploughshares, you'll beat them into swords.

As the world gets hotter, the hotheads grow angrier. According to a 2009 study published in the *Proceedings of the National Academy of Sciences*, there are 'strong historical linkages between civil war and temperature in Africa, with warmer years leading to significant increases in the likelihood of war. When combined with climate model projections of future temperature trends, this historical response to temperature suggests a roughly 54 per cent increase in armed conflict incidence by 2030, or an additional 393,000 battle deaths if future wars are as deadly as recent wars.'

Migrants come to work because they can't work at home. Heatwaves took almost a million people out of the global workforce in

2016, half of them in India alone. They come to eat because they can't eat at home. For every degree Celsius increase in temperature, wheat yields have been falling by 6 per cent and rice yields by 3 per cent. At 1.5 degrees, corn yields shrink by 10 per cent.

They come to drink because they can't drink at home. In 2018, India experienced the worst water crisis since it became a country. Six hundred million Indians – half the population – deal with high to extreme water scarcity. Every year, 200,000 Indians die because of a lack of water or unsafe water. And it's only going to get worse; by 2030, Indians will need twice the amount of water that is available. The deficit in water for irrigation, the government projects, will lead to a 6 per cent drop in the country's GDP by 2030. India's going to get a lot thirstier, a lot poorer.

A recent study in the journal *Science Advances* makes a horrifying prediction. The Indian mortality rate from heat-related deaths rose two and a half times in fifty years, due to a temperature increase of under 1 degree Fahrenheit. But this is just the beginning. India's going to get hot – very hot; some experts predict that its temperature will increase by anywhere from 4 to 10 degrees Fahrenheit by the end of the century. The choice, for many Indians, will be between staying in place and roasting to death or moving.

And where should they move to? To their former colonizers, or to the country most responsible for the heating of the planet? Americans are only 4 per cent of the world's population but are responsible for one-third of the excess carbon dioxide in the atmosphere. Next comes the European Union, which puts another quarter of the existing CO2 in the atmosphere. America creates a third of the world's solid waste and consumes a fifth of the world's energy. The average American uses as much energy as 35 Indians, or 185 Ethiopians, and consumes as many goods and services as 53 Chinese.

But America is the first and only country to walk away from a global attempt at a solution: the Paris Agreement. The Trump administration is an existential threat to life on the planet today. The most damning indictment against Americans: we ruined the planet and then elected a government that will stop any last chance we have of saving it. Climate migration is not new. It has happened throughout history. People have followed their families to greener pastures. In the 1800s, climate change caused a series of disastrous crop failures in south-western Germany. A year of extreme cold would be followed by one of extreme heat; barley, rye and oats withered in the fields. Five million Bavarians decided they'd had enough and got on ships to America. Among them was an illiterate sixteen-year-old who arrived in New York in 1885, speaking no English. His name was Friedrich Trump. Yes, grandfather to Donald.

But the situation we are facing now is much more dire. Entire island states may disappear under rising seas as soon as the middle of this century. After Hurricane Maria, half a million Puerto Ricans – one in seven people on the island – are expected to move to the mainland. By the end of the century, land that is currently home to 650 million people may be underwater. At the other extreme, by 2050, much of the world – up to 30 per cent of the earth's surface, home to 1.5 billion people – could be a vast desert, according to a study in the journal *Nature Climate Change*.

No force on earth is going to keep their desperate inhabitants from moving. And, logically, they should be given a home in the countries that are most to blame for the inundation. 'Twenty million people could be displaced in Bangladesh by the middle of the century,' the Bangladeshi finance minister pointed out. 'We are asking all our development partners to honour the natural right of persons to migrate. We can't accommodate all these people – this is already the densest-populated country in the world.' He called for the UN convention on refugees to give climate refugees the same protection as those fleeing political repression.

According to the UN high commissioner for refugees, since 2008, 22.5 million people have had to flee their homes because of climate-related extreme weather events, like hurricanes or droughts. El Salvador, for instance – the source of many of the people desperate to come to the United States – has been badly affected by climate change. Since the 1950s, the average temperature in the country has risen by 2.5 degrees Fahrenheit, leading to severe droughts; the seas have risen three inches and are going to rise another seven inches by 2050. The region has also been battered by increasingly frequent hurricanes. In the 1980s, Central America experienced fifteen hurricanes. Between 2000 and 2009, there were thirty-nine.

And it's going to get worse, much worse, for all of us. Research published in the *Journal of Climate* shows that, under middle-of-the-road estimates of global warming, Category 3, 4 and 5 hurricanes will increase by 11 per cent in frequency between now and 2035, and 20 per cent by the end of the century. Hurricanes of super-intense force, which might call for a new designation, Category 6, with winds above 190 miles per hour, will become much more common. The research also shows that hurricanes will jump in intensity, bringing us a number of storms that will speed up by over 115 miles per hour within twenty-four hours, leaving very little time for people to be warned and evacuate.

Climate change is a 'threat multiplier': it makes a bad problem, like ethnic conflict, worse. Between 2008 and 2014, 184 million people had to run away from their homes because of floods, earthquakes, tropical storms and volcanic eruptions – an average of one human being per second. With continued climate change, this number is set to rise dramatically. For each metre of sea level rise, 150 million people will have to flee their homes.

The water in Lake Chad has shrunk by 90 per cent since 1963. This has had disastrous consequences for the countries that depend on it for water, like Nigeria. The disappearance of the water is a key factor in the Boko Haram bloodbath, which made 3.5 million people take to their heels.

Twelve million people are at risk of starvation in Kenya, Somalia and Ethiopia right now. The region has suffered four massive droughts in two decades, and has dried faster than at any time in the last two millennia. A drought every five years is the new normal; three-quarters of Kenya is 'water-stressed'. What does this mean for the people on the ground? 'Pastoralists have walked these lands for centuries,' reports Somini Sengupta of the *New York Times*.

> The older ones among them remember the droughts of the past. Animals died. People died. But then the rains came, and after four or five years of normal rains, people living here could replenish their herds. Now, the droughts are so frequent that rebuilding herds is pretty much impossible ...
>
> These days, shepherds ... range further and further, sometimes clashing with rivals from Turkana over pasture and water, other times risking a confrontation with an elephant or a lion from the national park next door. Almost every night, park rangers can hear gunshots. Herders raid each other's livestock to replenish their own. At the Isiolo health center, everyone kept precise count of their losses. One woman said she lost all three of her cows last year and was left now with only three goats. A second said her husband was killed a few years ago in a fight with Turkana herders over pasture, and then, last year, the last of her cows died. A third said she lost twenty of her thirty goats in the last drought.

In China, the desert has advanced south and east 21,000 square miles since 1975. Hundreds of thousands of the people living where there were fields have been resettled by the government farther south. Most of them are culturally quite distinct from their new neighbours. Something's going to blow.

In Peru, as the Andean ice caps melt under the increasing heat, there's less and less water available for local farmers. So they move, down to the river, to the Amazon, to prospect for gold and grow coca, and join armed gangs for survival. Or move into Lima; or directly to Queens, New York.

Climate change affects everyday life, in every area of life, big and small. In the sweltering summer of 2018, daytime temperatures in the Colombian coastal city of Santa Marta regularly climbed past 40 degrees Celsius (104 degrees Fahrenheit). Hospitals in the city of 600,000 were overwhelmed with people complaining of heatstroke and nausea. So the city's health secretary issued an unorthodox appeal: to avoid heat exhaustion, please don't have sex in the daytime.

Whether it's Somali fishermen turning to piracy because there are fewer fish now that the oceans are boiling over or Latin Americans growing coca because the coffee crops are withering in the heat, a large percentage of the world's conflicts – and the flight to the cities – are happening because of climate change.

The Pentagon acknowledged as much in a 2014 study:

> The impacts of climate change may cause instability in other countries by impairing access to food and water, damaging infrastructure, spreading disease, uprooting and displacing large numbers of people, compelling mass migration, interrupting commercial activity, or restricting electricity availability. These developments could undermine already-fragile governments that are unable to respond effectively or challenge currently-stable governments, as well as increasing competition and tension between countries vying for limited resources. These gaps in governance can create an avenue for extremist ideologies and conditions that foster terrorism.

Australia is the world's largest exporter of coal. Per capita, Australians are among the biggest polluters on the planet; at 0.3 per cent of the world's population, they emit 1.8 per cent of its greenhouse gases. The Indian mining magnate Gautam Adani, a close friend of Prime Minister Narendra Modi, is expected to open a giant new coal mine in Australia. It will cost $16.5 billion and proposes to extract 2.3 billion tons of coal. It is shit coal – low quality, high ash – and will pump 130 million tons of carbon dioxide into the atmosphere every year. The emissions from the coal out of that one single mine will be larger than the entire carbon emissions from fuel combustion in entire nations, including the Philippines, Qatar and Vietnam.

And guess where most of the Australian coal will be burned? India, where Adani is building many of the fifty-five coal-fired plants that are under construction. So Australia partners with a notorious Indian businessman and sells the product that destroys the Indian environment – causes little Indian children to develop the highest asthma rates on the planet – and then puts refugees fleeing from the results of such sales in hellish camps in Papua New Guinea.

Prodded by statistics showing that their cities are the most polluted on earth, India (Adani notwithstanding)and China (which is currently the world's biggest polluter) have not only acknowledged that climate change is man-made, but they've also made substantial progress in controlling their emissions. China has met its goals under international climate agreements years ahead of schedule; its emissions have probably already peaked, according to the Brookings Institution.

'That China, still an emerging economy with per-capita income significantly lower than the long-affluent Western economies, is undertaking and delivering on such ambitious climate goals demonstrates that development and environment do not form a zero-sum equation,' according to Brookings. 'The progress and prospects of China's climate change mitigation could serve not only as a credible example to other developing countries struggling to balance the economy and the environment, but also to affluent countries that are wavering in their commitment to one of the most pressing challenges facing the world today.'

Even as these policies affect India's and China's economic growth, they let their people live longer. One of the rare bits of environmental good news in our time is that both countries have *increased* their forest cover in the past few years, because of their commitments to the Paris Agreement – and because they want their urbanites to enjoy breathing.

The threat isn't sometime in the future; it is here with us today. Environmental pollution kills nine million people a year – fully 16 per cent of all the deaths on the planet. That is more deaths than caused by hunger, smoking or natural disasters; that is 'three times more deaths than from AIDS, tuberculosis and malaria combined and fifteen times more than from all wars and other forms of violence', according to a recent report in *The Lancet*. And who exactly is dying? Ninety-two per cent of the deaths are in low- and middle-income countries. The creditors.

PART III
Why They're Feared

9

The Populists' False Narrative

The West is being destroyed, not by migrants, but by the fear of migrants. In country after country, the ghosts of the fascists have rematerialized and are sitting in parliaments in Germany, in Austria, in Italy ... They have successfully convinced their populations that the greatest threat to their nations isn't government tyranny or inequality or climate change, but immigration. And that, to stop this wave of migrants, everyone's civil liberties must be curtailed. Surveillance cameras must be installed everywhere. Passports must be produced for the most routine of tasks, like buying a mobile phone.

Take a look at Hungary, where Viktor Orbán has forced out the Central European University and almost destroyed the country's free press and most other liberal institutions, using immigrants and George Soros as bogeymen. Or Poland, whose ruling party purged the judiciary, banished political opponents from government media, greatly restricted public gatherings, and passed a law, modified only after an international outcry, making it a crime to accuse Poland of complicity in the Holocaust. Or Austria, where the neo-Nazis in the governing coalition want to fail kindergarteners for not knowing German. Or Italy, where a fanatically anti-immigrant coalition that won power is now going after the Roma. All these rode to power, or intensified their grip on it, like Orbán, by stoking voters' fear of migrants, promising to ban new immigrants and to take away the rights of immigrants already in the country. Once in power, they energetically set about depriving everyone else of their rights, migrants or citizens.

It's a successful strategy for the fearmongers. Driven by this fear, voters are electing, in country after country, leaders who are doing incalculable long-term damage. And some liberal politicians blame not the fearmongers or the people who vote for them – but the migrants. 'Europe needs to get a handle on migration,' declared Hillary Clinton in November 2018. It 'must send a very clear message – "We are not going to be able to continue to provide refuge and support" – because if we don't deal with the migration issue it will continue to roil the body politic.'

The economist Jennifer Hunt tells a story about visiting Germany recently and listening to people making the liberal argument against letting in refugees: 'If we let these people in, we'll have the far right in government.' Hunt's response: 'If you don't let these people in, you've already become a far-right government.'

Jews fleeing Nazi-occupied Europe were the harbinger of today's global migrants; many of today's covenants that protect refugees came into existence in response to their predicament. So it's particularly painful to hear that the first army in our time to shoot at people crossing the border looking for asylum was the Israeli army. In 2015, Israeli soldiers fired on African migrants crossing the Egyptian border, wounding a number of them. In December 2017, the Knesset passed a law under which the 40,000 asylum seekers in the country 'will have the option to be imprisoned or leave the country'.

It was fear of migrants, principally, that led the British to vote for Brexit, the biggest own goal in the country's history. A You-Gov poll in the days before Brexit found that 56 per cent of Britons named 'immigration and asylum' as the biggest issue facing the country. Tabloids with headlines such as 'Migrants Rob Young Britons of Jobs' and 'Britain's 40 per cent Surge in Ethnic Numbers' stoked fear of outsiders, day after day. From 2010 to 2016, the *Daily Express* ran 179 front-page anti-immigration stories and the *Daily Mail* 122 similar front-page jeremiads.

In the lead-up to Brexit, the far-right member of the European Parliament Nigel Farage unveiled a poster showing a horde of non-white males attempting to cross into Slovenia, with the slogan 'Breaking point: the EU has failed us all'. It turned out that the photograph was of a column of refugees, not economic migrants, and was similar to an image used in a Nazi propaganda film. But it worked, and Brexit passed. In the year after the Brexit vote, hate crimes in England and Wales jumped by 29 per cent. The young Brits who were gobsmacked by Brexit – even though a majority of them didn't vote for it – will soon experience firsthand the rigours of border control that their forefathers made people like my mother endure.

In the United States, voters motivated by an utterly irrational fear and hatred of immigrants elected in 2016 a leader who might end up being the most destructive in the country's history. In surveys, Trump's promise to build a wall was the single most important factor cited by crossover voters, including women. When Congress refused to fund his wall, he shut down the government itself for the longest period the nation had ever known, causing enormous economic and political damage.

For much of the twentieth century, America's greatest threat was from outside: Japan, the Soviet Union. Then from al-Qaeda. Now we realize that the greatest peril comes from within, from the heartland: Queens, New York. Only a year into his presidency, Donald Trump had succeeded in making the country I call home the most polarized I have ever seen it. Democrat versus Republican, Anglo versus Latino, urban versus rural, rich versus poor, men versus women: people are at each other's throats as never before.

A battle is being fought today in the public squares, in the political conventions, on the television, in the op-ed pages: a battle of storytelling about migrants. Stories have power, much more power than cold numbers. That's why Trump won the election; that's why Modi and Orbán and the Philippines' Rodrigo Duterte won power. A populist is, above all, a gifted storyteller, and the recent elections across the world illustrate the power of populism: a false narrative, a horror story about the other, well told.

The fear of migrants is magnified by lies about their numbers; politicians and racists train minds to think of them as a horde. In all the rich countries, people – especially those who are poorly educated or right-wingers – think that immigrants are a much bigger share of the population than they really are, and think that they get much more government aid than they really do. A recent study found that Americans think that the foreign-born make up around 37 per cent of the population; in reality, they are only 13.7 per cent. In other words, in the American imagination, we are three times as large as we really are. The French think that one out of three people in their country is Muslim. The actual number is one out of thirteen. British respondents to the poll predicted that 22 per cent of the people will be Muslim by 2020; the actual projection is 6 per cent.

A quarter of the French, one in five Swedes and one in seven Americans think immigrants get twice as much in government handouts as the native-born. This is not remotely true in any of these countries. Americans estimate that a quarter of all immigrants are unemployed; in reality, under 5 per cent are.

But there are also countertrends and counterexamples. Multiple studies have found that people who have direct contact with immigrants have much more positive views about their work ethic and reliance on welfare, and are much more open to increased immigration. And there are leaders who welcome migrants, however embattled they may be. Look at France, which elected the unapologetically pro-immigrant Emmanuel Macron, or Germany under Angela Merkel, which welcomed a million refugees in 2015. Above all, consider Canada, where the Justin Trudeau government has declared its intention to increase the flow of immigrants threefold, and whose economy had the strongest growth in the G7 in 2017 – 3 per cent a year, as opposed to the 2.2 per cent in Trump's America (although the gap disappeared in 2018, thanks to Trump's massive tax giveaways to the rich and to corporations). Hate crimes against Muslims actually went down in Canada in 2017; in its southern neighbour, they jumped by 5 per cent.

This shows that when countries safeguard the rights of their minorities, they also safeguard, as a happy side effect, the rights and economic well-being of their majorities, or other minorities within the majority. If a judiciary forbids discrimination against, say, Muslims, it is also much more likely to forbid discrimination against, say, gay people. The obverse is also true: when they don't safeguard the rights of their minorities, every other citizen's rights are in peril.

Every majority is composed of a set of discrete minorities. When you go after Palestinians and Africans in Israel, the Reform Jews are next. When you go after Muslims in India, the Christians are next. When you go after Muslims and Mexicans in America, the Jews and gays are next. The early targets are easy to hit, under the cover of nationalism. But hate, once fed, grows ever more ravenous. It is never satisfied.

But where does the hate come from? How was it generated?

10

A Brief History of Fear

Homo sapiens has always moved around the continents, and often been hated for doing so. Our time is one in which, after a postwar openness to migrants, that hatred has resurfaced. Where does this fear and loathing of migrants come from? It didn't start with the yobs on the street, the skinheads marching in leather, the torch-bearing white supremacists. The hatred has been manufactured. It's an Old World idea. While the colonizers ruled over the colonies – and the slave owners in the New World over the slaves – they also began to find it essential to distinguish themselves from their subject peoples, to hold themselves morally, intellectually and civilizationally superior to them. Otherwise, where would the colonial enterprise end? In intermarriage and race degradation. Since there were so many more of them than there were of the colonists, the tiny number of colonial officers would dissolve into a larger sea. Gandhi put the numbers in perspective: 'If we Indians [in 1947, 390 million strong] could only spit in unison, we would form a puddle big enough to drown 300,000 Englishmen.'

So, over the years, there's been a rich vein of hysterical European, particularly French, literature on the subject. Much of it is about Calcutta, epicentre of Western fears – and my birthplace. The legend began with the 'Black Hole', a small prison in which 146 British prisoners of war were locked up for three days in the stifling June of 1756 by an Indian nawab; only twenty-three survived. Ever since then, the popular image of Calcutta has been that of a giant urban black hole: overcrowded, hot, filthy.

Thus, the celebrated French anthropologist Claude Lévi-Strauss on Calcutta in 1955's *Tristes Tropiques*:

> What we are ashamed of as if it were a disgrace, and regard as a kind of leprosy, is, in India, the urban phenomenon, reduced to its ultimate expression: the herding together of individuals whose only reason for living is to herd together in millions, whatever the conditions of life may be. Filth, chaos, promiscuity, congestion; ruins, huts, mud, dirt; dung, urine, pus, humours, secretions and running sores; all the things against which we expect urban life to give us organized protection, all the things we hate and guard against at such great cost, all these by-products of cohabitation do not set any limitation on it in India. They are more like a natural environment which the Indian town needs in order to prosper. To every individual, any street, footpath or alley affords a home, where he can sit, sleep, and even pick up his food straight from the glutinous filth. Far from repelling him, this filth acquires a kind of domestic status through having been exuded, excreted, trampled on and handled by so many men ...
>
> In certain respects at least, these people, although tragic, appear childish to us. First, there is the engaging way in which they look and smile at you; then their indifference to propriety and places, which is forced upon your attention since they sit or lie about in any position; their liking for trinkets and cheap finery; their naïve and indulgent behaviour.

Lévi-Strauss's disgust wasn't directed just at Indians; it was at modernity in general, and its effects on the aboriginal peoples around the world that he loved. Lévi-Strauss loved tribal India, but not modern India, the India of the cities. Because cities contain a lot of people. And people like Lévi-Strauss don't like density. When confronted by masses of people, otherwise sober, non-racist professors experience a severe allergic reaction and start foaming at the typewriter.

The once-renowned environmentalist and Stanford biologist Paul Ehrlich begins his enormously influential 1968 book *The Population Bomb* (published by the Sierra Club) with another hysterical epiphany, this time in Delhi:

> I have understood the population explosion intellectually for a long time. I came to understand it emotionally one stinking hot night in Delhi a few years ago. My wife and daughter and I were returning to our hotel in an ancient taxi. The seats were hopping with fleas. The only functional gear was third. As we crawled through the city, we entered a crowded slum area. The temperature was well over 100, and the air was a haze of dust and smoke. The streets seemed alive with people. People eating, people washing, people sleeping. People visiting, arguing, and screaming. People thrusting their hands through the taxi window, begging. People defecating and urinating. People clinging to buses. People herding animals. People, people, people, people. As we moved slowly through the mob, hand horn squawking, the dust, noise, heat, and cooking fires gave the scene a hellish aspect. Would we ever get to our hotel? All three of us were, frankly, frightened.

Ehrlich and his family emerged from the taxi awakened to the peril: 'an utter breakdown of the capacity of the planet to support humanity'.

This epiphany led Ehrlich to advocate that the US condition its food aid to poor nations, like India, on those countries sterilizing their males.

> The United States could take effective unilateral action in many cases ... When we suggested sterilizing all Indian males with three or more children, we should have applied pressure on the Indian government to go ahead with the plan. We should have volunteered logistic support in the form of helicopters, vehicles, and surgical instruments. We should have sent doctors to aid in

the program by setting up centers for training para-medical personnel to do vasectomies. Coercion? Perhaps, but coercion in a good cause. I am sometimes astounded at the attitudes of Americans who are horrified at the prospect of our government insisting on population control as the price of food aid. All too often the very same people are fully in support of applying military force against those who disagree with our form of government or our foreign policy. We must be just as relentless in pushing for population control around the world.

Your belly or your dick: choose!

Ehrlich and his wife, Anne, were leading advocates for restricting immigration to the United States – because all those extra people would be bad for the environment – and for restoring ethnic quotas on immigration. He predicted that four billion people, including sixty-five million Americans, would die because the planet was incapable of feeding them. 'Sometime in the next 15 years,' Ehrlich predicted, 'the end will come.' This was in 1970.

None of this actually happened, of course – and India, Ehrlich's nightmare country, is actually reaping the demographic dividend of a workforce with a median age of twenty-seven. But there's something about brown and black people reproducing that has always horrified Western thinkers and leaders. Churchill, in 1945, opined that Hindus are 'protected by their mere pullulation [rapid breeding] from the doom that is their due.'

The *Mein Kampf* of the contemporary anti-immigrant movement in the West is a poisonous 1973 French novel called *The Camp of the Saints*. Its author, Jean Raspail, was nothing like Lévi-Strauss, the champion of aboriginal cultures, or Ehrlich, the environmentalist. He was a French adventurer in the tradition of the great pith-helmet-wearing white explorers who brought horrifying tales of native debaucheries back to Europe for the delectation of audiences like the Académie Française and the Société de Géographie, both of which gave Raspail awards for his books. *The Camp of the Saints* imagines a convoy of 800,000 migrants from my birthplace, Calcutta, on course to land in France in the year 2000. On board, they copulate promiscuously, including with their own children, and eat each other's excreta. As they prepare to land in France, the country is torn between liberals who are ready to welcome the new arrivals and the gallant native whites who have the moral fibre to fire on the unarmed men, women and children of the boat.

The prose of the novel is a whiter shade of purple. This is how the Indians – like me, my parents, my children – are described: 'First to land were the monsters, the grotesque little beggars from the streets of Calcutta. As they grovelled through the wet sand like a pack of basset hounds, or a herd of clumsy seals exploring an unfamiliar shore, with their snorts and grunts of joy, they looked like an army of little green men from some remote planet.'

It is an out-and-out, unapologetically racist book, as Raspail states in his 1982 preface to a reprinting: 'Our hypersensitive and totally blind West ... has not yet understood that whites, in a world become too small for its inhabitants, are now a minority and that the proliferation of other races dooms our race, my race, irretrievably to extinction in the century to come, if we hold fast to our present moral principles.'

The novel's influence has only grown over time. It set off a wave of other (mainly French) imaginings of this alien invasion, such as Renaud Camus's theory of 'the Great Replacement', in which Europeans will be replaced by immigrants, mostly Muslim, all at once. Michel Houellebecq's 2015 novel *Submission* imagined a north African Muslim winning the presidency of France.

In 1995, Raspail's disease-ridden book crossed over the ocean and landed in America, where it was reprinted by a malevolent ophthalmologist and eugenicist in Michigan named John Tanton, the *fons et origo* of today's anti-immigration movement in America. Tanton founded the anti-immigrant groups the Federation for American Immigration Reform (FAIR), the Center for Immigration Studies and Numbers USA; and he was a board member of US English and, not incidentally, the head of the Petoskey, Michigan, chapter of Planned Parenthood and a Sierra Club official. (There's often been a troubling alliance between extreme environmentalists, the zero-population growth crowd and racists, based on a common fear of density.) *The Camp of the Saints* has had an enormous influence on both Steve Bannon, who has called current immigration to Europe 'a Camp of the Saints-style invasion', and Marine Le Pen, who keeps a signed copy at her desk.

Tanton republished *The Camp of the Saints* in 2001, writing,

> Over the years the American public has absorbed a great number of books, articles, poems and films which exalt the immigrant experience. It is easy for the feelings evoked by Ellis Island and the Statue of Liberty to obscure the fact that we are currently receiving too many immigrants (and receiving them too fast) for the health of our environment and of our common culture. Raspail evokes different feelings and that may help to pave the way for policy changes. *The Camp of the Saints* takes the world population explosion and the immigration debate in a new direction. Indeed, it may become the *1984* of the twenty-first century.

Tanton's correspondence with a white donor reveals his truest colour. 'One of my prime concerns is about the decline of folks who look like you and me.' The godfather of today's anti-immigration movement also declared, 'For European-American society and culture to persist requires a European-American majority, and a clear one at that.' He was, like many racists, a eugenicist. 'Do we leave it to individuals to decide that they are the intelligent ones who should have more kids? And more troublesome, what about the less intelligent, who logically should have less. Who is going to break the bad news to them?'

11

Culture: Shitholes Versus Nordics

From *The Great Gatsby*:

'Civilization's going to pieces,' broke out Tom violently. 'I've gotten to be a terrible pessimist about things. Have you read "The Rise of the Colored Empires" by this man Goddard?'

'Why no,' I answered, rather surprised by his tone.

'Well, it's a fine book, and everybody ought to read it. The idea is if we don't look out the white race will be – will be utterly submerged. It's all scientific stuff; it's been proved.'

'Tom's getting very profound,' said Daisy, with an expression of unthoughtful sadness. 'He reads deep books with long words in them. What was that word we—'

'Well, these books are all scientific,' insisted Tom, glancing at her impatiently. 'This fellow has worked out the whole thing. It's up to us, who are the dominant race, to watch out or these other races will have control of things.'

'We've got to beat them down,' whispered Daisy, winking ferociously toward the fervent sun.

'You ought to live in California—' began Miss Baker, but Tom interrupted her by shifting heavily in his chair.

'This idea is that we're Nordics. I am, and you are, and you are, and—' After an infinitesimal hesitation he included Daisy with a slight nod, and she winked at me again. '—And we've produced all the things that go to make civilization – oh, science and art, and all that. Do you see?'

> There was something pathetic in his concentration, as if his
> complacency, more acute than of old, was not enough to him
> any more.

America, a nation of immigrants, offers the welcome mat to newer immigrants; and periodically, yanks it out from under their feet. A look at its complicated history shows that the anti-immigrant story is long in the making.

In 1751, Ben Franklin wrote about the alien menace: the forefathers of America's current president. 'Why should the Palatine Boors be suffered to swarm into our Settlements, and by herding together establish their Language and Manners to the Exclusion of ours? Why should Pennsylvania, founded by the English, become a Colony of Aliens, who will shortly be so numerous as to Germanize us instead of our Anglifying them, and will never adopt our Language or Customs, any more than they can acquire our Complexion.'

In the 1850s, the American Party, or the 'Know-Nothings', sent over a hundred people to Congress and eight to occupy governors' mansions. They were formed as a populist Protestant reaction to the Irish fleeing the potato famine, and were anti-Catholic and anti-moneyed elites. They tried to change the laws so that only immigrants who had been in the country for twenty-one years could become citizens; this would ensure that recent immigrants, like the Irish, wouldn't be able to vote for many years. Eventually, the party collapsed in a split over slavery.

It wasn't just outright racists and nativists who engaged in such rhetoric, or even policy. In 1925, Franklin Delano Roosevelt editorialized, 'Californians have properly objected' to Japanese migrants 'on the sound basic ground that ... the mingling of Asiatic blood with European or American blood produces, in nine cases out of ten, the most unfortunate results.' When he became president, he put 120,000 Americans of Japanese descent in internment camps, suspecting them of dual loyalties.

Occasionally, nativists formed unlikely alliances with African-American groups for economic reasons. In 1924, the civil rights leader A. Philip Randolph came out against immigrants: 'We favor reducing immigration to nothing ... shutting out the Germans ... Italians ... Hindus ... Chinese and even the Negroes from the West Indies. The country is suffering from immigration indigestion.'

A perennial strain in thinking about immigration says, we're not against immigration, but some immigrants are better than others. The definition of 'better' changes according to the season. Earlier, it was about cranial size or IQ. The 'Goddard' in *Gatsby* is a reference to Lothrop Stoddard, a Harvard Ph.D. and Klansman whose 1920 book, *The Rising Tide of Color against White World-Supremacy*, was an immediate sensation. Stoddard warned, 'Non-white races must be excluded from America ... The red and black races if left to themselves revert to a savage or semi-savage stage in a short time.' Shortly after the book was published, Margaret Sanger, the founder of Planned Parenthood, invited Stoddard to be on the board, where he joined a roster of other well-known eugenicists.

These days, the debate is about culture.

In January 2018, according to the *Washington Post* and NBC News, Trump spoke out at a cabinet meeting about what kind of people should and should not be welcomed in the United States. 'Haiti? Why do we want people from Haiti here? Then they got Africa. Why do we want these people from all these shithole countries here? We should have more people from places like Norway.'

An essential prerequisite to denying entrance to the migrant is to posit a dualism, a clash of civilizations, in which one is far superior to the other, and is therefore entitled to dominate the other.

In July 2017, Trump delivered a speech in Poland, written by his advisor Stephen Miller, about what distinguishes Western civilization:

> Today, the West is also confronted by the powers that seek to test our will, undermine our confidence, and challenge our interests ... The world has never known anything like our

community of nations ... We write symphonies. We pursue innovation. We celebrate our ancient heroes, embrace our time-less traditions and customs, and always seek to explore and dis-cover brand-new frontiers. We reward brilliance. We strive for excellence and cherish inspiring works of art that honour God. We treasure the rule of law and protect the right to free speech and free expression. We empower women as pillars of our soci-ety and of our success. We put faith and family, not government and bureaucracy, at the centre of our lives ... And above all, we value the dignity of every human life, protect the rights of every person, and share the hope of every soul to live in freedom. That is who we are. Those are the priceless ties that bind us together as nations, as allies and as a civilization.

All hail Western civilization, which gave the world the genocide of the indigenous Americans, slavery, the Inquisition, the Holocaust, Hiroshima, and global warming. How hypocritical this whole debate about migration really is.

In 2004, Samuel Huntington, a Harvard professor who'd pre-viously predicted a 'Clash of Civilizations' on Islam's borders, now warned against Latino culture in a *Foreign Policy* cover story bearing the title 'Jose, Can You See?' 'There is no Americano dream. There is only the American dream created by an Anglo-Protestant society. Mexican-Americans will share in that dream and in that society only if they dream in English,' Huntington wrote. He asked readers to think of the United States not so much as a melting pot but as a tomato soup: 'The base of the tomato soup is the aboriginal Anglo-Protestant culture.' And what about everyone else who came later? 'Onions and croutons and parsley and spices.'

Huntington explained the differences between the base and the add-ons by quoting a Texas entrepreneur on 'Hispanic traits (very different from Anglo-Protestant ones) that "hold Latinos back": mistrust of people outside the family; lack of initiative, self-reliance, and ambition; little use for education; and acceptance of poverty as a virtue necessary for entrance into heaven'.

The republic is in peril, wrote Huntington.

> The persistent inflow of Hispanic immigrants threatens to divide the United States into two peoples, two cultures, and two languages. Unlike past immigrant groups, Mexicans and other Latinos have not assimilated into mainstream US culture, forming instead their own political and linguistic enclaves – from Los Angeles to Miami – and rejecting the Anglo-Protestant values that built the American dream.

Huntington was the most respectable exponent of the cultural theory of the world: that it is divided between seven or eight civilizations locked in perpetual conflict. 'These include Western, Confucian, Japanese, Islamic, Hindu, Slavic-Orthodox, Latin American and possibly African civilization,' he claimed. 'The most important conflicts of the future will occur along the cultural fault lines separating these civilizations from one another.'

So who are the 'good' immigrants these days? In discussions of illegal immigration to the United States, people mostly focus on Latinos. While it's true that half of the undocumented are Mexicans, what about, say, Canadians? 'I've never met an illegal Canadian,' declared South Carolina senator Lindsey Graham, explaining why the government focuses on undocumented immigrants from the southern border. 'People come in from poor countries to work here. They come to Myrtle Beach, Canadians do. They enjoy themselves, they go swimming in March, and they go home.'

In 2015, the same year Graham said this, 93,000 Canadians overstayed their US visas – more than any other nationality. That was twice the number of Mexicans who overstayed their visas. There are over 100,000 illegal Canadians living in the United States today. No force of Minutemen is zealously guarding the northern border, standing watch for Canadians coming in through the snowy wastes of the Dakotas.

Periodically, US congressmen of Irish descent fought for legislation that would benefit their ethnicity. Such as the first diversity visa programme, in 1987, created as a response to the 1965 Immigration Act, which lifted quotas on non-Europeans. It was sponsored by the Massachusetts congressman Brian Donnelly and passed at short notice and with little publicity – except in the Irish community. House Speaker Tip O'Neill ensured that the bill would pass, and Ted Kennedy did the same in the Senate.

Ten thousand visas to countries adversely affected by the 1965 bill were to be awarded on a first-come, first-serve basis, and people were allowed to file an unlimited number of applications. This benefited groups with knowledge of the process. All over America and Ireland, the Irish held 'Donnelly parties', filling out as many as 500 applications per person. Ireland chartered special planes to ship the applications to the United States. As a result, more than 40 per cent of the visas – 4,161 of the 10,000 – went to the Irish.

The terms of the diversity programme were changed in 1989, and it became a random lottery, with only one entry per person permitted. By 1990, the top three countries receiving visas were Bangladesh, Pakistan and Egypt. The Irish share, though, dropped from 40 per cent to 1 per cent. This wouldn't do. So the programme was changed again in 1991 by the Connecticut representative Bruce Morrison. The programme would give out 120,000 green cards, but 48,000 of them would be reserved for Irish immigrants. 'For the Irish, the most important part of the Morrison bill is the section that gives virtual amnesty to all the illegal Irish immigrants in the country, and to aliens from some other Western European countries,' the *New York Times* reported.

Again, in 1995, the Irish had priority for visas unclaimed under the programme between 1991 and 1993. They received almost all – 1,303 of the 1,404 visas – under the scheme.

In 2012, the Massachusetts Republican senator Scott Brown introduced a bill that would grant 10,500 special work visas exclusively for Irish immigrants. A 2018 NPR report states, 'Ireland estimates as many as 50,000 unauthorized Irish are living in the shadows in America. Their government is so concerned that the prime minister has appointed a member of Parliament, John Deasy, to be special envoy to the US Congress. His mission is to work out an immigration earmark for the unauthorized Irish, to find them a pathway to citizenship and get more work visas.' On his way out of office at the end of 2018, Speaker Paul Ryan pushed a bill through the House of Representatives that would award Irish citizens thousands of additional work visas every year. Even the right-wing *Breitbart News* called this bill 'amnesty for Irish illegals'. Ryan has publicly expressed his hope that he would be made ambassador to Ireland in his sixties.

The 50,000 Irish undocumented immigrants are all over the country, but particularly in New York, in neighbourhoods like Woodside, Queens, working in construction, or as bartenders or nannies. In 2017, ICE deported 128,765 Mexicans – and 34 Irish.

America, like much of Europe today, seems to have a problem with Muslims. When liberals bring up immigration, there's one group that nearly everyone agrees is unassimilable: Muslims. A rich Persian, nominally Muslim émigré friend was talking about the problems with Muslims in Europe. 'They shouldn't be allowed to have minarets in Switzerland! It ruins my Swiss-chalet vibe.'

This view is given scholarly sanction by people like Stanford University's Thomas Sowell:

> Not all cultures are compatible with the culture in this country that has produced such benefits for the American people for so long. Not only the United States, but the Western world in general, has been discovering the hard way that admitting people

with incompatible cultures is an irreversible decision with incalculable consequences. If we do not see that after recent terrorist attacks on the streets of Boston and London, when will we see it?

The op-ed columns and airwaves are filled with pundits like Sowell who proclaim that most migrants assimilate – except Muslims. Just like their intellectual ancestors, who made the same claim about Papists and Protestants.

Fuelled by this ideology, the United States, and some European countries, are being led by a bunch of Islamophobes who are already in power, like Viktor Orbán, or have a significant presence in parliament, like Geert Wilders in the Netherlands. Muslims are the only group that you can publicly hate and get away with it. In 2016, the Slovakian parliament passed a law essentially outlawing Islam as a state-recognized religion in the country, by raising the number of followers that a faith needed for such recognition from 20,000 to 50,000. The law was proposed by the Slovak National Party, whose chairman declared, 'Islamization starts with a kebab ... We must do everything we can so that no mosque is built in the future.' Even though the law was later vetoed by the president, Islamophobia runs rampant in the country's political establishment. 'Islam has no place in the country,' said Prime Minister Robert Fico in May 2016. Soon after, Slovakia assumed the presidency of the EU Council, with influence over the entire continent's policies on Islam.

All over Europe, there is an insistent drumbeat in the right-wing tabloids: the migrants are terrorists. Muslims are terrorists.

Again, the chain of historical responsibility must be followed. Millions have already died – in Muslim countries. We bomb them from the air, from the ground and from our warships. We kill indiscriminately, and then lie about it – as a 2017 *New York Times* investigation of the casualties from coalition airstrikes in Iraq showed, the death rate is thirty-one times greater than officially acknowledged. But when, having no other option, they flee for their lives to the very countries that are bombing them, we throw up our hands in horror.

'Europe is committing suicide,' declared the British neoconservative writer Douglas Murray, in his 2017 book, *The Strange Death of Europe*. 'Europe – the home of the European peoples – gradually became a home for the entire world ... Streets in the cold and rainy northern towns of Europe filled with people dressed for the foothills of Pakistan or the sandhills of Arabia.' The book is an all-out attack on Muslim immigrants in Europe, who, in Murray's view, have come to Europe not to work but to rape and pillage.

Earlier, in a 2006 speech to the Pim Fortuyn Memorial Conference in the Netherlands, Murray thundered, 'All immigration into Europe from Muslim countries must stop ... Conditions for Muslims in Europe must be made harder across the board: Europe must look like a less attractive proposition. We in Europe owe – after all – no special dues to Islam. We owe them no religious holidays, special rights or privileges. From long before we were first attacked it should have been made plain that people who come into Europe are here under our rules and not theirs. There is not an inch of ground to give on this one. Where a mosque has become a centre of hate it should be closed and pulled down. If that means that some Muslims don't have a mosque to go to, then they'll just have to realize that they aren't owed one.'

Murray later walked back from the speech. But the fact that an Eton- and Oxford-educated man could say these words, not after having a few pints too many in a pub, but from the floor of the Dutch parliament, and then continue to be taken seriously as a public intellectual (Clive James, Michael Gove, Sam Harris and Lord Sacks have praised his work), speaks volumes about the quality of the anti-immigrant discourse in Europe today.

12

The Colour of Hate

For many years, it seemed that foreign cultures had replaced dark-skinned races as permissible objects of loathing and contempt. But lately, the pendulum of hate has swung back to race. 'You will not replace us,' read the posters held aloft by the white supremacists marching in Charlottesville, Virginia. There is one number that fills the nativists with horror: 2044. That is the year when America is projected to stop being a majority white nation. Whites will become just one of many minorities.

An analysis by the *Washington Post* found that Trump's immigration policies, if implemented, would keep out twenty million immigrants over the next decades, and push back the Rubicon five years, to 2049. 'You can shut the door to everyone in the world and that won't change,' said Roberto Suro, an immigration and demography expert at the University of Southern California. 'The president can't do anything about that. If your primary concern is that the American population is becoming less white, it's already too late.'

In 2013, America reached a different racial landmark. For the first time, half of the babies under the age of one were non-white. In 2018, deaths among whites outnumbered births in more than half the states – twenty-six, up from seventeen just two years earlier. (Partly, this was driven by drug overdoses. Whites, particularly, are turning to heroin, fentanyl and opioids, just as African Americans in the 1980s and early '90s turned to crack.)

The United States, in the future, will look increasingly like Latin America, and also like India and China.

Hispanics in the United States have an average age of twenty-eight, in their prime for making babies. White Americans have an average age of forty-three. From 2010 to 2016, the population of native-born Hispanics grew by five million; the population of native-born whites fell by 400,000. The 18 per cent of the population that are Hispanics are the biggest minority group in the country today; by 2060, they will be 28 per cent.

Although Latinos still make up half of all the foreign-born in the country, and Asians only 31 per cent overall, that ratio has been changing in recent years. The fastest-growing race in the country is now Asian; we are increasing by a rate of 3.4 per cent a year. The second-fastest growing group? The mixed-race: those who are descended from two or more races. And the slowest-growing racial group? Whites, who are ambling along at 0.5 per cent a year.

There's also the fear that, once the non-whites are let in, we'll do better than them. The 2016 median US income for Indian Americans was $110,026, the highest of any group. Palestinian Americans earned $65,170; Syrian Americans, $63,096. 'White' Americans, as a group, earned $61,349 – lower than Pakistani Americans, Egyptian Americans, Iranian Americans, and a whole slew of immigrants from Muslim-majority countries.

When it comes to education, African immigrants are more accomplished than the average American: 43 per cent of those older than thirty have a college degree, versus 29 per cent of native-born Americans over thirty. While some groups of immigrants, such as refugees from Latin America, are less educated and earn less than the average American, immigrants overall are much better educated. Thirty per cent of native-born Americans have college degrees. The immigrants arriving between 2000 and 2009 were of the same grade: 30 per cent of them were college educated. But of the immigrants arriving after 2010, a full 45 per cent have college degrees.

Counties that voted for Hillary Clinton account for 64 per cent of US GDP, twice that of the many more counties that voted for Trump. That's because her voters are clustered around cities and universities, both of which attract immigrants, who help make the places they settle flourish. For this they are hated. Fifty-eight per cent of Republicans now think that universities are bad for America. As the economist Paul Krugman points out, 'One way to think of Trumpism is as an attempt to narrow regional disparities, not by bringing the lagging regions up, but by cutting the growing regions down. For that's what attacks on education and immigration, key drivers of the new economy's success stories, would do ... They won't make America great again – they'll kill the very things that made it great.'

But even if whites lose their majority, and their educational pre-eminence, they're not about to lose power anytime soon. That's because whites vote, even if they haven't finished school. In 2020, whites without a college degree will still be 44 per cent of eligible voters, and they vote solidly Republican; Clinton lost them by 31 points in 2016. According to the political scientist Ruy Teixeira, their support will enable Republican presidential candidates to keep winning the electoral college until 2036 even as they lose the popular vote, other factors being equal. 'This is a real sea change,' Teixeira said. 'This is why Republicans have been able to weather these demographic changes, entirely on the backs of white non-college voters.'

And it's those non-college voters who care most deeply about immigration. So the appeals to their xenophobia, by Trump and his successors, are a logical electoral strategy. Keep immigrants out; and if they must be let in, keep them from being naturalized; and if they're naturalized, keep them from voting. Hence the barrage of new voter ID laws in Republican-controlled states with a lot of Hispanic voters, like Texas and Arizona. Fifty-four per cent of all legal immigrants get naturalized within a decade, and are thus eligible to vote; among certain groups of immigrants, the rates are even higher: 78 per cent of Africans and 65 per cent of Asians get naturalized within ten years. And they vote – Democrat. In the 2018 mid-terms, 69 per cent of Latino voters voted for Democrats; for Asian voters, that preference was even stronger, shooting up from 50 per cent in 2016 to 77 per cent in 2018. Immigrants don't like the Organization Formerly Known as the Party of Lincoln.

So, the expelling of undocumented immigrants, the vast majority of whom are non-white; the severe limits on legal migration; and the types of migration that the Trump coalition wants to put an end to – the diversity lottery and family reunification – have a clear end in mind: to keep whites in power.

And what would this plan cost? What would it really cost to throw out all the undocumented? A total of $4.7 *trillion*, according to the Center for American Progress. That's how much the GDP would be lowered over a decade if such an expulsion were carried out, plus $900 billion in lost revenue for the government. All this is not including the cultural and human cost of the ethnic cleansing.

Half of all federal prosecutions already involve immigration. With the Trump administration's 'zero tolerance' policy of treating all undocumented immigrants as criminals, this is going to consume a greater share of federal prosecutorial resources. The Justice Department has become, above all, the Department of Immigrant Hounding.

We are seeing a new Red Scare, except this time the enemy isn't communists; it's immigrants. The ICE and Border Patrol raids, grabbing mothers on the streets and hustling them into government vans in front of their screaming daughters, are reminiscent of the Palmer Raids in 1919 and 1920, when hundreds of suspected leftists who were foreign or looked or sounded foreign were rounded up and deported. Obama was better in his language than Trump, but not much better in his policies. He was called the 'deporter in chief' by immigrant advocates because of his record of forcibly removing three million people without proper papers – a far higher number than Bill Clinton or George W. Bush had removed. Obama expended little serious political capital to make life easier for the undocumented during his eight years in office, pleading political gridlock under a Tea Party-controlled Congress, although he did sign executive orders protecting the Dreamers in his second term.

What are whites so afraid of?

In 2007 I sought a meeting with a man who, at the time, came across as a wild-eyed extremist on race and immigration. He turned out to be something of a prophet. His name was Ron Cutlip, and he was the head of the New York chapter of the Minutemen (Jim Gilchrist wing). A ragtag bunch of nativist vigilantes, they had been in the news for going down to the US–Mexican border and harassing people they thought were illegal immigrants. I had wondered what a group like that was doing in New York City.

Cutlip agreed to meet me at a Starbucks below his office, on Eighth Avenue.

'How will I recognize you?' I asked.

'I'm five feet eleven. White male, obviously. And you're Japanese?'

I looked for him in the Starbucks. He was forty-seven, with slightly greying brown hair and a tight, angry mouth. He was angry about many things, but he was angriest about being called a racist. He spent the first fifteen minutes of our interview defending himself against a claim that I had not made.

He gave me a card. It said 'R. Stuart Cutlip' in a Gothic font, with a Highland-plaid ribbon and a coat of arms to its left, and underneath, the title:

Golf Course Architect
Land Planner

'Did you say you're Indian?' he asked.
'Originally, yes, but now I'm American.'

'I'm gonna speak to you as a white male. For the majority of the population, which is white, the pendulum swung too far the other way … You keep calling me a racist and it has no effect on me anymore,' he said, addressing his invisible opponents. 'I've travelled the world and seen racism in Africa, one tribe against another. You could be any race in the world, you could be racist. White America has bent over backwards not to be racist.'

He grew up in Maryland, in the DC suburbs, going to school with the children of ambassadors in the 1960s and '70s. He has an MSc in real estate development from Columbia, where he recalled a political event he attended, put on by the Young Republicans and Minutemen. The audience was filled with students opposed to the event. 'They were racist, ignorant.' An African-American speaker took the stage. 'The black student body was yelling very bad racial slurs.' Mahmoud Ahmadinejad, the president of Iran, had recently been invited to speak at Columbia; according to Cutlip, even he hadn't faced such opposition. Cutlip decided that the students were completely ignorant, and he joined the Minutemen.

In New York, the Minutemen did things like turn undocumented immigrants in to the IRS for committing tax fraud or report them to ICE. 'The Minutemen are common people like me and you. They fought the British, on a moment's notice.'

Cutlip considers himself a true American. 'I have Cherokee blood in me,' he said. The white part of his family has been in the country since 1740. There were Minutemen in his family more than once: they fought in the Revolutionary War and in the French and Indian War. But another side of his family came in through Ellis Island, from eastern Europe at the turn of the century, 'on those ships, getting examined, documented, quarantined. We don't even have a system like that today – that would be called racist. They said, just like you did, "I'm an American now."'

He explained how he viewed immigration: 'We need to know who's coming into the country and why they're here. Just like if someone knocks on your door, you're like, "Excuse me, how can I help you?" There are times you let the electric man come in or the plumber, but you don't let him live there.'

'This nation is made up of immigrants,' Cutlip allowed. 'I don't care if you're a Native American, you came from somewhere else. Minutemen are not against immigration. This is about the rule of law. Come here legally.'

The immigration issue, he noted, 'is as broad as a quilt'. It includes issues such as terrorism, drugs and gangs. 'There is a huge number of illegal immigrants in our prison system for serious felonies. On the southern border it's completely out of control – if you are a farmer or rancher, you're afraid of going on your property unless you have a rifle,' he told me. 'In New York City the problem is a taxpayer problem. If you go down to the Medicaid office, you will find all the people there not speaking English. I'm paying their way. My taxes go up ... There's problems with illegal immigrants from China, from Arab countries, wherever ... There's issues probably from your own country – from Pakistan.' It's the third country he's identified me with, so far.

But he has a particular problem with Latinos. 'I'm gonna talk specifically about Hispanics. La Raza doesn't care about Ron Cutlip, the white man,' he said, pausing to look at me and adding, 'may not even care about you.' When white people band together as a group, they end up in federal prison for racketeering. 'None of the rules apply to Hispanics to come here – this race has preference over others.' He was mad that at Latino rallies, some people claim that part of the United States is part of Mexico. 'I'm not gonna let it be a Spanish-speaking country,' he vowed. 'I work in the golf course architecture industry. I've told the foreman I don't want anyone driving heavy equipment that doesn't speak English.' He didn't say whether or not he imposed the same requirements on the workers not driving heavy equipment.

And how would he solve the problem of undocumented immigration? 'Once you go after the employers for tax evasion and fraud, within a period of a year or two you could have this situation nipped in the bud. You crack down on him and give him a jail sentence.'

I asked him whether he had to hire undocumented immigrants, since the golf course industry is labour-intensive.

'Fifty per cent or sixty per cent of the workers in golf courses are illegal,' he admitted, not answering my question.

In a 2018 column, the paleoconservative commentator Pat Buchanan pointed out the political ramifications of today's immigration: 'In US presidential elections, persons of color whose roots are in Asia, Africa and Latin America vote 4–1 Democratic, and against the candidates favored by American's [sic] vanishing white majority.' Then he painted a picture of the looming apocalypse: 'Mass immigration means an America in 2050 with no core majority, made up of minorities of every race, color, religion and culture on earth, a continent-wide replica of the wonderful diversity we see today in the UN General Assembly.'

Today, these jeremiads against migrants are given vent full-throated on Fox News. The Fox anchors claim they're not anti-immigrant; they just want immigrants to come lawfully. The commentator Tomi Lahren often tweets imprecations at immigrants: 'We are indeed a nation of immigrants. We are also a nation of laws. Respect our laws and we welcome you. If not, bye. #DACA.'

An amateur genealogist named Jennifer Mendelsohn dug up a 1917 court case featuring Lahren's great-great-grandfather, a Russian immigrant named Constantin Dietrich. He was indicted on two counts of 'willfully, unlawfully, and knowingly' lying about a naturalization proceeding and forging a naturalization document 'with a knife or steel eraser or other instrument unknown to the Grand Jurors'. He'd failed to file his application in time, so he forged it to make it appear that it had been executed two years earlier.

'Migrant memoirs and other documents are full of examples of people who lied,' points out Hasia Diner, a professor of American

Jewish history at NYU. 'They lied about their ages, they lied about their occupations. The word went through immigrant ships and stations and ports of embarkation, to say that one had a particular skill. People lied to leave Europe, because they could be liable for military conscription.'

The most notorious immigrant hater in the Trump administration is his advisor Stephen Miller, who grew up Jewish in California. His great-grandparents Wolf and Bessie Glotzer were refugees fleeing the pogroms in Belorussia. They came over in 1903, without hindrance of extreme vetting or even an interview with the American embassy, with eight dollars in their pockets.

'For Miller to say his family came to America "legally" is simply a ruse,' the *Jewish Journal* points out. 'There was no illegal immigration at the turn of the century, because all non-Asian immigration was essentially legal until the 1920s. Then, as now, angry voices fought to keep these immigrants out. They organized the Immigration Restriction League, focused on shutting the ports to swarthy Italians and Jews. "The floodgates are open," wrote one anti-immigrant newspaper editor as the Eastern European Jews docked in New York. "The horde of $9.60 steerage slime is being siphoned upon us from Continental mud tanks." Such sentiments led to the Immigration Quota Act of 1924 – which effectively shut the door to Jewish immigration on the eve of the Holocaust.'

As the article notes, 'When an American Jew turns on immigrants, there is a whiff of head-scratching hypocrisy, if not something more clinical. It is taking the side of people who, in a historical blink of the eye, would have met your own great-grandparents at the docks with stones and spitballs.'

Miller's own uncle, David Glosser, posted a Facebook note: 'My nephew and I must both reflect long and hard on one awful truth. If in the early 20th century the USA had built a wall against poor desperate ignorant immigrants of a different religion, like the Glossers, all of us would have gone up the crematoria chimneys with the other six million kinsmen whom we can never know.'

In June of 1948, the MV *Empire Windrush* docked in Tilbury, Essex, and 500 Jamaicans stepped out on to British soil. They were citizens of the British Empire, responding to the mother country's desperate need to fill postwar labour shortages. Over the years, Britain recruited another half a million other citizens of Commonwealth countries like Jamaica, Trinidad and Barbados. They've been in the UK since then, working and paying taxes. The 1971 Immigration Act gave them indefinite leave to stay, but they never got to be UK citizens. They never thought they needed to.

In 2010, Theresa May, who was then home secretary, told the *Telegraph* that her aim 'was to create here in Britain a really hostile environment for illegal migration'. It was a set of measures intended to make life so miserable for people who were not in the country legally, that they would self-deport.

Because the Home Office had never issued documentation to the Commonwealth arrivals before 1971 – it had, in fact, destroyed their landing cards in 2010 – 50,000 of the 'Windrush generation' suddenly found themselves in a position of precarious legality. People who had come to the UK as children could lose their jobs and be deported at any time. They were denied access to medical care and kicked out of government housing.

Even though the government apologized after a series of reports in the *Guardian*, the scandal illustrates the precarious position of immigrants in countries like Britain, which have no written constitution to protect their rights. The country they've lived in legally most of their lives could throw them out at a moment's notice, without redress or apology. We'll invite you when we need your labour, then throw you out when we've done using you. It's only a coincidence that most of the Windrush generation happen to be black.

Fear of migrants earns politicians votes. Fear of migrants sells. Fox ratings have never been higher. The Springer newspapers in Germany, the Berlusconi papers in Italy, and *The Sun* and *Daily Mail* in the UK are flourishing, feeding their readers a daily diet of xenophobia.

But the greatest facilitator of race-hatred against refugees isn't a tabloid; it's Facebook. Researchers at the University of Warwick recently studied every anti-refugee attack – 3,335, over two years – in Germany. They found that among the strongest predictors of the attacks was whether the attackers are on Facebook. The social network aids the dissemination of rumours, such as that all refugees are welfare cheats or rapists; and, unmediated by gatekeepers or editors, the rumours spread, and ordinary people are roused to violence. Wherever Facebook usage rose to one standard deviation above normal, the researchers found, attacks on refugees increased by 50 per cent. When there were internet outages in areas with high Facebook usage, the attacks dropped significantly.

Facebook is today's Radio Télévision Libre des Mille Collines, the genocidal radio station that was the vehicle through which baseless rumours about Tutsis spread in Rwanda in the 1990s – rumours that roused Hutus to mass murder. In country after country – Myanmar, Germany, the United States – the social network has become the hate network, purveyor to a mass audience of the most outrageous falsehoods against migrants. And it is doing far too little to stop it.

The conversation about immigrants in America, too, is approaching incitement to genocide. Not just restraining or detaining the undocumented, but murdering them en masse. Virgil Peck, a Kansas state assemblyman, offered a solution to America's immigration problem in the legislature during a 2011 committee meeting on shooting wild hogs from helicopters: 'If shooting these immigrating feral hogs works, maybe we have found a [solution] to our illegal immigration problem.' He later said that he'd been joking, that he was just speaking like 'a southeast Kansas person'.

These comments were mirrored in February 2013 by a conservative radio show host and former US Navy SEAL named Carl Higbie. 'What's so wrong with wanting to put up a fence and saying "Hey, everybody with a gun, if you want to go shoot people coming across our border illegally, you can do it fo' free"?' Higbie said on his radio show, *Sound of Freedom*. 'And you can do it on your own, and you'll be under the command of the, you know, National Guard unit or a Border Patrol. I think stick a fence six feet high with signs on it in both English and Spanish and it says, "If you cross this border, this is the American border, you cross it, we're going to shoot you" ... You cross my border, I will shoot you in the face. I will go down there. I'll volunteer to go down there and stand on that border for, I don't know, a week or so at a time, and that'll be my civil duty. I'll volunteer to do it.'

What happened to this homicidal, hate-filled man? Four years later, Donald Trump appointed him to be head of external relations for AmeriCorps. After the comments came out in the wider media, he resigned.

In February 2018, the US Citizenship and Immigration Services (USCIS) removed the phrase 'nation of immigrants' from its mission statement. It will no longer secure 'America's promise as a nation of immigrants'; it will now merely 'administer the nation's lawful immigration system'. This was met with wide applause from anti-immigrant groups like FAIR and Numbers USA. The Peruvian-born head of USCIS, Lee Cissna, explained the change: that the agency now exists 'to ensure people who are eligible for immigration benefits receive them and those who are not eligible – either because they don't qualify or because they attempt to qualify by fraud – don't receive them, and those who would do us harm are not granted immigration benefits'. In other words, a sort of immigrant monitor, ever on the alert for criminals, terrorists, rapists, malingerers, deadbeats, cheats.

Even if they are observed more in the breach, these official catchphrases such as 'nation of immigrants' mean something: what the country's ideals are, what it aspires to. In changing the phrasing, USCIS removed even that aspirational ideal. It announced in no uncertain terms its idea of America: a nation of immigrant haters. The racists from my high school have grown up and they are celebrating. In Trump's America, they think they own the streets. I got a taste of this personally one night before Thanksgiving 2017 in Hoboken, New Jersey.

My sister, visiting from California, says, 'Let's go to Hoboken for a drink. They just elected a Sikh mayor.'

We park and walk down to the river. We cross an intersection and a beat-up black car pulls up with the windows open.

'Did you hear what they're yelling?' my sister asks.

'*Allahu akbar! Allahu akbar!*' a white man in the passenger seat yells out at us, grinning, rocking back and forth in his seat.

I turn, put up my middle finger at him.

The car is stopped at the intersection. He opens the door and walks fast towards us. He is dressed in a football jersey, in his twenties, heavily muscled; he would have beaten the shit out of us. There is a restaurant to our right, and my sister and I walk rapidly towards it.

'What's the problem?' my sister demands of the man coming at us.

'He gave me the middle finger!'

By now we're in the restaurant, and he stays outside, yelling curses at me. 'Wuss! Pussy!' Then he gets back into his car, and the car speeds off.

We sit in the restaurant and have a glass of wine. Then I decide to call the police, because the people in the car, amped up as they are, are probably looking for the next brown man to beat up.

Two cops show up: an older white cop with whiskers covering his jowls and a rookie Puerto Rican cop. The white cop interrogates me about the incident: 'Was he close to you? Was he yelling epithets when he was *out* of the car?' He's trying hard to demonstrate that it couldn't have been a bias attack; it was just drunk people in a car.

'He was yelling "*Allahu akbar*" at us,' I say.

The cop is nonplussed. 'What's that mean?'

'God is great.'

He throws out his hands. 'What's wrong with that?'

Then my sister explains that it's something often yelled at Muslims, implying that they're terrorists.

'But you don't even look Muslim!' the cop says. 'If I'm looking at you, I'd think you were Indian.'

I tell him that many Indians are Muslims.

The cops run through the logistics of the attack. I tell him we were crossing the street when we heard the insults.

'Did you push the crossing button on the signal?' he asks.

I say I didn't.

'Then you went against the light,' the cop declares, triumphantly. The sleuth has found the real crime: jaywalking.

'*I* pressed the crossing button,' my sister says.

I turn to the cop. 'What are you trying to get at?'

He gets on his radio and calls in a sergeant, a burly African-American man who turns out to be more sympathetic. 'I want to offer my sincere apologies. As a community, we're not like that.'

We walk carefully back to my car. A black car pulls up next to us, and we're both on our guard. The streets of Hoboken have never been so menacing.

As we're leaving, my sister says, 'I'm getting the tiniest taste of what it feels like to be black in America.'

It could have been worse for us, much worse. Two Indian engineers were having beers on the porch of a bar in Kansas earlier that year. A white Navy veteran came up to them. 'Where are you from?' he demanded. 'How did you get into this country?' Other people in the bar shooed them off. The questioner came back with a 9mm gun. 'Get out of my country!' he yelled, and shot both of them; one of them died. He was thirty-two and left a wife he'd been married to for just four years. She was waiting for her husband to come home so they could sip chai together in the backyard that unseasonably warm February evening.

Every year, extremists murder people for their views. The Anti-Defamation League notes, 'A majority of the 2017 murders were committed by right-wing extremists, primarily white supremacists, as has typically been the case most years. The white supremacist murders included several killings linked to the alt-right as that movement expanded its operations in 2017 from the internet into the physical world – raising the likely possibility of more such violent acts in the future.' Between 2008 and 2017, white supremacists accounted for 71 per cent of deaths in terror attacks in the United States.

The researcher Lyman Stone has calculated the ancestries of all 422 people charged with terrorism in America since 2001. More than half – 227 – have 'no foreign citizenship, parentage, or identifiable ancestry of any kind'. That is, they're Americans, in the generic sense. We have met the enemy, and he is us.

13

The Alliance between the Mob and Capital

Of course, resistance to immigration is not all about culture or race – at least not all the way down. It must be understood as well as an outgrowth of income inequality, which has been particularly grotesque recently.

The gap between rich and poor in Britain today is the highest it has been since the 1860s. Many working-class Britons see London as a playground of the global elite, and find themselves unable to afford a house or even a meal at a good restaurant. 'Given the recent evolution, one might have expected to observe rising political demand for redistribution,' wrote the French economist Thomas Piketty. 'However so far we seem to be observing for the most part the rise of various forms of xenophobic "populism" and identity-based politics (Trump, Brexit, Le Pen/FN, Modi/BJP, AfD, etc.), rather than the return of class-based (income-based or wealth-based) politics.'

In the last three decades, there was zero income growth in the bottom 50 per cent of American households. The income of the top 1 per cent, meanwhile, leaped by 300 per cent, and their share of the country's total wealth grew from 22 per cent in 1980 to 40 per cent by 2017. The bottom 40 per cent of Americans not only don't have any wealth to speak of, but they actually owe an average of $8,900 as of 2017. This concentration of wealth also leads to a concentration of political power and the redirection of outrage against inequality away from the elites and towards the migrants.

During the Trump campaign, Steve Bannon railed against Wall Street as loudly as he railed against immigrants. Soon after he won the election, riding a wave of immigrant-hatred, Trump stocked his administration with the very Wall Street elites Bannon had denounced – people like Steve Mnuchin, Wilbur Ross and Gary Cohn. A cabinet of billionaires, the wealthiest in American history. And eventually, Bannon was shown the door. The administration, and the Republicans in Congress – including people who had said 'Never Trump' during the campaign – then proceeded to enact a series of tax cuts and rollbacks on financial regulation that the wealthy had long dreamed about. It was a smart strategy. When the peasants come for the rich with pitchforks, the safest thing for the rich to do is to say 'Don't blame us, blame them' – pointing to the newest, the weakest: the immigrants.

Who are the people who fall for this, and why?

In summer 2016, I took an epic road trip with my son to drop him off at college in California. We saw the biggest country we'd ever seen. Endless mountains, endless roads. Cattle on the road, licking up water from the recent thunderstorm off the blacktop with their big fat tongues. Red sandstone ramparts on the Colorado–Utah border; who were these fortresses built for? What palaces adorned their summits? We passed small towns: Rachel, Warm Springs; nothing more than a collection of trailers and a motel, and maybe a general store. In the towns with more than one street, kids ran about in packs. On the road, trucks were piled high with bales of hay. These were not gentleman farmers.

On my way back, I set my Google Maps setting to 'Avoid Highways' and took a month to get back to New York. One morning, after driving through hours and hours of thick Allegheny forest in northern Pennsylvania, I found myself in Warren, a small town by a river. I was hungry and decided to stop for lunch. As I got out of the car, I noticed a sign saying 'Blair Company Museum' on a three-storey building. I walked in and found myself inside a clothing store selling casual wear. Behind the store was the museum, where I learned that the Blair Corporation got its start selling raincoats to undertakers in 1910. The exhibits told the story of the company's beginning and steady rise. Business really took off during the wars, when the company supplied raincoats to the military. There was a waxwork of the company founder standing with his trench coat at the entrance to his personal elevator. There were photos of all the people who had worked for the company on the wall: as long as the photos were in black and white, there were more people in the picture each succeeding year. The photos showed a prosperous, behatted, white America; men in cardigans swinging a golf club, women in long dresses and permed hair.

The company prospered, making garments and selling them all over the country. When the photos entered the colour era, sometime around the 1960s, the number of people in the pictures started dropping off. The company started seeing declining sales because of competition from China. The last of the executive portraits in the museum is of a plump-faced south Indian, who resigned as CEO in 2010. These days, the Blair Corporation is a mail-order supplier selling foreign-made garments, with a mixed record for quality: at least nine people died across the country when the Blair chenille robes they were wearing caught fire. In 2009, the company was sued, and the federal government ordered Blair to recall 300,000 garments made in Pakistan. It still employs a few hundred 'associates', but all its manufacturing in Warren has ceased, and its ownership regularly changes hands as a subsidiary of larger companies and investment funds. There are no pictures of whoever owns the company today in the Blair Company Museum.

I stepped outside the museum and walked around the ghosts of giant factories and down the main street with shuttered and abandoned shopfronts until I found a store that was open, an antique emporium. Inside were stalls where the townspeople were, literally, selling their family jewels. Except there were no people in the vast emporium other than the manager and his assistant. I picked up a beautiful set of Depression-era glasses and tray for $20, and felt bad about paying so little.

I chatted with the friendly manager, a white veteran who walked with a cane, about places to eat. He offered to personally walk me to the bar/restaurant that his friends ran. We stepped outside into the sunlight.

'It's a beautiful town,' I said.

'It used to be,' he said, and sighed. 'Nowadays the only industry left is the military or the drug trade.' There were very few people on the street this midday. Occasionally I would see a young white man or woman who looked strung out as they stumbled along the empty streets, zombies in a ghost town. The whole scene reminded me of Harlem or the East Village in the 1980s, young junkies wandering among abandoned houses and stores – except these people were all white. White people fled the cities to escape the inner city; the inner city followed them to places like Warren, Pennsylvania.

Warren housed 15,000 souls in 1940 and is now down to 9,478. For $45,000, you can buy a three-bedroom home in decent condition. There are very few immigrants in Warren; 99 per cent of the population is made up of US citizens, almost all of them white. Still, they fear immigrants. A few months after my visit, Warren County went for Trump en masse: 69 per cent, against the 27 per cent that voted for Clinton. The city of Warren voted for Trump by 2,219 votes over Clinton's 1,334 votes. In 2012, Obama had carried this same city over Romney by a thin margin.

I could understand the anger and confusion of the people in Warren. The twentieth century belonged to them; they worked in the town's factories and felt glad to be Americans. Now they were truly desolate in a way that they had seen only American blacks desolated: their young people were cannon fodder or junkies. What happened? Whose fault was it?

Today, the eight richest individuals on earth, all men, own more than does half the planet, or 3.7 billion people, combined. The top 1 per cent have more wealth than the bottom 99 per cent combined. There are 1,542 billionaires today, whose fortunes rose by a fifth in 2017, to $6 trillion – equivalent to the GDP of the UK and Germany combined. Such figures cause outrage in the rich countries; many of the Obama Democrats in the Rust Belt who voted for Trump did so because Steve Bannon convinced them that he shared their anger against Wall Street.

Income inequality in the United States rises, in part, from radically different systems of education for the rich and the poor. Only 20 to 30 per cent of the children of the poorest 10 per cent go to college; but 90 per cent of the kids of the top 10 per cent do.

Deregulation of the financial sector also gave an outsize share of society's most glittering prizes to the top 1 per cent. This was facilitated by a tax system that grows ever more regressive. At the end of 2017, the US Congress gave the biggest Christmas gift in history to the richest in the country: dramatically lowering their taxes while doubling the estate tax exemption. According to estimates from Union Bank of Switzerland and Pricewaterhouse-Coopers, 460 people will bequeath $2.1 trillion to their heirs over the next twenty years, which is larger than the GDP of India, a country of 1.3 billion people. It will be the greatest transfer of wealth in history.

So the way to wealth now isn't to work for a pay cheque, but to inherit Daddy's millions and then put your money in a hedge fund, where the structure of investment and tax laws allows for crazy returns – at least until it all goes crashing down, at which point, as with the financial bailout of 2008, the little people who pay taxes can be sent the bill.

As the people in Warren are slowly realizing, there's a tax on being poor. You pay more for everything, particularly to the money changers: the banks charge the poor higher interest rates on credit cards, mortgages and student loans – simply because they're poor and ill equipped to stay ahead of the schemes that are designed to fleece them. The rich get richer because they can hire the smartest people to grow their wealth.

The United States, at this point, cannot properly be called a capitalist society. It is a plutocratic society, a society of rent seekers. The 'moral hazard' that is supposed to be part and parcel of free enterprise – you can make as much money as you want, but if you fail, you're on your own – has been rendered moot by the government's willingness to catch you if you fail, as long as you're wealthy. The giant upward transfer of wealth, already unprecedented since the age of the robber barons, is set to accelerate. So the farmers and steelworkers who voted for Trump will find their taxes going up, their benefits slashed, their health insurance nonexistent, and they will be angrier still. But the news that they listen to – financed by the plutocrats – will divert them ever more energetically on to immigrants, the invisible enemy.

With the passage of the tax bill, America will look even more like an airliner: divided into first, business, premium economy and basic economy. It's not just the poor against the rich anymore; it's the poor against the middle class, the upper-middle class against the rich. The country is angry, and going to be angrier still once the economy starts going south again and the people in cattle class realize they've been sold a bill of goods.

Who benefits from populists railing against immigrants and greedy elites? The greedy elites. Who has benefited the most from Trump's election? Wall Street, the corporations that got the gargantuan tax cut, as well as free rein to let their industries pollute unchecked. Many of these same corporations were, earlier, publicly arguing against restrictions on immigration, because it would drive up wages when the supply of cheap foreign labour went down; but they stopped making a fuss once Trump took office and delivered the goods. The same is true of a number of other 'populists' around the world: the greatest beneficiaries of their assuming power have been the rich and the corporations in their countries. Environmental regulations have been eviscerated, banks have been freed to gamble with their customers' money, corporate taxes have been slashed beyond the CEOs' wildest dreams.

In *The Origins of Totalitarianism*, Hannah Arendt called it the 'alliance between mob and capital'. When the rich see that anger is building in their countries about economic deprivation, they inflame or create anger and resentment against scapegoats – like foreigners, during Arendt's time, and immigrants or Muslims or African Americans today – which makes the mob change direction, turn their attention from demanding redistribution of wealth, and focus on the politically weak, the newcomers, the minorities. The new robber barons have come to power, and intend to hold on to it, on the wings of xenophobia.

14

The Refugee as Pariah

The first time many Americans became aware of the family-separation policy was in spring 2018. After an epic journey, a Congolese mother and her six-year-old daughter, fleeing mass rape and war in their country, had turned up at the US–Mexican border in November 2017. They immediately presented themselves to border control officials and requested asylum. An officer interviewed the mother and determined that she had a credible case for asylum. They should have been released on parole. But the San Diego ICE field office has a policy of refusing to grant parole to asylum seekers, and so they were detained.

Four days later, the officers summoned the mother and child into a room. Then they dragged the little girl away, 'screaming and crying, pleading with guards not to take her away from her mother', according to the American Civil Liberties Union. The mother was handcuffed, jailed and not allowed to speak to her daughter for the next four days. In those four days, she had no idea what happened to her daughter.

What happened was this: the Department of Homeland Security shipped the child 2,000 miles north, to an immigration detention centre in Chicago, which might as well be the moon for the little girl, who only spoke Lingala. From November until March, the mother was allowed to speak to her daughter a total of six times, by phone. No video. In December the girl spent her seventh birthday far from her mother, far from any family, in an ICE jail for child migrants. Each time the little girl heard her mother's voice on the phone, she started crying uncontrollably; she was fearful about what would happen to her and her mother. The mother was sick with worry, and couldn't sleep or eat.

In an editorial, the *Washington Post* summarized the policy of separating parents from their children at the border: the mother and child 'could have been placed together in a family detention center. There has been no explanation of why the determination was made to separate them; nor is there any allegation that [the mother] is an unfit parent. The only principle at work, if it can be called that, is the idea that future asylum seekers might be deterred if they are convinced that the United States is actually a crueler and more heartless place than their native country.' It's a competition: you think rape and robbery on the freight train north was bad? You ain't seen nothing yet. We're going to take your children away from you when you get here.

The Congolese mother and child, of course, were only an augury of things to come. Over the next few months, the Trump administration officially instituted the family-separation policy. Children, no matter how young, were to be separated from their parents who showed up at the border while their case was being adjudicated. There was a grim legal logic to this. The Trump administration had decided to put parents applying for asylum in detention centres automatically – unlike in the past, when they were granted parole pending their asylum hearing. But it would be a violation of earlier court orders, the government argued, to imprison their children with them. So tens of thousands of children were taken from their parents and shipped to 'shelters', which were often across the country, with little or no access to their parents. It was a policy specifically intended to deter families fleeing violence and instability in their home countries. Why was it so draconian? What primal fear could these ragged families evoke in the hearts of the mightiest government in world history?

The refugee, as the Polish sociologist Zygmunt Bauman said, brings with him the spectre of chaos and lawlessness that has forced him to leave his homeland. He embodies the economic and political disorder that was caused by the orderly rich countries when they sloughed off their redundant populations into colonies and then retreated, leaving behind ill-defined 'nation-states'. The refugee, though, suffers from statelessness; today, ten million people are officially stateless, people without a nation. Or he cannot 'go home' because his home has been wrecked by banditry or desertification.

So, bearing the burden of his failed state, he comes knocking on the West's doors, and if he finds one of them ajar, he slips in, not welcomed but barely tolerated. He may have been a surgeon in his alleged nation, but here he is ready to perform any task – such as clean the bedpans in a hospital where he is more qualified than most of the doctors – but can never hope to be one of them because of the laws protecting their guild. He must be abject, renouncing claims to an equitable share of the wealth of his new habitation or to any kind of political franchise. All he can hope for is a measure of personal security and the opportunity to remit enough money back to his family so that they can send the eldest boy to a private school near the refugee camp in which they await their chance to be reunited with their father, brother, husband in his marginal existence.

It was only in the early twentieth century that the modern, convoluted superstructure of passports and visas came about, on a planet where porous borders had been a fact of life for years beyond count. So the refugee arrives at the border of the country he seeks to live in, bearing papers, many papers, all kinds of papers that could make his case: school transcripts; certificates from notables and grandees such as teachers, politicians, Rotary Club presidents; identity cards; photos of the crater left by the bomb when it hit his house. Papers that establish identity, accomplishment, victimhood.

The political refugee has, by binding international covenants, the right to asylum. But in the orderly nations of northern Europe, he is rejected as much as, and in some cases (like Germany today) even more than, the economic migrant, because he is the sum of their worst fears, the looming future of the twenty-first century brought in human form to their borders. Because he wasn't necessarily impoverished in the country he came from – he might have been a businessman or an engineer just a year ago, before everything changed – he is a reminder that the same thing could happen to them too. Everything could change – radically, irrevocably, suddenly.

What is the difference between a refugee and a migrant? It is a strategic choice of words, to be made at the border when you're asked what you are; etymology is destiny. The 'migrant' does not even enjoy the nominal rights that are the privilege of the refugee, because it is implied that his movement is voluntary. You could be sent back if you're just an 'economic' migrant, but you could also be shunned and feared if you're identified as a political refugee. Whether you're running from something or running towards something, you're on the run.

In summer 2016, I drove out to the Hungarian–Serbian border with a volunteer for a church-based organization providing supplies to refugees. I had been in Hungary for a week studying its attempt to win the crown of Europe's most hostile country for refugees. All over the country, there were blue posters bearing questions like 'Did you know? Since the beginning of the immigration crisis, more than 300 have died in terrorist attacks in Europe', and 'Did you know? Brussels wants to settle a whole city's worth of illegal immigrants in Hungary', and 'Did you know? Since the beginning of the immigration crisis, the harassment of women has risen sharply in Europe'. The Orbán government was urging its citizens to vote in a referendum against accepting an EU quota of refugees: 1,294 refugees in 2016, for a country with almost ten million people.

We crossed the Serbian border at Röszke and spent four hours looking for a road to get to the cluster of tents we'd seen right by the side of the highway near the border. We drove on dirt roads in the depopulated countryside, past orchards of apple, peach and plum trees. From the car window, I picked a purple plum off a branch. It wasn't quite ripe yet.

A woman told us which road to take to the 'Pakistani camp'. We rattled down a rutted road by the superhighway and came up to the camp. It was an instant south Asian slum, but with back-packing tents instead of plastic sheets, just like the Sziget music festival I'd just come from on the Danube in Hungary. The festival had been filled with Instagram-ready teens, who, on payment of the $363-per-person entry fee, could luxuriate in their own tent city for a week.

There were children in the refugee tents, too, but younger and brown: pre-teens and toddlers on the run with their families. They played cricket amid the garbage. It cost a euro to use the toilet at the border. So people from the long lines of cars waiting to cross used the bushes instead, which served as the migrants' temporary home, where they slept and ate, waiting for the doors of Europe to open.

We opened the boot of our car and handed out water bottles, chocolates, socks and underwear. A group of men came over; when they identified me as Indian, they shook my hand and spoke to me in Urdu about their travels. One of them was from the Pakistani city of Lahore, where there were bombings and killings. He'd been here for just a few days. The Hungarians wouldn't let him in even though he had no desire to stay in that country; he wanted to go on to Germany, Sweden. The Serbians wouldn't let him go back to Macedonia. 'It's closed in the front. It's closed from the back,' he said.

A large black vehicle pulled up, and two big Serbian policemen dressed in black stepped out. 'Please go,' they told us; we didn't have official permission to visit the camp. They reminded us that the Hungarians were worse than the Serbians: 'They have drones and cameras,' they said, monitoring the camp from the other side of the border fence.

For the few refugees who make it over the fence, it's no promised land. At the time, any migrant caught within roughly five miles of the border would be arrested and deported. The Hungarian provision has since been expanded to include migrants detained in any part of the country. In November 2015, Orbán told a press conference, 'All the terrorists are basically migrants.' Like much else coming out of his mouth, this statement was factually wrong: many of the perpetrators of terrorism, in Europe and elsewhere, are native-born, like Timothy McVeigh and Anders Behring Breivik. Eight months later, he turned the statement on its head, broadening it: 'Every single migrant poses a public security and terror risk.'

If Hungary has elevated the anathematization of refugees to a new level, Denmark has gone one step further – rendering its own legal residents pariahs. In 2018, Denmark adopted an initiative called One Denmark without Parallel Societies: No Ghettos in 2030. According to the initiative, one of the three criteria for designating an area a 'ghetto' is if half or more of the inhabitants are from non-Western countries. The government classified thirty largely Muslim and immigrant neighbourhoods containing a total of 60,000 people as 'ghettos', in which parents will have to abide by an entirely different set of laws from those in the rest of the country.

The initiative includes twenty-two separate measures, some of which have been passed, and others that are still pending in parliament as of autumn 2018. Starting at the age of one, 'ghetto children' will be separated from their 'ghetto parents' for a mandatory twenty-five hours of instruction a week – not including nap time – in 'Danish values', which include celebrations of Christmas and Easter, even if the children are Muslim. If they don't obey, their welfare payments stop. Non-ghetto children can stay home until they're six. If ghetto parents compel their children to make extended trips to their homeland, which the government has dubbed 're-education trips', the government wants to jail them for two to four years, because the 'schooling, language and well-being' of the children would be harmed. They will also lose their residency rights. But if white Danish parents decide to send their kids to, say, America or Britain for boarding school, then no worries.

The government, with the broad support of most Danish parties, will also double the punishment for a crime committed in a ghetto – designated a 'special punishment zone'. A proposal that was seriously entertained was to confine ghetto children to their homes after 8 p.m., and have them monitored by electronic bracelets affixed to their ankles.

There is a war going on in Denmark – what the Danes call a 'meatball war'. It is a bloody war, but the blood is pig blood. Denmark has five million people and thirteen million pigs, and politicians in the country want to redress the imbalance. In 2013, Prime Minister Helle Thorning-Schmidt railed against Danish childcare centres dropping pork from their menus because they felt it might offend Muslims. A survey by a newspaper found that of the country's 1,719 childcare centres, exactly 30 had stopped serving pork or switched to halal food. But the meatball war had begun in earnest. That year, the far-right Danish People's Party (now part of the ruling coalition) announced that it would drop out of a closely fought mayoral campaign if the incumbent promised to serve more pork meatballs in public canteens.

In 2018, the immigration minister, Inger Støjberg, asserted that Muslims observing Ramadan were 'a danger to all of us', and demanded that those persisting in fasting during Ramadan stay home 'to avoid negative consequences for the rest of Danish society'. She pointed to bus drivers and people working in hospitals; a fasting bus driver might become faint and crash his bus. A spokeswoman for one of the country's main bus operators said they'd never had an accident with a driver who was fasting. If the minister's dark fears were true, the entire Muslim world would be awash in traffic accidents and medical malpractice during Ramadan.

In 2016, the pro-meatball side won a battle in the central Danish city of Randers. Its city council decreed that all public buildings *must* serve pork. 'We will ensure that Danish children and youth can have pork in the future,' a councillor stated. But another councillor said that the idea of defining a 'Danish food culture' is absurd. 'This is a pseudo-problem that doesn't exist in Randers. We don't have any institutions where you can't eat a hot dog if you want.'

The war over what real Europeans eat has a long history. During the Spanish Inquisition, an easy means of identifying Jews and Muslims for torture and forced conversion was if they shunned pork. When Indonesian migrants from the Netherlands' former colony began arriving in Holland in the 1950s, Dutch government officials regularly made unannounced inspections of their homes to make sure they were eating potatoes, not rice, and were thus assimilating into Dutch culture.

In 2016, the Danish parliament passed a law under which newly arrived refugees would be subject to a police strip search, and any valuables, including family jewellery, worth over 10,000 Danish kroner ($1,250 at the time) would be confiscated as advance payment for whatever support the state might provide them later. I remember the Hasidic Jews who would troop through my parents' diamond office on Forty-Seventh Street in New York, and their tales of how they'd got into the diamond business: they fled Nazi Germany after having converted their assets into loose diamonds, which they could carry on their person. If they were to have the misfortune to be in the same situation today, they would have their assets forfeited if they showed up in Denmark.

The world's richest countries can't figure out what they want to do about migration; they want some migrants and not others and will demean their own image to keep the latter out. In 2006, the Dutch government tried to make itself unattractive to potential Muslim and African migrants by creating a film, *To the Netherlands*, that included scenes of gay couples kissing and topless women sunbathing. The film was a study aid for a $433 compulsory entrance exam for people immigrating for family reunification. Except those making more than $54,000 a year, or citizens of rich countries like the United States or the European Union, for whom the requirement was waived. The film also showed the run-down neighbourhoods where immigrants might end up living. There were interviews with immigrants who called the Dutch 'cold' and 'distant'. The film warned of traffic jams, problems finding a job, and flooding in the low-lying country.

In 2011, the city of Gatineau, Quebec, published a 'statement of values' for new immigrants that cautioned against 'strong odors emanating from cooking', which might offend Canadians. It also informed migrants that, in Canada, it was not OK to bribe city officials. Also, that it was best to show up punctually for appointments. It followed a guide published by another Quebec town, Hérouxville, which warned immigrants that stoning someone to death in public was expressly forbidden. The warning was duly noted by the town's sole immigrant family.

In the twenty-first century, we will all have to suffer neighbours we dislike. I've been living in lower Manhattan on and off since 1980, when I studied at NYU, where I majored in Greenwich Village. I have a lot of immigrants coming into my neighbourhood now. They are wealthy invaders from Europe, China, Russia – as well as California, Florida, Oregon. They bring their tastes for food, which are quite different from mine. Most of the bagel shops and bodegas have disappeared, to be replaced by restaurants featuring $300 tasting menus. I don't like what these newcomers have done to my neighbourhood. They are a real economic threat to the people who live there: they've forced out the artists, the writers, the musicians that made this neighbourhood what it is. The newcomers have only the power of their money. But they're there. And I have to live with them.

The distaste for immigrant manners and mores so evident in Denmark and the Netherlands is spreading quickly. Often, a sexual panic is involved. In Germany, the country's 'welcome culture' changed in one season, from the guilt-expiating September 2015 – when the Merkel government opened its doors – to 'rapist refugees go home' after the Cologne attacks on women that same New Year's Eve. Of all refugees, the most frightening is the single male migrant, his eyes hungrily scanning the exposed flesh of the white woman. The words the tabloids and right-wing politicians use to describe these Afghan or Moroccan men are similar to the terminology used to describe black men in the United States in the early twentieth century: as sex-hungry deviants. In 1900, the South Carolina senator Benjamin Tillman spoke from the US Senate floor: 'We have never believed him [the black man] to be the equal of the white man, and we will not submit to his gratifying his lust on our wives and daughters without lynching him.'

Fast-forward to 2017: 'Pro-rata, Sweden has taken more young male migrants than any other country in Europe,' said Nigel Farage. 'And there has been a dramatic rise in sexual crime in Sweden – so much so that Malmö is now the rape capital of Europe.' This claim was quickly debunked: by 2015, the year Sweden took in a record number of asylum seekers, sex crimes decreased by 11 per cent from the year before.

While it is true that there are horrific stories of organized rings of rapists with immigrant backgrounds – such as a group of Pakistanis in Rotherham, in the UK, who groomed teenage girls for sex, or the north African men who assaulted German women en masse on New Year's Eve 2016 – there's no evidence that immigrants overall rape or steal at rates higher than the general population. In fact, there's plenty of evidence that immigrants commit less crime than the native-born. Mug shots of dark-skinned criminals, whether Moroccan or Mexican, somehow strike more terror in the Western imagination than those of home-grown white rapists. The fear is primal, tribal: they're coming for our women.

Salman Rushdie has written about the perverse reversal of history as depicted in books (and their screen incarnations) such as *A Passage to India* and *The Jewel in the Crown*, which have as central events the rape of an Englishwoman by an Indian: 'If a rape must be used as the metaphor of the Indo-British connection, then surely, in the interests of accuracy, it should be the rape of an Indian woman by one or more Englishmen of whatever class … not even Forster dared to write about such a crime. So much more evocative to conjure up white society's fear of the darkie, of big brown cocks.'

In situations of social stress, there's a long history of empires forcing entire populations to move: the Koreans that Stalin moved to what is now Uzbekistan; the Cherokee Trail of Tears; the massive population exchanges and massacres that followed the hasty British exit from India in 1947. Trump wants to deport some twelve million to twenty million people, the majority of them non-whites, because they are 'criminals' – simply for seeking a better life for themselves and their children. This is not immigration control. This is ethnic cleansing. What else do you call the planned forcible transfer of millions of men, women and children – three million of whom have known no other home since childhood?

If we are talking about crime, consider that the most ruthlessly efficient elimination in our species' bloody history was the extermination, by design or oversight, of the native peoples around the world by European migrants. So, when Americans or Australians talk about 'the rule of law' or 'jumping the line', it is an argument rank with hypocrisy.

Nobody asked the Aboriginals if Britain could dump its wretched refuse on their shores. Eighty-four per cent of the Aboriginal population died out after British colonization. When the British arrived in Tasmania in 1803, there were over 6,000 Tasmanians in nine culturally and linguistically disparate nations. There was conflict between them and the settlers, who accused them of stealing their sheep. The natives were put beyond the reach of colonial law; you could legally hunt them down like vermin. Thirty years later, only a hundred of them were alive. The survivors were transported to other islands, and in 1876, the last surviving full-blooded Tasmanian Aboriginal died, and with her, her race.

From its founding in 1901 until 1973, Australia had a 'white Australia' policy. Now it's a hotbed of immigrants; half of Australians are immigrants or their children, many from non-white countries – two of the three top sources of recent immigrants have been India and China. But there are still people who'd like to go back to a white Australia, including Peter Dutton, the home affairs minister and architect of the policy of locking up mostly Muslim refugees in offshore internment camps. In March 2017, he offered emergency visas to white South African farmers who were facing legal action to redistribute their lands to black farmers, because they 'need help from a civilized country like ours'.

When non-white refugees flee to Australia by boat, they're intercepted by the Australian navy and dumped in Papua New Guinea, in a hellhole called Manus Island. Conditions there are made deliberately inhuman, so that other asylum seekers are deterred.

The boatloads of refugees afloat on the seas are a human version of the famous New York garbage scow, the *Break of Dawn*, that roamed the Caribbean and the Gulf in 1987, looking for a place to unload its 230-foot-long, 18-foot-high mountain of the city's trash. It was originally supposed to do so in North Carolina, where officials rejected it, suspecting it of having toxic waste. It was then turned away by Louisiana, Mississippi, Alabama and Texas, which is when the boat decided to slip into Mexican waters. The Mexican government dispatched its navy and air force to keep a watch on the barge. The navy, such as it was, of Belize was also ordered to put it under surveillance. The Bahamas, too, refused to take NYC's garbage.

After travelling 6,000 miles and spending a million dollars trying to find safe harbour, the *Break of Dawn* returned to New York and disposed of the trash in a Brooklyn incinerator.

PART IV
Why They Should Be Welcomed

15
Jaikisan Heights

Teddy Roosevelt declared, in a 1915 speech to the Knights of Columbus, 'There is no room in this country for hyphenated Americans ... The one absolutely certain way of bringing this nation to ruin, of preventing all possibility of its continuing to be a nation at all, would be to permit it to become a tangle of squabbling nationalities, an intricate knot of German-Americans, Irish-Americans, English-Americans, French-Americans, Scandinavian-Americans or Italian-Americans, each preserving its separate nationality, each at heart feeling more sympathy with Europeans of that nationality, than with the other citizens of the American Republic ... The only man who is a good American is the man who is an American and nothing else.'

If Teddy Roosevelt were around today, I'd take him on a walk around Jackson Heights. To those who say, 'Should immigrants assimilate?' I have two words in response: 'Jaikisan Heights', the south Asian way of pronouncing the name of the Queens district.

When my family first came to New York in 1977, we found a dangerous city, a bankrupt city, a city from which the white middle class was fleeing. I got mugged twice when I was a teenager; our car got stolen regularly. Jackson Heights was not glamorous or welcoming. Assuming that, like in India, the best schools were the 'convent' schools, my parents put me in the nearest Catholic school, where I was one of the first minorities. One of the teachers called me a pagan. I was a senior during the Iranian hostage crisis, in 1980. One day I was walking down the hallway with my friend

Ashish, the only other Indian in school, when an Irish boy yelled at us, 'Fucking Ayatollahs!'

We stopped and turned around, and I corrected him. 'Hey! We ain't Iranians. We're Indians.'

The boy considered this new information. 'Fucking Gandhis!'

When we were there, most of the south Asians in this neighbourhood were Indians, beneficiaries of the 1965 Immigration Act, which lifted racial quotas and encouraged family reunification. They were professionals: engineers, doctors. Now, it's a much more diverse mix of south Asians: Bangladeshis, Nepalis, Tibetans, Bhutanese. They are shop owners, taxi drivers, garment factory workers.

Very few of the Indians I knew when I was growing up in 1970s New York are still in this neighbourhood. With one exception: some of the children of those families, friends of mine who are artists, writers and journalists, who lived in the East Village in the '80s and in Park Slope in the late '90s, are increasingly moving to Jackson Heights. There's something about the diversity of these streets that is attractive to people from all over – piano players from Paris and software engineers from Kansas. Increasingly, creative people want to live in the kind of city where they can hear many languages spoken on the street, and have a choice between *pupusas* and *parathas* for dinner. Diversity isn't just a nice thing to have; it is actively essential to attract the kind of people who create wealth.

If Teddy Roosevelt were walking with me, I'd invite him to take a look at the directories in the buildings of Jackson Heights. The names in the lobby of the building I grew up in on Eighty-Third Street range from Abbasi to Winfred, passing Balyuk, Bruschtein, Basu. My neighbours were Indians and Pakistanis, Jews and Muslims, Haitians and Dominicans; the building was owned by a Turkish man but the super was Greek. Many of them had been killing each other just before they got on the plane. But in Jackson Heights they lived next door to their ancient enemies, and their kids dated each other. It's not that we loved each other. Behind closed doors, at our dinner tables, our parents still said horribly racist things about the other nationalities; some of us still sent money back to the most nationalist and far-right parties or militias back home, to attack the groups that our neighbours in New York belonged to.

But we were in a new country now, making a new life. And we could live side by side and interact in certain demarcated ways. We could exchange food; our kids could play together; they could go to school together. We discovered that we are more alike than different. South Asians in the West, for instance: Indians and Pakistanis and Bangladeshis who have been warring at home discover, in Jackson Heights, that they are 'desi', and share a love of samosas and Bollywood. If we still didn't like our neighbours, we would not burn and riot as we might at home; we would suffer them, because the hate-crime laws in New York are enforced vigorously, unlike at home. It's been years since there was any major ethnic conflict in the city. Because no one ethnicity dominates, no one community gets blamed if the economy goes south. A walk around the extraordinarily safe metropolis illustrates the data: places with more immigrants have lower crime. Thirty-eight per cent of New York's population is foreign-born, and crime rates have fallen to what they were in the 1950s.

The immigration divide is also an urban–rural divide. In country after country, rural voters elect xenophobes. The majority of people who voted for Brexit lived in the British countryside; multicultural London was the Tower of Babel for them. The areas that have the fewest immigrants are the ones most afraid of them. People in cities tend to like immigrants more, because they have everyday experience of them. This kind of density, living in the same space, having to share courtyards and grocery stores, forces you to interact more than you otherwise would. You go outside your comfort zone and find that you're not uncomfortable.

Soon after Trump announced his ban on Yemenis and other Muslims entering the country, my friend Somak, a New Yorker and

THIS LAND IS OUR LAND

venture capitalist, decided to go to Bay Ridge to eat at a Yemeni restaurant, in solidarity. 'There was a line out the door,' he recalls, of other New Yorkers with the same idea.

It's astonishing how little ethnic strife there is in New York. It's astonishing how safe New York has become, while encountering some of the biggest waves of immigration in its history. It's astonishing how free the immigrants are to follow their own culture, language, religion. It's astonishing how rich immigrants have made New York. If there's a poster city for demonstrating that immigration works, New York is it. But it's not the only one – 60 per cent of London, where 38 per cent of the population are immigrants, whose children speak over 300 languages at home, and whose economy accounts for a quarter of Britain's GDP, voted to remain in the EU. They understood that immigrants had helped the city flourish, economically and culturally.

In 2010, the bigots brayed in full chorus against a group of Muslims who wanted to put up a religious centre near Ground Zero. They smeared the organizers as terrorists. Very few politicians came to the organizers' defence; most attacked them. 'It's insensitive and uncaring for the Muslim community to build a mosque in the shadow of Ground Zero,' said the Nassau County congressman Peter King, who had earlier held hearings in Congress to brand American Muslims as terrorists. Earlier still, he was one of the most active supporters of the Irish Republican Army in Congress, raising money for its terror attacks through the front group Irish Northern Aid Committee (Noraid). 'If civilians are killed in an attack on a military installation, it is certainly regrettable, but I will not morally blame the IRA for it,' he declared in 1985.

Mayor Michael Bloomberg, not known for his oratorical prowess, took a different tack. He went to Governors Island to talk about the Ground Zero centre. He had been thinking about his own childhood, when his family had difficulty buying a house in the Boston suburbs because they were Jewish.

We've come here to Governors Island to stand where the earliest settlers first set foot in New Amsterdam, and where the seeds of religious tolerance were first planted. We've come here to see the inspiring symbol of liberty that, more than 250 years later, would greet millions of immigrants in this harbour, and we come here to state as strongly as ever: this is the freest city in the world. That's what makes New York special and different and strong. Our doors are open to everyone – everyone with a dream and a willingness to work hard and play by the rules. New York City was built by immigrants, and it's sustained by immigrants – by people from more than a hundred different countries speaking more than 200 different languages and professing every faith. And whether your parents were born here, or you came yesterday, you are a New Yorker.

He brought up previous incidences of religious bigotry in the city's history, such as when the Dutch governor Peter Stuyvesant prohibited Quakers from holding services, and a group of non-Quakers signed the 'Flushing Remonstrance', as ringing a defence of religious liberty as the world has ever seen. He cited examples of persecution against Catholics. Then he came around to the present emergency.

On September 11, 2001, thousands of first responders heroically rushed to the scene and saved tens of thousands of lives. More than 400 of those first responders did not make it out alive. In rushing into those burning buildings, not one of them asked, 'What God do you pray to?' 'What beliefs do you hold?' ... There is no neighbourhood in this city that is off limits to God's love and mercy.

All manner of transactions happen on the sidewalks of Jackson Heights. Mexican *abuelas* sell tamales out of shopping carts lined with black bin liners; day labourers stand under the elevated route 7 Subway tracks waiting for work. The municipal authorities seem to have agreed to suspend many of the laws that they might enforce in Manhattan. That's also part of the vibrancy and part of the accessibility for immigrants. Because you don't need a permit to sell food in Jackson Heights; you can just stand on a street corner and sell it. Occasionally, a cop might come along and tell you to move. So you wait for the cop to pass and then resume. In neighbourhoods like this, the line between formal and informal is thin to the point of invisibility.

Every fifth store in the district is a place where you can send money back. The remittance economy is omnipresent – there are barbershops where you can get a haircut and send money back home, whether the money, like the sender, is documented or undocumented.

Remittances in places like Jackson Heights are an example not so much of 'untapped capital' but of 'undocumented capital', along with the people who produce it. We have no way of knowing precisely how much these unofficial, informal, illegal sectors of a city's economy actually produce – because many of these people don't file tax returns (even though they may pay social security taxes, and do pay sales taxes). They aren't counted by the census, and economists don't speak all of their languages. But they show hard evidence of one fact: these migrants are not lazy; they're not sitting around collecting welfare cheques. They're working, very hard, for themselves and their families back home.

A few years ago, representatives of the giant warehouse shopping club Costco had come to New York City's planning office with a question: Would it be economically viable to open a Costco in Sunset Park, in Brooklyn? There were executives at the chain who thought it might be profitable in the long term, but there were doubts. The economic data of the region wasn't encouraging. There were lots of immigrants in the district, and their median income was on the lower end of the scale. There didn't seem to be much money there.

The statisticians in the city planning office, who know about the hidden cities of New York, told Costco, 'Go in there – just trust us.' There was money in those undistinguished blocks of apartment buildings and wood-frame houses, they said; more money than met the eye. Being an immigrant area – it used to be full of Scandinavian longshoremen, who have now been replaced by Chinese and Vietnamese and Mexicans – it has a thriving underground economy. The official data underestimates the number of people living in the illegally subdivided units, and the large flows of start-up capital that some of the immigrants bring with them. 'In those areas, income tends to be underreported,' as the planners put it. The store opened in November 1996, and immediately turned a profit in its first year. A decade later, it is among the highest-grossing Costcos in America, even though it's half the size of the average Costco.

16

Jobs, Crime and Culture: The Threats That Aren't

The arguments against immigration are most often about jobs, crime and culture: that immigrants take away native jobs; that they increase the crime rate; that they are an alien culture.

The first two arguments are demonstrably false.

When people first immigrate, they compete most not with the native-born, but with immigrants who got off the boat just before them. But the previous year's immigrants don't mind, because many of the newcomers are related to them. And in any case, the difference it makes in their wages is minuscule.

In 2006, Mayor Bloomberg, then a Republican, testified in the Senate right after the mayor of Hazleton, Pennsylvania, who wanted landlords who rented to undocumented immigrants to be locked up.

Bloomberg said there were half a million undocumented immigrants in New York City. 'And let's be honest: they arrive for a good reason – they want a better life for themselves and their families, and our businesses need them and hire them! Although they broke the law by illegally crossing our borders or overstaying their visas, and our businesses broke the law by employing them, our city's economy would be a shell of itself had they not, and it would collapse if they were deported. The same holds true for the nation.'

The self-made billionaire laid out the business case for immigration: many other countries are growing their economies faster than the United States is, reversing the century-long advantage

America has enjoyed. Baby-boomers are retiring, America's birth rate is slowing, and there aren't enough young workers to pay for the old folks' pensions. 'The economics are very simple: we need more workers than we have.'

He called for increasing immigration, because it's good for the economy, and for legalizing those who're in America already. 'There is only one practical solution, and it is a solution that respects the history of our nation: offer those already here the opportunity to earn permanent status and keep their families together.' It is a moral argument. 'For decades, the federal government has tacitly welcomed them into the workforce, collected their income and social security taxes, which about two-thirds of undocumented workers pay, and benefited immeasurably from their contributions to our country.'

But just as there are climate change sceptics, there are immigration sceptics. There's a global consensus among 99 per cent of legitimate economists that immigration is good for the economy. Then there's George Borjas, an economist at Harvard. He is among the very few to have presented any kind of serious evidence that it is not so. 'Although immigration makes the aggregate economy larger, the actual net benefit accruing to natives is small, equal to an estimated two-tenths of 1 per cent of GDP. There is little evidence indicating that immigration (legal and/or illegal) creates large net gains for native-born Americans.'

Borjas further argues that immigration has harmed those Americans who were already least able to withstand harm. He estimates that immigration has cut the wages of American high school dropouts by 3 to 5 per cent, or an average of $1,800 a year. And, yes, for many, that $1,800 is a significant amount.

In 2015, Borjas published a study claiming that the arrival of the 'Marielitos', the 125,000 prisoners that Castro emptied from his jails in 1980 and put on boats to Florida, made the wages of high school dropouts in the area plunge by 10 to 30 per cent. This study was cited by none other than Trump's senior advisor Stephen Miller in support of his draconian restrictions on immigration.

But later analysis showed that Borjas's study was, at the very least, deeply flawed – in part because it used sample sizes as small as seventeen to twenty-four people per year, and focused on the people who could confirm his hypothesis. Borjas eliminated Hispanic dropouts, women and workers who're not between the ages of twenty-five and fifty-nine – who constitute a combined 91 per cent of low-skilled workers in Miami – in his samples of people affected by the Marielitos. According to the UC Berkeley economists Giovanni Peri and Vasil Yasenov, the new immigrants may have actually had a positive effect on the local job market because they created a demand for services, from supermarkets to car repair shops. In any case, the Marielitos are thriving, and the Florida job market quickly recovered from whatever short-term effects the influx might have had.

Do immigrants steal jobs from the natives? Çağlar Özden, a lead economist for the World Bank's Development and Research Group, maintains that they don't. 'In general Özden found that migrants often take jobs that locals don't want or can't fill ... Özden also found that unskilled migrants tend either to have no impact on local wages and employment or to increase wages and employment,' summarizes the analyst Ruchir Sharma, the chief global strategist at Morgan Stanley. If you can have an immigrant nanny mind your children, you can go to work as a writer or a dentist and make more money than if you were home minding your children.'

The economist Michael Clemens makes a similar point. As *The Atlantic* explains,

> he [Clemens] and his co-authors, through study of all the available economic literature, have found that decades of immigration of tens of millions of people to the United States has reduced real wages for the average American worker by fractions of a percent, if at all ... Clemens's research also challenges the notion

that immigrants take away jobs from Americans. In agriculture, for example, he has estimated that for every three seasonal workers who are brought in, one American job is created across all sectors. Directly, workers need managers, and more often than not those managers are Americans. Indirectly, workers buy things, which means more Americans are needed to sell and produce those things. And yet, Clemens told me, 'when a bus of 60 Mexicans is coming up from the border, nobody looks at it and says "Ah, there's 20 American jobs"'.

Close to half of American farm workers are in the US illegally. Expelling them will not only decimate American agriculture; it will make no difference to the wages of native farm workers. When the Bracero 'guest worker' programme ended in 1964, and Mexican farm workers, who had done backbreaking work in the fields to replace Americans shipped off to the battlefields of Europe, were asked to go back, they were not replaced by American workers. Their bosses simply shifted to less labour-intensive crops and introduced more machines in the fields.

Instead, the nation would be better served if the farm workers and most of the other undocumented who're already in America, like the Dreamers, got amnesty. There's a precedent for this. In 1986, Ronald Reagan signed the Immigration Reform and Control Act, also known as the 'Reagan amnesty', which gave green cards to 2.7 million undocumented people. After it passed, the wages of the legalized workers went up, tax revenues increased as they started filing tax returns, and the crime rate fell by 5 per cent, as property crimes decreased because the undocumented could work legally.

There will be winners from free trade and free movement of people – like technology corporations. And there will be losers, for a while – like the unskilled. But the winners could be made to give away a part of their winnings to the losers through taxes. One way to do this would be to make the earned income tax credit much more generous. This would help both immigrants and the high school dropouts whose prospects are most hurt by immigration. More federal funds should be made available for areas such as border towns that are struggling with the impact of rising migration, in the form of aid for schools and hospitals. These funds could also be raised through a fee that would be charged to companies for each skilled immigrant they sponsor.

Ultimately, whatever the merits of Borjas's argument, the solution isn't to keep low-skilled workers out, which would be catastrophic for entire sectors of the economy. (For example, four out of eight of Maryland's crab-picking businesses closed in 2018 because of the difficulty of finding seasonal migrant labour after Trump's restrictions.) It's to get more students through high school. Then the migrants with lower skills can begin their climb on the ladder of economic opportunity working as apple pickers and nannies, while those born in America can work as clerks and in call centres. And both can dream of their children becoming doctors and presidents.

If you want to make the economy grow, let in more immigrants – and legalize the ones who have already arrived.

Immigrants, particularly the undocumented, are presented by politicians and Fox anchors as a feral horde of drug dealers and rapists. How criminally inclined are immigrants, really?

Alex Nowrasteh of the Cato Institute analysed crime statistics in Texas for 2016. Native-born Americans were convicted of crimes at a rate of 2,116 per 100,000 people. For legal immigrants, that number plunged to 292 per 100,000; for illegal immigrants, 879. 'The native-born criminal conviction rate was thus 2.4 times as high as the criminal conviction rate for illegal immigrants in that year and 7.2 times as high as that of legal immigrants,' writes Nowrasteh.

A 2018 study in the journal *Criminology* studied the correlation between levels of undocumented immigration in American states and the prevalence of crime, from 1990 to 2014. The conclusion was unambiguous: 'Increases in the undocumented immigrant population within states are associated with significant decreases in the prevalence of violence,' the study found. For every 1 per cent increase in the undocumented population, there were 49 *fewer* violent crimes per 100,000 people. 'Immigrants are driven by pursuit of education and economic opportunities for themselves and their families,' said Michael Light, one of the study's co-authors. 'Migration – especially, undocumented migration – requires a lot of motivation and planning. Those are characteristics that aren't correlated with a high crime-prone disposition.'

According to a 2018 Yale survey, the number of undocumented immigrants in America now stands at 22.1 million – and could be as high as 29.5 million. This may mean that the undocumented commit crimes at half the rates originally attributed to them. 'You have the same number of crimes but now spread over twice as many people as was believed before, which right away means that the crime rate among undocumented immigrants is essentially half whatever was previously believed,' said Edward Kaplan, a co-author of the study.

If you want to make the country safer, let in more immigrants – legal or otherwise.

The third complaint, that immigrants bring in a culture different from an existing one, is the most valid. So, if you're living in a kind of Norman Rockwell America, you might not like a cantina to open up next door blaring salsa music. But your neighbour, bored out of his mind by the sterility of Norman Rockwell's America, might welcome it. You don't get to define what a national culture is. Americans don't; even Europeans don't, because go back a few decades and the definition of French, or British, or German culture – what religions and foods and ethnic origins constituted it – was radically different from what it is today.

Might you consider that by our moving here we will make things better – not just economically but also culturally? That there is something worthwhile in the cultures we bring with us – all of us, not just the Asian model minorities – and some of it is something that you can learn from? It could be our work ethic, it could be our love of family, it could be our gorgeous dresses or soulful music; it could be our richly spiced cuisine or our complex myths. Our old gods will meet your newer gods and produce a hybrid better suited for worship by all.

The unofficial national dish of Germany is doner kebab; of Great Britain, chicken tikka masala; of France, couscous. The most exciting music in Paris isn't Edith Piaf but the Afropop playing in dozens of clubs in and around the city.

We were also drawn here by your songs. My father moved himself, and his wife and three children, to America to expand the family diamond business. But there was a deeper, more longstanding attraction, which had begun in college in Calcutta, in the 1950s. It was when my father was first exposed to the great rock 'n' yell of Chuck Berry and Elvis – music that the Jesuit deans of St Xavier's tried to ban because they couldn't bear to see their students gyrating their pelvises. My father had never heard such an awesome caterwaul before, and – along with America's decadent movies and books – it seeded the young man's desire to go and live there someday.

And isn't that, after all, what makes America work: this messy mix, this barbaric yawp, this redneck rondeau, this rude commingling? Isn't this what permeates its films, movies, books; and isn't it the principal product it can still export? It is American culture's permissiveness, openness and vigour that still attracts the masses to the Golden Door, not its rigidity.

An argument that's been resurfacing is that this new crop of immigrants, unlike previous waves of migrants, doesn't assimilate. 'The vast majority of past immigrants changed *their* values, not America's, when they came to this country. They came to America to become American, not only in terms of language, citizenship, and national identity, but also in terms of values,' wrote the radio host

Dennis Prager in *National Review*. 'But while some immigrants still do, the majority does not. They want to become American citizens in order to better their lives – a completely understandable motivation – not to embrace American values and identity. The majority of today's immigrants from Latin America, for example, wishes to become wealthier ... Latin Americans.'

On this question, a lot of people on both sides throw around facts and figures out of their own hats. What was needed was an authoritative, thoroughly researched study conducted by a respected, impartial organization.

In 2015, the federal government – the US Department of Citizenship and Immigration Services and the National Science Foundation – asked the National Academy of Sciences to undertake just such a study. It was, and remains, the definitive word on the subject. The 500-page report looked at forty-one million immigrants and their thirty-seven million children. It assembled research from eighteen leading economists, demographers and migration scholars – including immigration sceptics like George Borjas.

English-language learning 'is happening as rapidly or faster now than it did for earlier waves of mainly European immigrants in the 20th century', the report found. According to a 2013 Gallup poll, 95 per cent of immigrants think learning English is essential or important. By the second generation, educational achievement catches up to the children of the native-born. By the third generation, most immigrant children speak only English. Only 41 per cent of third-generation Mexican-American children, for example, speak exclusively Spanish at home. The report also found that incarceration rates for immigrant men in the eighteen-to-thirty-nine age group are a quarter of those for native-born men. 'Cities and neighborhoods with greater concentrations of immigrants have much lower rates of crime and violence.'

As for jobs, 86 per cent of first-generation immigrant males participate in the labour force, which is a higher rate than the native-born. 'Immigrant men with the lowest level of education are more likely to be employed than comparable native-born men, indicating that immigrants appear to be filling low-skilled jobs that native-born Americans are not available or willing to take.'

The study found that in almost all categories, immigrants do better than the native-born. 'Foreign-born immigrants have better infant, child, and adult health outcomes than the US-born population in general and better outcomes than US-born members of their ethnic group. In comparison with native-born Americans, the foreign-born are less likely to die from cardiovascular disease and all cancers combined; they experience fewer chronic health conditions, lower infant mortality rates, lower rates of obesity, and fewer functional limitations. Immigrants also have a lower prevalence of depression and of alcohol abuse.' They also get divorced less.

There were some caveats. The first to arrive need more government help than they contribute in taxes, such as public schooling for their children, as have newly arrived immigrants in the past. The total annual cost to all levels of government is $57 billion. But the children of these immigrants, by the second generation, contribute $30 billion in taxes; by the third generation, $223 billion.

By the third generation, immigrants assimilate into America – in all ways. Their crime, health, divorce and education rates are the same as the native-born. They sit around on the couch and watch TV and grow obese; work or not work; study or not study; commit crimes; and dislike learning languages other than English at the same rates as the native-born. In other words, they've become fully American.

The report came down resolutely on one side of the debate:

Immigration is integral to the nation's economic growth. The inflow of labor supply has helped the United States avoid the problems facing other economies that have stagnated as a result of unfavorable demographics, particularly the effects of an aging work force and reduced consumption by older residents. In addition, the infusion of human capital by high-skilled immigrants has boosted the nation's capacity for innovation, entrepreneurship, and technological change.

Sometimes America isn't even aware of the talent coming to its shores, or the way somebody let in for one skill can later demonstrate another. A farm worker could become a political activist; an engineer could open a restaurant. And their children ... do what children of immigrants have always done. Although a Mexican migrant may start out mowing lawns, his children quickly move up, according to the report:

> Second generation children of immigrants from Mexico and Central America have made large leaps in occupational terms: 22 percent of second generation Mexican men and 31 percent of second generation men from Central America in 2003–2013 were in professional or managerial positions ... The occupational leap for second generation women for this period was even greater, and the gap separating them from later generation women narrowed greatly.

Immigrants also assimilate in other ways, less palatable to people like Iowa representative Steve King, who famously declared, 'We can't restore our civilization with somebody else's babies.' The primal fear of nativists like King is 'They're coming for our women!' Oh, yes, we are – and for your men, too. One out of every seven marriages in America is interracial or interethnic, twice the rate of the last generation. In 1970, only 1 per cent of American babies were descended from parents of different races. By 2013, that number had risen tenfold. In the next four decades, the number of interracial births will go up by 174 per cent.

I've always found American definitions of 'race' confusing. In India, I could understand categories of religion or caste. But what does it mean to be 'black' or 'white' in America? Is Obama half white or half black? The best answer to whites' fear of being over-run by 2044 may be this: by then, 'race' might not matter anymore.

'More than 35 percent of Americans said that one of their "close" kin is of a different race,' says the National Academy of Sciences report. 'Integration of immigrants and their descendants is a major contributor to this large degree of intermixing. In the future, the lines between what Americans today think of as separate ethno-racial groups may become much more blurred. Indeed, immigrants become Americans not just by integrating into our neighborhoods, schools, and workplaces, but also into our families. Very quickly, "they" become "us".'

If you want to keep the culture vital, let in more immigrants.

The value of ethnic diversity, like culture, is one of those intangibles that is difficult to measure in economic terms. But it can revitalize old industrial cities across the richer countries, make downtown central again.

The mayor of Schenectady, New York, realized this in 2002. Schenectady was a depressed industrial city of 66,000 in upstate New York, heavily polluted by smokestack factories. When the factories left, so did the city's energy. A third of its population, mostly Italian, German and Polish, fled. Its downtown looked like a disaster area. Then the mayor, Albert Jurczynski, heard about the enterprise of immigrants from the South American country of Guyana in New York City when he assisted a local Guyanese man in constructing a temple in vacant public housing. The Guyanese man said to the mayor, 'We don't believe in public assistance.' The mayor, himself the grandson of Polish immigrants, responded, 'You're singing my tune.'

So Mayor Jurczynski started inviting busloads of Guyanese from Queens to Schenectady, showing them around the city, taking them to his in-laws' house for homemade wine. Occasionally, he personally went to Liberty Avenue in Richmond Hill, glad-handing the Guyanese, eating their spicy goat curry, and drinking their rum.

It cost the city of Schenectady $16,500 to demolish a home; it was better policy to offer it to the industrious Guyanese for $1, on the condition that they refurbish it.

Now there are 10,000 Guyanese living and working in downtown Schenectady, fully 12 per cent of the city's population. They've refurbished abandoned and burned-out homes and, with little or no government assistance, rehabilitated them with sweat equity, with neat brick-and-metal fences around them. They created their own economy, opening little grocery stores, insurance and money-transfer businesses, and restaurants. Schenectady has a cricket league and Guyanese members on the city council. Every year, Guyana Day is celebrated by its German and Irish and Guyanese citizens. They've helped the city turn around. Because the city accommodated a new spice in the mix.

And it's not just Schenectady. A number of down-on-their-luck upstate New York cities have been similarly revitalized by immigrants, particularly refugees. New York State took in 40,000 refugees over the past decade, and settled almost all of them upstate, in Buffalo, Utica, Syracuse and Rochester. The refugees are Vietnamese, Burmese, Bhutanese, Bosnians, Somali Bantu, Iraqis, Syrians and Ukrainians; they joined the earlier Irish, German, Italian and Polish residents.

A little over an hour's drive from Schenectady is the city of Utica, where a quarter of its 62,000 population are immigrants, including 7,000 Bosnian refugees. As the native-born in Utica started leaving – 3,100 fled the city between 2000 and 2015 – the foreign-born started coming in, attracted by cheap housing; 3,500 of them moved into Utica in the same period. The Bosnians bought hundreds of shabby homes and rehabbed them. An old Methodist church downtown would have cost the city $1 million to demolish; the Bosnians took it over, fixed it up, and turned it into a thriving mosque.

Detroit is an enormous city, 139 square miles, big enough to fit Manhattan, Boston and San Francisco. But one-third of the houses in Detroit are empty. It has lost 60 per cent of its population since 1960, and people are still leaving. But zoom in and you'll find the antidote: an enclave called Hamtramck, which is a 2-square-mile independent city inside the city of Detroit. In 1980, when Chrysler shut down the Dodge factory, which employed most of its residents and provided a quarter of its operating revenue, Hamtramck went into a decline like the rest of Detroit.

Today, it has a density of around 10,000 people per square mile – Detroit has half that. Since Hamtramck is just over 2 square miles, people don't need a car to get around. The residents of Hamtramck come from Bangladesh, Yemen, Poland, Albania and Bosnia. Twenty per cent of the population is African American. Poles, who were 90 per cent of the population in 1970, are now down to 13 per cent. Over half the residents' mother tongue is not English, and over two dozen languages are spoken in the city's schools. A guide to the city's social services is printed in five languages. In 2015, Hamtramck became the first American city to elect a city council in which the majority of the councillors are Muslim.

Immigration is the city's bread and butter, according to Shahab Ahmed, a member of the city council. 'We want to attract more immigrants.' The city has recently come out of receivership and is running its own affairs. 'Back in 2000, you used to see one car in two minutes,' a Bangladeshi named Shaker Sadeak, who'd left New York for Hamtramck that year and eventually opened a clothes store, reminisced to the Voice of America. 'Now we have thousands of cars driving on the streets. All the immigrants came into this town and rebuilt the whole thing.'

Cities that are losing population should get special exemptions from the immigration laws to attract migrants. Canada's Provincial Nominee Program allows individual provinces to fast-track residence permits in their states for overseas immigrants – so, in effect, Saskatchewan and Ontario are competing for immigrants along with British Columbia and Quebec. Might American cities offer

visas? Immigrants, who are 13 per cent of the American population, account for 40 per cent of the home-buying market, according
to a study by the Mortgage Bankers Association. If you want to
come to America, start by staying in a shrinking city like Baltimore
or Buffalo or Camden, refurbish an abandoned house, live there
five years. And you get a green card. Cities need warm bodies for
cold houses.

There is enough land to accommodate the newcomers, and not just
in the cities. There are enough houses. There is enough space in the
United States alone to hold all seven billion of our species. The
United States contains 3.8 million square miles, with a density of
86 people per square mile. Now let's look around the world. Macau
fits in 52,000 people per square mile; Singapore, 20,000; Bangladesh, 2,980. The United States ranks 191st in the world in terms
of density; its most crowded state, New Jersey, comfortably accom-
modates 1,200 people per square mile. We won't turn into
Bangladesh if we let in double or even triple that number. Elbow
room is still abundant on our endless frontier.

As the conservative *New York Times* columnist Bret Stephens
points out, 'America is vast, largely empty and often lonely.
Roughly 80 per cent of Americans live in urban areas covering just
3 per cent of the overall landmass ... Much of rural or small-town
America is emptying out. In hundreds of rural counties, more people are dying than are being born, according to the Department of
Agriculture. The same Trumpian conservatives who claim to want
to save the American heartland from the fabled Latin American
Horde are guaranteeing conditions that over time will turn the
heartland into a wasteland.' Stephens exhorts immigrants to 'come
on in. There's more than enough room in this broad and fruitful
land of the free.'

It is immigrants' manifest destiny to spread out from the cities
and into the red states. 'And that claim is by the right of our manifest destiny to overspread and to possess the whole of the continent

which Providence has given us for the development of the great experiment of liberty and federated self-government entrusted to us,' said John L. O'Sullivan, the nineteenth-century journalist who urged the United States to annex Texas and California and Oregon and everything else.

I claim the right to the United States, for myself and my children and my uncles and cousins, by manifest destiny. This land is your land, this land is our land, it belongs to you and me. We're here, we're not going back, we're raising our kids here. It's our country now. We will not reassure anybody about their racist fears about our deportment; we're not letting the bastards take it back.

It's our America now.

Whether Trump or May or Orbán likes it or not, immigrants will keep coming, to pursue happiness and a better life for their children. To the people who voted for the populists: do not fear the newcomers. Many are young and will pay the pensions for the elderly, who are living longer than ever before. They will bring energy with them, for no one has more enterprise than someone who has left their distant home to make the difficult journey here, whether they've come legally or not. And given basic opportunities, they will be better behaved than the youths in the lands they move to, because immigrants in most countries have lower crime rates than the native-born. They will create jobs. They will cook and dance and write and play sports in new and exciting ways. They will make their new countries richer, in all senses of the word. The immigrant armada that is coming to your shores is actually a rescue fleet.

17

We Do Not Come Empty-Handed

It's not just down-on-their-luck urban areas that immigrants can revitalize – it's the entire economy. America has succeeded, and achieved its present position of global dominance, because it has always been good at importing the talent it needs.

Immigrants are 13 per cent of the US population, but they have started a quarter of all new businesses and earned over a third of all the Nobel Prizes in science given to Americans. One out of every four US tech companies established since 1995 was founded by an immigrant, and a third of Silicon Valley workers are immigrants. The numbers are even more impressive at the top: of the twenty-five biggest tech companies in 2013, immigrants or their children founded 60 per cent of them, such as Apple's Steve Jobs, son of a Syrian immigrant, and Google's Sergey Brin, who came from Russia at the age of six.

In 2008, Bill Gates stated before Congress that for every tech worker that the country lets in, five American jobs are created. Over half of all the billion-dollar tech companies have an immigrant founder. Today, they employ half a million Americans. Immigrants or their children founded 43 per cent of the Fortune 500 companies, which employed over twelve million people worldwide in 2017.

This record of success continues into the next generation. In 2016, 83 per cent of the winners in the Intel International Science and Engineering Fair were children of immigrants. Three-quarters of the finalists were children of parents who came over on the H-1B visa programme.

To shut off this incredible wellspring of talent would be to cut off America's brain to spite its muscles. Because that talent has an increasing number of countries vying to get it to come to their shores.

In 2000, Germany realized that it had a shortage of programmers and other IT experts and needed 75,000 more of them to keep German industry competitive. The Germans had heard that there were many skilled programmers in countries like India. So they decided, in their munificence, that they would grant a limited number of entry permits – 20,000, to be exact – to tech workers, on the condition that they not bring their families, return after five years, and learn German before going there. Even this was strenuously opposed by German nationalists. 'Kinder statt Inder' (children instead of Indians) was the slogan of the prime minister of North Rhine–Westphalia, Jürgen Rüttgers, urging Germans to have more babies, not import Indians.

Having opened the gates, the German government waited for the desperate techie hordes to come pouring in from Bangalore and Bombay. At the time, India produced 133,000 software professionals a year. A grand total of 160 Indians applied. Many countries were in need of their skills; why would they go under such restrictive conditions to a country whose welcome mat was studded with nails?

Countries like Canada realize this, and have seen the burgeoning American resistance to immigration as something to be exploited. 'If you guys cannot figure out your immigration system, we're going to invite the best and brightest to come north of the border,' said Jason Kenney, Canada's immigration minister for Stephen Harper's Conservative government, before a 2013 trip to the San Francisco Bay Area.

In 2017, Canada started the Global Talent Stream initiative, which lets highly skilled workers in fields such as artificial intelligence enter the country without a work permit, and obtain one in two weeks. The Canadian government was not acting out of a wish to uplift Indian and Chinese programmers, but because of one stark fact: by 2020, the booming Canadian economy will have a shortage of 220,000 tech workers. There aren't anywhere near enough native-born Canadians who can fill these jobs.

Canada's per capita immigration rate is three times that of the United States. In 2016, it welcomed 320,000 immigrants. One out of five Canadians today was born somewhere else. And the Canadian public loves it. Eighty-two per cent (and rising) think immigration is a good thing; two-thirds also love multicultural-ism, the idea that there isn't, nor should be, a uniform Canadian culture. Ninety-five per cent think someone born abroad will be as good a citizen as someone born in Canada. Even working-class white voters for populist parties like Harper's Conservative Party, which held power from 2006 to 2015, are in favour of immigra-tion; those who describe themselves as most strongly patriotic in polls are also most likely to support immigration and multicul-turalism.

As the authors of a 2015 survey noted, 'What the findings do tell us – through empirically grounded facts – is that, amid the noise of global ethnic conflict, grim warnings about domestic terrorism and a lethargic economy that is failing many, most of us are keep-ing the faith in Canada as the most welcoming multicultural society on the planet.' The Canadian experience shows that the more you experience immigrants firsthand, the more likely you are to want more of them.

As the populations of the developed countries get older, they need the vigour of immigrants all the more, because they are young. Four out of five immigrants to the USA are under forty, and the work they do will support the half of the country overall that is over forty. It's going to be a nation of old codgers as the baby boomers retire. And most immigrants don't move with their par-ents; so, their social security taxes go towards paying for others' parents. Immigrants also have more children than the native-born, so their children will also continue subsidizing both the greying native-born and their increasingly less fecund children.

Americans are retiring in larger numbers, and they're living longer. In 1960, there were about five workers paying social security taxes for every retiree or disabled person receiving benefits; by 2013, there were fewer than three. And Americans aren't making enough babies – or American women are choosing not to. In 2016, the US fertility rate fell to an all-time low of 1.8 babies per woman; the replacement rate is 2.1.

In 2018, for the first time in thirty years, the federal government gave out more money in social security than it received in payroll taxes: a shortfall of $2 billion, which meant it had to dip into the social security trust fund. At current levels, this fund will run dry by 2034. After that, social security recipients will only get 79 cents for each dollar they're owed.

One way this financial Armageddon can be averted, according to a report by the trustees of the Social Security Administration, is to increase immigration, illegal as well as legal. Immigrant workers are younger, and therefore will work longer and pay more into the system. Immigrants, both legal and illegal, will pay half a trillion dollars into the social security trust fund over the next twenty-five years. Over the next seventy-five years, they will pay $4 trillion. 'The numbers get much larger for longer periods,' explained the Social Security Administration's chief actuary, Stephen Goss, 'because that is when the additional children born to the immigrants really help.'

The issue is particularly acute when it comes to undocumented immigrants, most of whom pay into the system but are ineligible for benefits. According to the Social Security Administration, undocumented immigrants paid $13 billion in payroll taxes in 2010 and received only $1 billion in benefits. The rest of the money went into shoring up the social security trust fund.

Immigration reduces the social security deficit by hundreds of billions of dollars; the greater the number of immigrants that we let in to work and pay into the system, the more likely retirees are to not have to open cans of dog food for their dinner. America's problem, in the years ahead, isn't going to be that too many people are coming to America. It's going to be that too few might want to.

But this is a global problem. By the middle of the century, a quarter of the worldwide population outside Africa will be sixty or older. By then, there will be fewer than two workers for every retiree in twenty-four European, seven Asian, and four Latin American countries. Japan already has the lowest number of workers – two – for every person over sixty-five. African countries, by contrast, have thirteen.

Europe is actually shrinking, in real numbers. Fertility rates in every European country are below the replacement rate of 2.1 babies per woman. Today, there are 740 million people in Europe and Russia combined, and 1.2 billion in all of Africa. Africans are younger, more able to work; 60 per cent are under the age of twenty-five, while only 27 per cent of Europeans are.

By 2050, the population of Europe and Russia will shrink to 700 million, while Africa's will double, to 2.4 billion – a quarter of the global population. By the end of the century, almost 40 per cent of humanity will be African. The future of our species, like our past, is African.

After the Brexit referendum, the UK is looking towards its former colonies, and the other fifty-two nations of the Commonwealth, to save itself. Some have suggested making a trade agreement with them, to replace the one between Britain the other European countries. But some of the former colonies, such as Singapore, have surpassed their former master in per capita income, and many others, like India, have vastly bigger domestic markets. Why should they make a deal with a cold, windswept bunch of islands in the North Sea?

In 1968, the Conservative Party parliamentarian Enoch Powell made his notorious 'Rivers of Blood' speech, warning against taking in brown- and black-skinned people. It was partly aimed against people like my mother – east African Asians who had migrated to the country of their citizenship. He forecast doom for a Britain that would be foolish enough to take them: 'It is like watching a nation busily engaged in heaping up its own funeral pyre ... As I look ahead, I am filled with foreboding; like the Roman, I seem to see "the River Tiber foaming with much blood".'

Half a century later, the Thames is not foaming over with blood. It's actually the opposite. The east African Asian refugee community – Christians, Hindus, Muslims, Parsis and Sikhs – is one of the wealthiest communities of any colour in the UK; their educational achievements eventually outrun those of native-born whites. Even though one of the biggest factors in the Brexit vote was fear of immigrants, it is immigrants and their descendants who will help their new country in making the deals it seeks with their ancestral countries. They are ambassadors, each one of them.

For many countries, immigrants are, literally, the future of the nation. As the Swedish government puts it on an official website, 'Sweden needs immigration to compensate for the decline in numbers of babies being born here.' Even as anti-immigration sentiment is on the rise in Sweden, because of fears of the strain it would impose upon its generous welfare state, the government recognizes that a certain level of immigration is also essential to that same welfare state's survival.

For Germany to maintain its current balance of working-age people to retirees, says Sharma, it would have to attract 1.5 million new immigrants *on top of* the 1 million that came there in 2015 – and would have to keep letting in 1.5 million migrants a year until 2030. 'That is not to suggest that Germany can or should simply accept more than a million refugees a year, because the challenges of integrating that many people into the economy quickly are real,' he says. 'It is only to dramatize the scale of Germany's ageing problem, in which the imbalance between old and young is unfolding even faster than the refugees were arriving in 2015. This situation is typical for many industrial countries: even a huge increase in the number of migrants they accept will only partially offset the depopulation bomb.'

Under 2 per cent of Japan's population is foreign-born – in nearly all other developed nations, that number varies from 10 to 15 per cent. For Japan to maintain its population balance, it would have to let in ten times the migrants it does now – from 50,000 a year to half a million per year.

Japan, particularly in the rural north, is becoming a country without people. The young have moved to the cities, and the old are dying out. By 2050, 40 per cent of Japan will be over the age of sixty-five. Where humans are absent, other animals step in; in some villages, wild boars outnumber people. There is no one to tend the rice paddies, and so the boars move in, aggressively, trampling the fields, eating everything they can. Some of them, weighing up to 280 pounds, attack humans, running through the village streets, barging into shops and schools. 'The lack of manpower here is a real problem,' an official in charge of the anti-boar campaign explained to the *Washington Post*. 'We need farmers to protect their own land and to take action against the boars, but it's difficult for them because most of them are old.' The average Japanese woman will give birth to 1.44 babies in her lifetime, well below the replacement rate. The average boar has 4.5 piglets a year; and those piglets start breeding at the age of two.

Japan can't afford to remain a fortress, it is clear, but what is the alternative? A new vision of immigrant integration. Imagine if the Japanese let in whole families – from Asia, Africa, Latin America – and the immigrant parents worked and paid taxes that would support the pensions of the elderly Japanese; and the elderly Japanese took care of the immigrant kids while the parents went to work. Everyone would have something to do, everyone's lives would be enriched.

António Guterres, the UN secretary-general, has proposed 'global skill partnerships', which are voluntary agreements between two countries – the one sending migrants and the one receiving migrants – to train migrants *before* they emigrate so they arrive with skills that are in short supply in their new country. If you can't beat 'em, train 'em.

UN figures, cited by Sharma, show that the number of countries that have publicly announced plans to increase immigration to fight population decline went from ten in 2010 to twenty-three in 2013. Countries that we think have been swamped by migrants have actually benefited from them. Turkey, which has seen its birth rates fall in recent years, gave residence rights to over a million refugees, most of them Syrian, in 2014. That year, a quarter of new businesses were started by Syrians, and the places where they settled had the fastest growth in the country.

Just as America mines bauxite or copper from foreign countries, it has, until Trump, been good at recruiting the skills it needs. Take India, for instance. The USA isn't directly implicated in India's plight, where levels of malnutrition among its children exceed those in sub-Saharan Africa. But it benefits, like Britain did, by having Indians move there. We are the second-largest immigrant group after Mexicans – there are almost four million of us in America. From 2013 onwards, more Indians have been entering the country each year than Mexicans. We are recent arrivals; only 13 per cent of us were born in America. But we have made up for lost time. In 2017, India sent more immigrants to the United States than did any other country on the planet.

Indian Americans are the most successful group of any kind in the United States: we have the highest per-capita incomes, the highest educational attainment and the lowest crime rate. Seventy-seven per cent of us over the age of twenty-five have a college degree (which is two and a half times the American average); more than half have a postgraduate degree. We are 8 per cent of America's doctors. Around a fifth of all start-ups in Silicon Valley were founded by Indians.

As a minority, we are the model. But it's not because Indians are some sort of master race; if that were the case, what explains India? America skims off the 'creamy layer', as we used to call the elite of the lower castes in India, from other nations. Most of the immigrants who come to America are substantially better educated and richer than the countrymen they left behind. We do not come empty-handed, mine host!

18

Immigration as Reparations

Ta-Nehisi Coates has written about what America owes its black citizens: 'Now we have half-stepped away from our long centuries of despoilment, promising, "never again". But still we are haunted. It is as though we have run up a credit card bill and, having pledged to charge no more, remain befuddled that the balance does not disappear. The effects of that balance, interest accruing daily, are all around us.'

Globally, too, a giant bill is due. But the poor countries aren't seriously suggesting that the rich send sacks of gold bullion or bitcoin every year to India or Nigeria. They're asking for fairness: for the borders of the rich to be opened to goods and people; to Indian-made suits as well as Nigerian doctors.

If the rich countries *don't* want the poor countries to migrate, then there's another solution. Pay them what they're owed. Pay the costs of colonialism, of the wars you imposed on them, of the inequality you've built into the world order, and the carbon you've put into the atmosphere. Settle the account, and the creditors will have no reason to come to your house. Reparations or migration: choose.

Some twelve million Africans were enslaved and carried across the Atlantic by European powers. Should not twelve million people from present-day Africa now be allowed to live in the countries enriched by the labour of their ancestors? For each African forcibly expatriated to make money for a rich country, should there not be an African now who's allowed to migrate to that same country, to make money for himself as well as his hosts? Both will be better off: the African still suffering from what slavery has done to his country, and the rich country, which will now get more benefits from African labour, but this time without enormous pain and for a fair wage.

Migration today is a form of reparations. But the countries that are paying aren't necessarily the ones that are directly linked with the people they are absorbing; the vast majority of migrants move from a poor to a less-poor country, not a rich one. Fair immigration quotas should be based on how much the host country has ruined other countries. Thus, Britain should have quotas for Indians and Nigerians; France, for Malians and Tunisians; Belgium, for very large numbers of Congolese. The Dominican Republic, for instance, where the United States propped up the homicidal dictator Rafael Trujillo for three decades until his assassination in 1961, should be high on the American preference list. Michael Gerrard, of the Sabin Center for Climate Change Law at Columbia, proposes a just response to climate change in the title of his 2015 *Washington Post* op-ed: 'America Is the Worst Polluter in the History of the World. We Should Let Climate Change Refugees Resettle Here'.

In the text, he points out:

> Climate change results from the cumulative emissions of greenhouse gases all over the world, because the gases stay in the atmosphere for a century or more. International law recognizes that if pollution crosses national borders, the country where it originated is responsible for the damages. That affirms what we all learned in the schoolyard: If you make a mess, you clean it up. The countries that spewed (or allowed or encouraged their corporations to spew) these chemicals into the air, and especially the countries that grew rich while doing so, should take responsibility for the consequences of their actions.

He proposes a formula for migration as compensation: assuming 100 million climate refugees need to be resettled by the middle of the century, the United States takes in a quarter of them, since it's contributed at least a quarter of the excess carbon in the atmosphere; Europe takes in another quarter, China takes in 11 per cent, and so on.

Just as there's a 'carbon tax' on polluting industries, there should be a 'migration tax' on polluting nations.

The anti-immigrant French writer Alain Finkielkraut is an exponent of the theory that European countries have some sort of *ur*-culture that incoming immigrants should be expected to follow, rejecting the culture they brought with them (particularly if it's Islam). But he unwittingly put his finger on another issue when he whined in an interview to *Der Spiegel*, 'Some say that France was a colonial power, which is why those who were colonized could not be happy. But why has Europe been subjected to this massive immigration from former colonies over the past half a century? France still has to pay for the sins of colonialism and settle its debt to those who vilify it today.'

Indeed, a huge bill due to the West is coming. And it is one that the West is not only morally obliged to pay, but one that it should also look forward to paying.

In almost every case, as we have seen, immigrants make the countries they move to better. They work and contribute to the economy. Their social security taxes pay the pensions of the rapidly increasing ranks of old people in the rich countries, who are living longer than ever. The fastest way to make the world a better place may be to ease barriers to migration. According to Michael Clemens, 'The gains from reducing emigration restrictions are likely to be enormous, measured in tens of trillions of dollars.'

This is true even in non-Western countries. A provocative 2014 article in the *New Republic* argues that global inequality would be sharply reduced if only the Western countries became more like the Gulf countries. The inequality in the UAE is vast: 85 per cent of the population, who are resident foreigners, live on under $5,000 a year; their Emirati overlords make over $300,000 a year, 'greater economic inequality than existed even in Apartheid South Africa or the antebellum South'.

But, as the law professor Eric Posner and the Microsoft researcher Glen Weyl point out, the migrants make five times as much as they might in their home countries, even as they are being stripped of their dignity. By allowing in workers from the poorest countries, the Gulf nations get cheap maids, construction workers and prostitutes; and also do more for the poor nations than the foreign-aid programmes of the rich nations, because of the volume of remittances the migrants send back. The countries of the Gulf do not demand – in fact, actively discourage – assimilation. You can be who you are, work – however degrading the work conditions may be – make money and go back; or stay and have children, who will never be citizens. You will always be inferior to the Emiratis, who can always go straight to the front of a queue in a supermarket or bank, but your family back home will live in dignity, even if you don't.

Migrants are the creators of some of the biggest and most liquid capital flows anywhere. They send back some $600 billion in remittances every year, which amounts to three times more than the direct gains from abolishing all trade barriers, four times more than all foreign aid, and 100 times the amount of all debt relief.

Migrants from poor countries alone sent $481 billion in remittances to the global south in 2017, mostly in $200 and $300 payments, which make up an average of 60 per cent of the family income back home. Almost half of this – $240 billion – is sent to people in poor rural areas. But this is almost certainly an underestimate, because many migrants carry money back in cash or use unofficial networks to transfer it, rather than use banks or Western Union.

Between 2015 and 2030, remittances sent to developing countries are projected to be over $6.5 trillion. With each year, migrants send even more back. Over the past decade, while migration from the developing countries has increased by 28 per cent, remittances have risen by 51 per cent.

For many migrants, the reason they moved was not to enrich themselves but to support those left behind. Ronaldo, the middle-aged Mexican deportee who I met in Tijuana, told me that most of what he did in the United States was work so that he could send money back to his grandmother, who was closer than his mother, and who he refers to as Mom. 'I sent one hundred dollars every week to my mom until the day she died,' he said with some pride. He lived every week on the hundred dollars he had left over. His grandmother kept saying, 'Come on! Come back! No more! I don't want you to stay there no more! Come back!'

But Ronaldo knew why he'd stayed on in the United States for twenty-five years and led a brutally hard life. 'I helped my mother till the day she died. That was my goal. That's why I left my country.'

Almost one in every seven humans – a billion people – receive or send remittances. So significant are remittances that the United Nations has declared 16 June the International Day of Family Remittances. In the Philippines, its ten million overseas workers are celebrated as national heroes. The wire transfer company MoneyGram even has an awards ceremony, the MoneyGram Idol Awards, during which a group of overseas workers are flown to Manila to be reunited with their families, 'to recognize the everyday struggles of families living and working abroad'.

One of the best ways of reducing global poverty is to reduce the fees on money transfers, which exceed $30 billion annually. Lacking the deposits needed for proper bank accounts, migrants pay an inordinately high percentage of the money they send back in fees to places like Western Union. They are disproportionately high for the poorest countries and remote rural areas. But the Trump administration is now considering extorting the poor; it is looking at ways to tax remittances sent to Mexico, to pay for a wall to keep other Mexicans out.

But it's not as if the migrants are just taking from the host countries and sending it all back. Total migrant earnings are estimated at $3 trillion annually, of which 85 per cent stays in the host country. The money sent home averages out to under 1 per cent of the host countries' GDP.

One of the most important forms of remittances isn't money, but knowledge transfer and charity. A US-trained doctor goes back to India for a spell and sets up a rural hospital. Muslims in Germany fund schools in Syria through *zakat*, the charity that every Muslim is religiously obliged to perform. This, too, is a kind of ordinary heroism.

Because of their history, are the rich countries obliged to take in any and all comers from the ones they have despoiled? There are reasonable opponents of open borders – of increased immigration in general – who are not motivated by white fear or bigotry. Philosophers such as Michael Walzer and David Miller point out that a collective has a right to accept or decline members based on criteria that it formulates. As Walzer puts it, 'The state's right to control immigration derives from a cultural group's right of cultural preservation.' Miller has a theory of 'weak cosmopolitanism', which holds that while a state should demonstrate moral concern for, say, refugees, it does not have an obligation to let in anybody who asks. Members of a nation who have enhanced the value of the nation through their hard work and talent are entitled to reject migrants from other nations that have not been similarly enhanced.

There are serious arguments against open borders: that a nation is defined by its borders. That the United States is a lifeboat in an ocean of poor nations, and we can't let too many people into the lifeboat, otherwise it sinks and everyone dies. That, even if we owe reparations to people we've dispossessed, those reparations can come in the form of cash payments, or to resettlement in another territory.

But there are no serious arguments that demonstrate long-term economic damage to countries that accept immigrants, even large numbers of them all at once. During the age of mass migration, for example, a quarter of Europe moved to the United States – and the United States survived, and thrived. A world with more open borders would have a brief spasm of mass movement, and then migration might actually decrease, because money and happiness would be more equitably spread around, and more people would stay at home.

The long-term benefits of migration accrue not just to the countries people are migrating from (in the form of remittances), but also to the countries they're migrating to, and not just because immigrants work harder. (Migrants are 3 per cent of the world's population but contribute 9 per cent of its GDP.) Yet few people think of the long term when they see a sudden mass of foreigners at their borders.

To avoid paying the 'migration tax', and not be swamped by migrants from the countries they've ruined, the rich countries should, for their own good, be nicer to other countries. They should stop propping up dictators. They should keep a check on their own corporations, stop them from amassing profits through bribing local officials, stop them from starting polluting factories and mines. They should make sure that trade is more equitable.

You want to go in and start a war that costs, according to *The Lancet*, 600,000 Iraqi deaths? OK, the consequence should be that you'll be taxed; you'll have to let into your country an equal number of living persons – 600,000 Iraqis. For each person that you kill in an overseas adventure, you give one person a chance at a new life.

What might appear to be 'good' immigration policy for a country – one that focuses on what it has to gain from its immigrants – doesn't necessarily line up with what is just and moral. For example, America might want to let in more skilled Indians and fewer unskilled Latinos; but America has hurt Latinos much more than it has hurt Indians. America owes them more, and so it should open its doors more to them. History is not 'bunk' in the words of that famous American and anti-Semite Henry Ford. History is what has happened and can never un-happen; history is happening right now. Attention needs to be paid.

The whole system of visas and borders is less than a hundred years old; it only came into force in most places after World War II. Why not reclaim the right to travel, the right to migrate?

It is every migrant's dream to see the tables turned, to see long lines of Americans and Britons in front of the Bangladeshi or Mexican or Nigerian embassy, begging for a residence visa. My mentor, the distinguished Kannada-language writer U. R. Ananthamurthy, was once invited to Norway to give a talk at a literary festival. But the Norwegian government wouldn't give him a visa until the last minute, demanding that he produce testimonials and bank statements and evidence that he wasn't going to stay in the country. When he finally got to Oslo, the Indian ambassador threw a party for him.

'Is it easy for Norwegians to get an Indian visa?' Ananthamurthy asked the ambassador.

'Oh, yes, we make it really easy for them.'

'Why should it be easy?' my mentor demanded. 'Make it difficult!'

Perhaps the most selfish reason that Americans or Europeans should keep their borders permeable is that someday soon – or even today – the traffic of people in search of economic opportunity might reverse. The fiercest debate that is raging in these nations today is about whether immigration takes jobs away from people already here. But maybe one solution is emigration *from* America. Today, there are nine million Americans living abroad, not counting those in the military – up from four million in 1999. Up to five and a half million Britons live outside Britain – a full 8 per cent of the population. In the twenty-first century, the West's greatest export could be ... Westerners.

Just as India's greatest export has long been Indians. In 1990, fewer than seven million Indians lived overseas. By 2017, over seventeen million did. When my grandfather was sixteen, he had to support his five younger siblings in a village in Gujarat. So, in 1936, his father sent him to Nairobi, to join his uncle's accounting office. In turn, his children moved, to America, to England, to Australia, going where the work took them, and it wasn't easy for them either. In the 1970s, my father stood for nine hours a day at the Diamond Dealers Club on Forty-Seventh Street because he couldn't afford an office. My grandfather's descendants are doctors, lawyers, public servants and corporate executives. We kept in mind the lesson he learned at an early age: mobility is survival.

Somehow, Americans (more so than other Westerners) have always thought that the rest of the world should want to come to them; many recoil at the idea that they should have to go out there, for anything more taxing than sightseeing. The number of Americans working abroad is very low compared to that of other developed countries. A little over a third of Americans own a passport; three-quarters of Britons do, and 60 per cent of Canadians. If you were to believe Trump, and even some of the Bernie supporters, you would think that this is because every American has a God-given right to a well-paid job, right there in their country.

The twentieth century was the American century; the twenty-first, not so much. A young person in Denmark or New Zealand has a better quality of life, by almost any metric, than a young person in America. If you're fortunate enough to live in those advanced countries, you can go to college for free, not have to worry about money when you're sick, and enjoy two months' holiday even if you're only an intern. Part of the reason for this differential is a massive underinvestment by the American state in education, healthcare and the arts.

When I'd just arrived at my American high school from Bombay in the 1970s, I was surprised at how ignorant my American classmates were about world history. That ignorance, I later realized, was an American luxury, like a Cadillac, the grandest car in the world in the 1960s. Americans competing with Chinese, Nigerian and Brazilian youths for the same multinational jobs can't afford the same luxury.

Americans who work abroad do quite well; American pilots working in Chinese airlines, for example, make $300,000 a year. All around the world, legions of Americans make a good living as engineers, corporate executives, English teachers.

There is much talk these days about the American resistance to losing 'home', and its ancillary concern, the white fear of being replaced, re-placed. I certainly understand why Americans might be attached to their house, their friends and family, their home country. I've made New York my home, the last home for those who have no other. It's a beautiful country, a safe country and, for most people, a comfortable country. It's true that we should fight for better-paying jobs at home; companies that are relocating their plants abroad are engaged in a race for the bottom dollar.

But nobody asked my family how they felt about losing 'home'. After Trump's election, there have been endless stories about the plight of the small-town American who's forced to give up his town, where his ancestors are buried, and move to the cities of the plain, New York or Los Angeles. What they are demanding is the right not to change. They gave the rest of us no such choice.

American jobs are disappearing not so much because they're moving to Mexico or China, but because they're being done by robots rather than humans of any nationality. What we need is not a tariff, but training. We also need to gently teach our children: you have a right to a home, but not to fixed abode. You might prefer to stay in the house you were born in all your life, but it's not a constitutional right.

Immigrants know this. According to Berkeley's Giovanni Peri, immigrants are more willing to move to fast-growing, high-income, dense cities than natives are. If the native-born lose a job, they tend to stay where they are. If immigrants lose jobs, whether they're skilled or unskilled, they move. Once you're set in motion, you get used to moving.

As my family's example has shown, you can leave home and take it with you; find other homes, without losing your own. We had to move because there was no future in rural Gujarat; 200 years of British colonialism had left the Indian economy in ruins. When we moved, we missed the trees, the language, the spicy vegetarian food of Gujarat; the festival of the winter millet; the dance of the nine nights in the autumn; the sweetened fragrance of the earth after a heavy rainstorm.

Some of it we could take with us – no Gujarati travels anywhere without a stack of flatbreads and mango pickle. Some of it we couldn't, and so we went back to Gujarat as often as we could, or not at all. My aunt in England, whose family moved from India to Uganda three generations ago, has never been to India and still speaks fluent Gujarati and eats mostly Gujarati food.

Americans are more fortunate; the whole world looks like America now. Americans who emigrate don't have to go without McDonald's or CNN, their language, their dress, their customs. When they are abroad, they are much better protected than my family was when we left India. When I had an Indian passport, border officials all around the world treated it like the mark of Cain. After I became an American citizen, I once lost my passport in London; the American embassy gave me a new one in an hour, in time to catch my flight. American embassies and consulates will take care of you, bail you out if there's trouble; the Indian missions never had the money or clout to do the same for their citizens.

Some of my former American students are employed in the booming Indian media world, even though they don't speak the local languages, because they have writing and editing skills honed at NYU. In India, their salaries can buy them an apartment, or a shared room, nice dinners, domestic help. Meanwhile, most of their peers in New York are still struggling in unpaid internships, supported by loans or parents. The best way to start a journalistic career is to move to a small country and establish yourself as a local stringer for American news organizations who are ditching their foreign bureaus wholesale.

Many of my students have become accustomed, through a lifetime of vacations abroad and study-abroad programmes, to the possibility of making a life anywhere on this beautiful blue planet. It doesn't mean they love their country less; it's just that they see that other countries are loveable, and liveable too. A globalist is a nationalist who's bothered to get a passport.

My family's trek around the world has come full circle.

For my college-going sons, there is no guarantee that there will be a job waiting after graduation in America. But they have already worked, with confidence, in Jakarta, Brazil and India. Growing up in New York – where two out of three people are immigrants or their children, and where one out of every five people in Manhattan is a tourist – has made them comfortable with the idea of living anywhere in the world. The other day, my son Gautama, who wants to be a journalist, told me he was thinking about looking for a job ... in India.

Epilogue: Family, Reunified – and Expanded

In 1871, Walt Whitman foresaw the way human beings would relate to each other in our times. As he put it in his poem 'Passage to India': 'Lo, soul, seest thou not God's purpose from the first? The earth to be spann'd, connected by network.'

Whitman's lines explain, for me, how an immigrant can come to a big, expensive city like New York or San Francisco, without papers, without money, without housing, and make a new life. Or how other immigrants come in at the top of the scale and find jobs whose salaries start at several times the median income. The answer lies in the network: they go to their tribes, their communities in the city. Whether it's an association of software engineers or an alumni association or a church group, immigrants live and die, work and marry, pray and play, within the network.

As a result, there isn't always a great need to assimilate – even if, in the long term, most immigrants, and particularly their children, do. There are whole neighbourhoods in New York where you can spend your entire day working, eating, playing and dealing with the government without knowing a word of English. All you need is access to a network that speaks your language; and for the network to be broad enough to provide the goods and services of a decent life. New York City today has 270 magazines and newspapers in 36 languages, catering to 52 separate ethnic groups. But it's not just New York. There are entire towns in Maine and Minneapolis that have been re-energized by Somalis. There are farming towns in Iowa that could be small towns in Mexico.

How does an immigrant network spring up? An Asian engineer may be admitted for his skills and given an employment-based work visa, such as an H-1B. He works for several years, gets a green card, and then brings his parents and sisters over. Thus, a skills-based network becomes a family network, which is stronger and more lasting. The concept of 'family' can be very broad among immigrants; with Indians, it can include the entire caste group; with Latinos, it can include the entire village. My own caste group, of several hundred Indians in the New York metropolitan area, holds regular picnics and dances; cricket is played, marriages arranged, and leads on housing and jobs exchanged over Gujarati food in state parks in New Jersey and Italian wedding palaces in Queens.

The definition of an 'immigrant network', and its function, is wide-ranging. For a couple of years, I used to meet a group of south Asian writers every Tuesday in a South African café in Brooklyn. They were Indians such as Amitav Ghosh, Kiran Desai and Jhumpa Lahiri, and Pakistanis such as Mohsin Hamid, and the great poet Agha Shahid Ali, who identified himself as Kashmiri. Other south Asian writers who passed through town came and stopped by; we occasionally met at each other's houses or studios and ate our curries, drank and gossiped.

Such a trans-south Asian gathering would not be possible in south Asia; it would be too difficult to get a visa for a fellow writer from the enemy country to meet in Delhi or Lahore. So we met in Brooklyn, where ancient tribal hatreds were soused in good Stellenbosch wine. The normal writerly jealousies and rivalries of the subcontinent do not apply here, where we are small fish in a big pond. We read and commented on each other's work; exchanged tips on editors and agents; and blurbed, publicized and celebrated each other's achievements. It was as much of a network as a bricklayers' union or a medieval guild; we came together for work and, incidentally, found companionship in what is an otherwise solitary endeavour.

Old-school ties are now transnational. The first foreign group that came in large numbers to Silicon Valley to work in technology industries were Taiwanese, many of them graduates of the island's elite National Taiwan University. In the late 1970s and the early '80s, up to 80 per cent of the graduates went abroad, mostly to Silicon Valley. They were followed by graduates of the Indian Institutes of Technology, who came in comparable numbers.

And it's not just university networks that are global. I know of a group of young women in New York, all graduates of an American international school in Hong Kong. The women are of different ethnicities, from Irish American to Swedish; they went to different places for college and graduate school, then migrated in batches to New York. They do all the things that Latin American restaurant workers or Pakistani cabbies might do for people from their home villages: they find apartments for their school friends, check out potential dates, tell them where to shop for lingerie and good cheese. Most of all, the network makes these young women feel less alone, less vulnerable in the big anonymous city. So they meet almost every weekend; their school network is the strongest constant in their lives in the big city, across the globe from the big city where they first met.

Other kinds of immigrants form other kinds of enclaves. Immigrants today see no need to follow an imagined, idealized 'American way'; because of the strength and regular reinforcement of their ties to the old country, they can live in America, in many ways, as they did in the land left behind.

You network with people in the new world you wouldn't give a second glance to in the old country. Over brunch, a young Nigerian couple, an investment banker and a lawyer at top firms in New York, told me about how they discovered their fellow Africans. They live much as others of their education (boarding school in Britain, business and law school in Boston) do: summer shares in the Hamptons, expensive meals on expense accounts.

Then the wife got pregnant, and they bought a large apartment in a section of Harlem where they come into daily contact with African street vendors, people they would have interacted with only as servants in Nigeria, where both their families are tribal nobility. The top banking and legal firms are supposed to be a meritocracy; anybody who can make money for the firm is supposed to be welcome. But as they tried to become partners, they saw more and more evidence of the caste system of haute New York, and found more in common with the street vendors than they'd ever have imagined. As they struggled to find a place in New York City, they ended up rediscovering Nigeria.

In their professional lives, the Nigerian couple have to emulate the culture and manner of the elites in the same way that their Jewish and black predecessors had to when they first entered the WASP banking and law firms, in the twentieth century. But in their personal lives, the Nigerian couple and their child have more choices: they can speak their language, eat their food, enrol the child in cultural events, much as they might have done in Nigeria. Because a part of Nigeria is right there on their doorstep, in Harlem.

A network is made up of individuals in a collective. A city is the most hospitable of collectives, since it has room for multiple individual networks. Because of the polyglot nature of New York, the city sees some strange intersections of networks, including people who band together in the face of a common enemy. A young Gujarati man from Queens told me about belonging to a street gang in Jackson Heights called the Punjabi Boys Network. Its members come from India, Pakistan, Afghanistan and Bangladesh – countries that, at any given time, are at war with one or more of the others. But in Queens, their commonalities outweigh their differences as they fight the Latinos and the African Americans in the high schools. When a fight gets particularly violent, he said, they call on some Brooklyn-based members of the Bloods gang – African Americans, not a group they normally associate with. And so, united in strife, the south Asians and the African-American gangs go forth to do battle with all comers.

Will the new immigrants fully assimilate? Does it matter if they don't? Immigrants should have the freedom to not melt entirely into any sort of pot; to speak in their language as well as their host country's, worship their god, marry as they choose. That is the meaning of being American, and that is why the Quakers came to Pennsylvania. They didn't have to become Calvinists – or worshippers of the Great Spirit.

Austria now wants to fail kindergarteners if they don't know German. My son's preschool teacher had a better idea.

It is 1996, and my son Gautama's first day of school, at the YMCA on Fourteenth Street in Manhattan. The entire class of two-year-olds is speaking English, all except my son, who we have raised speaking Gujarati. He comes into the class and sees a toy yellow school bus and runs towards it. But someone else snatches it from him. The teachers lead the kids through a drill, telling them when to raise their hands; they sing songs. My son cannot understand. I sit with him feeling miserable. The kids in my apartment building say about him: 'He can't talk.' He looks up at them hopefully, but they don't invite him to play with them. When he sits in the little garden downstairs, eating his *khichri*, the girl across the hall says, 'Eeeuww.'

I switch him to a new school, the Third Street Music Settlement (which is actually on Eleventh Street), where the medium of instruction is music. When I first speak to his teacher, a woman sitting behind a piano in front of a class of little Japanese, little French, little American kids, I caution her that Gautama doesn't speak English; there would have to be a transition. 'Don't worry,' she says. 'When you bring him here, come with a tape of a song he knows in his own language.'

So I make a tape, of a lullaby that I have been singing to Gautama almost every night:

Lalla lalla lori
Doodh ki katori
Doodh me batasha
Munna dekho tamasha

Gautama enters the new schoolroom, apprehensive, wondering if all these kids would talk to him, play with him. The teacher listens to the tape. Then she turns to the classroom. 'Children, this is Gautama. Let's all sing a song in Gautama's language.' She plays it on the piano, leading the chorus. And my son watches in amazement as all the little American and Japanese and French and Indian kids sing this song that he knows so well, this song that soothes him to sleep. My son discovers that his language is no longer unspeakable. If they're willing to learn his language, then ...

Within a month, Gautama was speaking English.

How does a new immigrant learn a new language? Not at gunpoint. As new immigrants, we gravitate toward the middle world: the ethnic neighbourhoods of cities where there is something of the country we've left behind, amid the standard American landscape of drugstores and strip malls – its foods, its festivals, its language. If we welcome the newcomers in Gujarati or Spanish – if we are willing to respect them, ease their fears, by learning *their* language, then, well ... If you're willing to become a little bit Indian, then I'll be much more willing to become a lot more American.

Why should new Americans have to speak English immediately? In many cities like Nueva York or Los Angeles, you can work, date, eat, take public transit, and attend civic functions speaking only Spanish, Bengali or Fujianese. In this, they're following the grand American tradition. A 1911 committee set up by Congress studied 246,000 immigrants working in mining and manufacturing for three years. Just over half – 53.2 per cent – spoke English. These immigrants weren't highly skilled and needed handouts. The commission found that 38 per cent of all national charity was given to immigrants. In some of the studies it cited, immigrants constituted over half of all charity recipients. They worked hard, like today's immigrants, and, like today's immigrants, they needed a helping hand their first few years in the new country as they were learning the new country's language. And when they did learn to speak English, which helped them find better jobs and participate in the country's civic culture, they did not lose the languages they had come over with. That was a choice for their children to make.

Latinos are 18 per cent of the population – fifty-seven million Americans. By 2065, there will be 107 million – one out of every five Americans. And the vast majority of them won't be immigrants, but American-born. For many of them, New York is Nueva York and America is Estados Unidos. It is no longer a monolingual country.

Gujaratis, Lebanese and Chinese are some of the most successful trading communities around the world. We can travel because we don't lose ourselves entirely where we go. We're not going to become British in Britain – come on, are you joking? Did the British become Gujarati when they ruled over us? No, we'll watch our Bollywood movies, and eat our *dal-bhaat*, and, at least initially, marry mostly among ourselves; but we will speak English, run for Parliament, operate pharmacies, write books. We will contribute, without becoming complaisant.

In India we were brought up to idealize the nineteenth-century European nation-state; if only our quarrelsome heterogeneity could be assembled into a patriotic parade, how much better off, like the British or the French, we would be! It was only later on that I came to realize that the Scots and the Irish and the Welsh were almost as fissiparous as the Assamese and the Sikhs; that France had its Breton and Corsican secessionists too. In fact, at the time of the French Revolution, half the people living in France didn't even speak French.

Can you belong to a country without belonging to a nation? The state insists that you belong to a nation. I would rather belong to a community. Or more than one community. Many of us who are lucky enough to have the right papers live not in one place or the other, but in a continuum of our birthplace and the place we've migrated to. Where is home for people like us? Are we Indian or American? Are we Bombayites or New Yorkers? We are both, and neither. The communities of people that move these days between two or more localities, as I do between south Bombay and Greenwich Village, might be called 'interlocals'. The dictionary defines the word as 'situated between, belonging to, or connecting several places'. So I propose a new way of looking at migrants: not as people who go in one direction and stay there, but as people in continuous transit between two or more *places*, not nation-states. Let's look at migration as not an arrow but a circle.

Immigrants feel the need for family most keenly when they first get here. Every immigrant I know misses, most of all, the family left behind. Humans have traditionally migrated in tribes, not alone or just with their spouses and children.

When I go back to Mahudha, where my father's people are from, I find a house with durable Burma teak cabinets, an orchard of mango trees in the courtyard, watered from a well in which my father swam as a boy, and a sense of peace behind high walls. But the village has become a town; Mahudha now has some 16,000 residents, its own Facebook page and an organization that brings together people hailing from the town – mostly Patels, whom my family would look down upon – in New Jersey. There's an invitation on the Facebook page: 'Mahudha Gaam Summer Picnic. We will be grilling and chilling at this Annual Mahudha Gaam Summer Picnic. So come join us with your family to enjoy this fun time.'

I immigrated over with not just my immediate family, not just my extended family, but a large part of my subcaste, the Dashanagar Vaniyas. It's a subcategory of Gujarati merchants from the villages around Ahmedabad, 'the merchants of the ten towns'.

It was a fine day at the subcaste picnic. All my caste-fellows, young, old, were playing cricket, eating, strolling by the New Jersey lake; and the old ladies were pleased that not one of us had yet married an American. What we had not known when we arrived there in the morning with our trays of *puris* and dry fried potatoes was that the Mahwah kennel club was also having its annual dog show in that very same park.

My caste-people were, on the whole, noisier than the dogs. We threw a ball back and forth, and this excited the dogs, which did not perform the tricks demanded of them by their owners with the requisite precision, because they were distracted by our shrieks. They complained to the park warden, who came over with his assistant. 'Hand over that ball,' he demanded. All the subcaste gathered around him, and he didn't know whom to argue with.

No one in my subcaste owned a dog, either in India or in America. Dogs are unclean animals, they bring in pollution from the outside, said the old ladies. But everyone in India plays with dogs – the streets teem with strays, and they show up at the kitchen door after lunch and eat up the leftovers in the blink of an eye. Dogs don't like to eat fruit; this was noticed by the old ladies, and this is what they said to each other at the subcaste picnic. Among other things. As they strolled round and round the lake, they spoke of many things – their grandchildren and who among them was likely to marry an American; the Pakistani soap operas they were watching on cable; and the *paan* they would eat every day with their departed husband in Ahmedabad. Meanwhile, the men and boys played cricket, and the girls went for walks in twos, and the mothers had a nap. Often the boys would, out of the corner of their eyes, notice the nice way a girl's hair swayed. At four o'clock everybody had tea, and at noon we all ate a big lunch with ten different varieties of curried potatoes. Because when we had arrived, in the morning, some of us had eaten up the *katchoris* that we were supposed to save for later.

In the West we think of migrants as a mass, fungible; but each one of them has a place in a much larger network as an uncle, a second cousin, a daughter-in-law, with individual mannerisms, hairstyles, favourite foods, which are known in intimate detail to the dozens of people who are close to them. And when one of them goes, that entire network goes, grieves, is broken.

How do migrants collect themselves after dislocation? One way is through the gathering of food. We bring spices and smuggle mangoes in our bags on the 8 p.m. Air India plane from Bombay, also known as the 'dada-dadi bus'. The vast majority of the gifts the migrants are carrying from their home countries is food: ham, *za'atar*, chilies, custard apples. Customs officials and agricultural inspectors are our enemies. There's no earthly reason the US government should confiscate, say, cheese at the borders – other than the possibility that if Americans were to taste truly good cheese, there would be an insurrection and Kraft would go out of business.

We bring these strong-smelling foods from our villages to the city, lay them out on the kitchen table as soon as we get home from the airport. As we eat, we weep. Our tears moisten the bread, which has been baked by our grandmother, who will never get a visa to join us. We send her a giro every month, Skype with her every week. It all feels unsubstantial – but this, this *arepa* she baked just this morning before we got on the plane, and that we are holding to our faces, to our noses, afraid almost to eat, to consign to our bellies – this is home, this is love, this is truth, this brings back memories of happier times. Abuela: *gracias*.

The greatest sorrow, said Dante, was to recall in misery the time when we were happy. The sadness of a lost happy time.

The migrant's dream: to build good houses for herself and each of her children, a family compound in the hills above the city, in her ancestral village, where all the family will gather, cousins and uncles and old people and children running about, and we will spread a sheet under the fig trees and there will be a freshly slaughtered sheep baked in a hole in the ground and the women will have been cooking for three days and there will be the good wine from the north in jugs and everybody will be there, the neighbours that we have been fighting with for generations too, and after we have eaten and drunk our fill there, we will join hands and dance in a circle to the old songs and laugh and laugh and laugh as if we never had to leave ... And everybody will be there, and we will laugh so much, we will dance so much, we will eat so much, as we did in the Before.

I am here – I am writing this book – as a result of chain migration. First came Anilmasa, my uncle who struck out from a small town in Gujarat to Kent State University in Ohio to train as an engineer. Then came his wife, his brother, his mother and his wife's siblings. I am in the United States because of 'family reunification', or what Trump calls 'chain migration'. We haven't taken a dime in welfare. When we needed the money, we borrowed from family. For immigrants, the family isn't a chain. It's a safety net.

In 2017, two-thirds of the 1.1 million green cards that America gave out went to relatives of US residents; only 12 per cent got them through employment. If America's immigration system were to be based on 'points' – if it lifted its lamp only to the highly skilled – then my family would never have been allowed in. My mother went to America because her sister in Detroit, a US citizen, sponsored her and her husband and three small children. My mother wouldn't have got a visa based on her skills. Because, as I discovered when I was thirty-six years old and in a car with my parents coming up to the George Washington Bridge, my mother never finished her college degree.

In March 1963, in Bombay, my mother was in the back of a taxi with two of her friends from the elite Sophia College, going to her uncle's house for dinner. In a month, she was to get her bachelor of arts, in philosophy and French, after taking her final exams. She was confident of the results; she was a good writer, and her essays would be shown around as a model for other students. She had married my father the previous year, and I was five months growing inside her.

The taxi pulled into a petrol station to refuel, and her friends insisted that she move to the middle because she was pregnant. The taxi drove out of the station, and a drunk Marwari came speeding down, broadsiding the taxi. Her friend sitting near the window had multiple fractures. The friend sitting on the other side was also hurt, and the taxi was a write-off. But my mother was largely unhurt, except for some bleeding around the hip.

The doctor told her this. He also said, 'If it was my own sister, I would tell her not to sit for the exams.' Because the exams involved sitting for six hours at a stretch. 'You can take the exams if you want, but it could be risky for the baby.' So my mother rested in bed for some time, and then went to Calcutta and had me, but of course studying was impossible for the new mother. She never became Usha Mehta, BA. She had never mentioned this incident to me. Once, around the time my wife was pregnant, my mother had said something about being in an accident when she was younger and asked my wife to be careful when travelling in cars. I had recently asked my mother about the full story – since I was writing a book about Bombay and our life in it – and she related it to me.

So I said it, in my parents' Lexus, as we were coming up to the George Washington Bridge, thirty-six years later: 'You gave up your college degree for me.'

'Yes,' she replied. 'But it was worth it, because I got ... you.'

America opens its doors to a million legal immigrants a year. Four hundred thousand of them come in to reunify with their families. Four million more are on the waiting list. In the UK, the number of foreigners allowed to join their British-resident families plummeted by 73 per cent from 2006 to 2017.

Countries should not be opposed to this kind of migration. When you have your extended family around you, you are more likely to prosper. When your son is flunking out of high school, your brother will speak to him, understand him as you cannot, and keep him off the streets. When you need to go to work and can't afford daycare, your mother will look after your child and feed her and tell her stories. When your daughter is looking for a job, your sister will tell her about an opening in the hospital she works in. E pluribus unum.

We new immigrants need it, need our extended family. We don't have the luxury of a legacy network, three or four generations deep in the country, that will get our daughter into a good college or loan us money when insurance doesn't cover the cost of hospitalization.

What frightens migrants most: the idea that you should come to America and Europe, and your extended family should dissolve into a nuclear one, and then disappear entirely, as you join the solitude of urban America, where half the inhabitants live alone. That you should forget the different terms for 'maternal uncle' and 'paternal uncle'; that you should be unaware of your grandparents' siblings' grandchildren; that your family shouldn't be extended, it should be excluded; the excluded family.

Even Donald Trump is on earth because of chain migration. His mother, Mary Anne MacLeod, moved from a village in Scotland to New York to join her two sisters and work as a maid. So, on both sides, Trump is a direct beneficiary of everything he campaigns against: chain migration and climate refugees, like his grandfather Friedrich. But this has happened often with different waves of immigrants: last one in shut the door.

I spent my first fourteen years in a country that had very few foreigners. The first time I had any sort of significant encounter with people who weren't Indian was when a delegation of Japanese university students came to my school in Bombay, when I was in the ninth grade. I had only the slightest of encounters with them; one of the female students asked to see my notebook and giggled at the doodles I'd made instead of my schoolwork. But for the longest time afterward, I was in a daze, enraptured by the foreignness of her. She could have been Zambian or Paraguayan; what mattered was that she was different, mysterious. I wanted to know people who weren't like me. The next year my family left for New York.

In my last year of college at NYU I discovered that I was part of a set of triplets. My siblings were an Italian-American boy named Chris and a Bavarian Szechuan girl named Ming. Ming was a dancer. Chris had a comic book store in Queens. I was trying to evade the family diamond business.

We met in a writing class, and after the class everybody went out drinking and lived the life of writers in Manhattan – without actually doing much writing. We spent a little too much money on drinks and dinner, and then looked the other way when the bill came at the end and we were short. We made literary jokes, imitating Hemingway: 'I went to Paris. And it was good.' We had love affairs, and embellished them in the telling, like when Chris went out with the daughter of an undertaker and she asked him to make love in a coffin in the mortuary. We were under the impression that Jill Clayburgh, then at the peak of her acting career, was stalking us, since we saw her twice in the same week at two separate restaurants where we were dining on the Upper West Side.

Chris and Ming made fun of me for my accent (since they were born in America, I couldn't do the same with them) and my driving. 'Did I just see you drive the wrong way down Queens Boulevard?' Chris asked incredulously early one Sunday morning as I was coming to pick them up.

They were the first real American friends I had, and they were very ethnic, in the way those who are born in New York can be. Ming's father, a thrice-married refugee in his seventies from China and then later Chiang Kai-shek's Taiwan, tried to get me interested in investing in a shoe factory with him. Christopher ('Christ-bearer', he explained the meaning of his name) was the son of Joseph and Mary; Joe was an artist who knew exactly how to cook eggplant parmigiana. ('Just use any olive oil. Never understood what "extra virgin" means. You're a virgin or you're not – how can you be extra?!') They invited me to their homes; I invited them to mine and fed them spicy *bhelpuri* for breakfast. Chris introduced us to the Italian-American terms 'Fugeddaboutit!' and 'Bada bing, bada boom' long before we heard the cast of *The Sopranos* say them.

We would go on weekend trips into the countryside together ('do Sylvan') to Massachusetts, upstate New York – places where everyone was white, and not white like Chris either. I remember, coming back after one of those trips, that we drove straight to Veniero's Pasticceria in the East Village to eat their ricotta cheesecake. Sitting in the packed room, with the transgendered, the blacks, the punks, the Italian families, I felt a tremendous sense of ... safety. Belonging. There, nobody was turning their heads around to look at our unlikely group. We were different, just as everyone else was different in their own way. As an Indian, I was the least strange person there.

I have close friends in Bombay too, but they're all Indian. They are diverse in the Indian way: Farrokh is Zoroastrian, Naresh is Catholic, Manjeet is Hindu. They speak different languages. But they are all Indian. They're the same colour.

In Bombay I can travel to the different states of India; in New York, the different countries of the planet. In New York now I can eat at a restaurant from a different region of the world every day for a year and not repeat. It's not about the food; I'm vegetarian and there's very little for me in a Nigerian or Moldovan restaurant. But it's the sense that I can go abroad at home, travel all the world for the price of a MetroCard. It expands my sense of myself. When I feel sad or lonely, I get on the subway and take it to the end of the line, walk in the lanes of a neighbourhood that is the representation or simulacrum of a faraway land, with its grocery stores, its drinking dens and eateries, and temporarily forget my dolour, which is overwhelmed by curiosity, and a healthy hunger. For that is the beginning of the end of sadness: when you are hungry again.

This is the American exceptionalism: it's a country made up of all the other countries. This is why I'm proud to call it my country. It may not be the reason I came, but it is the reason I stay. Today's immigrants might have come as the creditors, but they have become a credit to the country.

*

In spite of Trump, Americans, and their northern neighbours, are still the most welcoming people in the world for immigrants. According to a 2018 Ipsos poll of 20,000 people in twenty-seven countries, Canadians and Americans were first and second in the world, respectively, in believing that an immigrant could be a 'real Canadian' or 'real American'. The UK, by contrast, was ranked tenth. Only four non-Muslim countries surveyed by the poll had majorities who thought that a Muslim could be a real national of the country: South Africa, France, the United States and Canada.

America has been good to my family. And we have been good to America. In my extended family, we are engineers, writers, doctors, businessmen, prosecutors, infantrymen, teachers; and as of 2017, unexpectedly, a state senator.

My sister Sejal met her future husband, Jay, while they were campaigning for a half-Japanese, half-Indian candidate for Congress in rural Tennessee in 1994. The campaign, unsurprisingly, went nowhere (my recollection is that he came in fifth of four candidates) but led to their marriage ten years later, and two lovely children. They settled in a nice block close to downtown Raleigh, North Carolina, of single-family houses quite close together, where the neighbours can see what you're cooking as they walk by, and often invite themselves over.

In 2016, Jay called me to say he was giving up his safe government job to run for state senate.

'How are you going to support my sister?' I demanded. Jay is Indian; subcategory Bengali, and was born in Fayetteville, North Carolina. He'd never held elected office before and wanted to run against a gentleman with the fine old Southern name of Ellis Hankins, who was the executive director of the North Carolina League of Municipalities. It seemed an impossible endeavour – most of his constituents couldn't even pronounce his last name. In Fayetteville, Jay's father's patients called him 'Dr Chadhoori' because they couldn't pronounce 'Chaudhuri'.

But, since we are family, my sons and I went down to Raleigh to campaign for Jay. We knocked on doors, hundreds of them. Most people were friendly, in the Southern way. Most of them. One man pulled his gun on my son and told him to get out of his yard. I had a dog run at me. (All right, it was a small dog, a vicious poodle named Chewy. 'Chewy! Chewy!' I could hear his owner, a blowsy African American woman in a housecoat smoking a cigarette, calling while standing next to a pile of butts. 'You get back here, Chewy!')

And all the neighbours on Jay's block – Laurent from Martinique, Suzanne from Massachusetts, Bill from right there in Raleigh – rallied to support Jay, handed out flyers, put up yard signs, knocked on doors. Jay is a progressive Democrat, against the 'bathroom bill', which officially discriminated against the LGBTQ community, and for gun control. I wondered about what this meant for his chances in a state like North Carolina, which Trump carried in 2016.

Jay won his senate seat, in a landslide: by twenty-seven points in the Democratic primary and by thirty-one points in the general election.

'Seventy per cent of them voted for a candidate that's not of their own race,' Jay reflected, in wonderment. They didn't care about Jay's race; they didn't care that he would become the first Indian-American state senator in North Carolina history. They just liked what he had to say: that teacher's salaries, decimated by the Republicans, need to be raised. They liked that he came to their door, again and again, through blizzards and rainstorms, to ask for their vote, while his opponent seemed to take their vote for granted. One of them posted a picture on Instagram, of Jay making his way to her doorstep in a blizzard, to ask for her vote. He knocked on 10,000 doors; all told, his campaign knocked on 14,000. All politics is local.

After the election, Gautama and I and my sister and Jay are invited for dinner at Suzanne's house; she is celebrating the marriage of Fran, who was married to Bill, a carpenter who lives down the block, and is now remarried to Henry, an amiable accountant. Afterwards, we sit around the living room. I see a couple of guitars propped up against the wall, and I ask Gautama to play. He begins, with a Caetano song in Portuguese, which he learned in his gap year in Brazil. Then Suzanne's son Matt follows, and Laurent from Martinique's son Noah.

Then the master takes the stage: Suzanne's husband Rod, who is a very well-preserved rock musician approaching sixty, who has had to raise a family and so makes music for video games, and sometimes plays with a band in the Raleigh bars, but now these are his closest friends and his wife and his son, and he has had quite a bit of whiskey. So he picks up the guitar and fixes a harmonica around his neck, and sings a song for two women named Frances, one of them his mother-in-law. As he plays, he coaxes an intricate web of sound out of this ancient contraption of wood and strings, and we are transfixed. There, in that room with the good modernist furniture, after we've all eaten our fill of pie, with the newlyweds on their second or third marriage, with the boys I've known since they were children, now approaching full-grown manhood, this community of people on Graham Street in Raleigh, who've rallied to help their Bengali-American neighbour get elected because they believe in his politics, and because he is their neighbour and they know he is a good and honest man, wherever he may be from. He is now family, and his family is their family. This is my America. It is my land – and our land.

Notes on Sources

I. A PLANET ON THE MOVE

4 *I am now among the quarter of a billion people*: United Nations, Department of Economic and Social Affairs, Population Division, *Trends in International Migrant Stock: The 2017 Revision*. United Nations Database (December 2017), p. 1. http://www.un.org/en/development/desa/population/migration/publications/populationfacts/docs/MigrationPopFacts2017s.pdf.

4 *in surveys, nearly three-quarters of a billion people want*: Neli Espova, Julie Ray and Anita Pugliese, 'Number of Potential Migrants Worldwide Tops 700 Million'. Gallup (8 June 2017). https://news.gallup.com/poll/211883/number-potential-migrants-worldwide-tops-700-million.aspx.

5 *Nine years earlier, Parliament had passed*: Commonwealth Immigrants Act 1968, *National Archives Legislative Record* (1968, ch. 9). https://www.legislation.gov.uk/ukpga/1968/9/pdfs/ukpga_1968000 9_en.pdf. Restrictions then further codified by Immigration Act 1971, *National Archives Legislative Record* (1971, ch. 77). http://www.legislation.gov.uk/ukpga/1971/77/pdfs/ukpga_19710077_en.pdf.

6 *the most diverse county in the United States*: Svati Kirsten Narula, 'The 5 US Counties Where Racial Diversity Is Highest – and Lowest'. *Atlantic* (29 April 2014). https://www.theatlantic.com/national/archive/2014/04/mapping-racial-diversity-by-county/361388/.

8 *Ninety per cent of Republicans*: Gallup, 'Presidential Approval Ratings – Donald Trump' (last accessed 5 December 2018). https://news.gallup.com/poll/203198/presidential-approval-ratings-donald-trump.aspx.

8 *Between 1960 and 2017, the overall number of migrants tripled*: Phillip Connor, 'International Migration: Key Findings from the US, Europe and the World'. Pew Research Center (15 December 2016). http://www.pewresearch.org/fact-tank/2016/12/15/international-migration-key-findings-from-the-u-s-europe-and-the-world/.

8 *By mid-century, migration will account for*: US projections from Pew Research Center, 'Modern Immigration Wave Brings 59 Million to US, Driving Population Growth and Change Through 2065' (28 September 2015). http://www.pewhispanic.org/2015/09/28/chapter-2-immigrations-impact-on-past-and-future-u-s-population-change/. U.K. projections from the Office for National Statistics, 'National Population Projections: 2016-Based Statistical Bulletin' (26 October 2017). https://www.ons.gov.uk/peoplepopulationand-community/populationandmigration/populationprojections/bulletins/national-populationprojections/2016basedstatisticalbulletin. Australia projections from Australian Bureau of Statistics, 'Population Projections, Australia, 2017 (base) – 2066' (last updated 22 November 2018). http://www.abs.gov.au/ausstats/abs@.nsf/mf/3222.0.

9 *Today, among the rich countries*: Organization for Economic Cooperation and Development, 'International Migration Outlook, 2018' (20 June 2018). http://www.oecd.org/migration/international-migration-outlook-1999124x.htm.

9 *The population of African cities is slated to triple*: All figures in this paragraph are compiled from the United Nations Department of Economic and Social Affairs, Population Division, 'World Urbanization Prospects: The 2018 Revision' (compiled 4 December 2018). https://population.un.org/wup/DataQuery/.

10 *In 2012, there were 930,000 newly registered asylum seekers*: Office of the United Nations High Commissioner for Refugees, 'Global Trends in Forced Displacement, 2017', Table 2, p. 40 (25 June 2018). http://www.unhcr.org/en-us/statistics/unhcrstats/5b27be547/unhcr-global-trends-2017.html.

10 *Not since the end of World War II*: Jason Beuabein, '5 Surprising Facts About the Refugee Crisis'. NPR (20 June 2017). https://www.npr.org/sections/goatsandsoda/2017/06/20/533634405/five-surprising-facts-about-the-refugee-crisis.

10 *Half are women*: United Nations Department of Economic and Social Affairs, Population Division, 'International Migration Report 2017: Highlights' (18 December 2017), p. 15. http://www.un.org/en/development/desa/population/migration/publications/migrationreport/docs/MigrationReport2017_Highlights.pdf.

10 *Eight out of ten Central American women*: Figures and information on *cuerpomático* from Deborah Bonello and Erin Siegal McIntyre, 'Is Rape the Price to Pay for Migrant Women Chasing the American Dream?' *Splinter*

(formerly *Fusion*; 10 September 2014). https://splinternews.com/is-rape-the-price-to-pay-for-migrant-women-chasing-the-1793842446.

11 **Well over half of all undocumented immigrants come into America not through the borders**: Robert Warren and Donald Kerwin, 'The 2,000 Mile Wall in Search of a Purpose: Since 2007 Visa Overstays Have Outnumbered Undocumented Border Crossers by a Half Million'. *Journal on Migration and Human Security* 5, no. 1, 2017, pp. 124–136. https://journals.sagepub.com/doi/pdf/10.1177/233150241700500107.

11 **In 2015, a group of immigrants, mostly Syrian refugees**: Rena Silverman, 'Syrian Refugees Biking to Safety'. *New York Times* (23 November 2015). https://lens.blogs.nytimes.com/2015/11/23/syrian-refugees-biking-to-safety/.

11 **Article 13 of the Universal Declaration of Human Rights**: United Nations, Universal Declaration of Human Rights (Paris: 10 December 1948). http://www.un.org/en/universal-declaration-human-rights/index.html.

2. THE FENCE: AMARGO Y DULCE

13 **It was inaugurated by First Lady Pat Nixon in 1971**: Background on Friendship Park from Yanan Wang, 'At One Border Park, Separated Immigrant Families Hug Across a Steel Divide'. *Washington Post* (1 May 2016). https://www.washingtonpost.com/national/for-families-divided-by-a-mesh-fence-a-rare-chance-to-embrace/2016/05/01/d0fdcf08-0b07-11e6-a6b6-2e6de3695b0e_story.html. More background and a time line from Randal C. Archibold, 'US–Mexico Border Fence Will Split Friendship Park'. *New York Times* (22 October 2008). https://www.nytimes.com/2008/10/22/world/americas/22iht-22border.17155357.html.

13 **the door was opened only six times after 2013**: Kate Morrissey, '"Door of Hope" Closed to Cross-Border Hugs, Weddings'. *San Diego Union-Tribune* (5 January 2018). https://www.sandiegouniontribune.com/news/immigration/sd-me-friendship-park-20180105-story.html.

14 **Scott also came out with a list of new restrictions**: Kate Morrissey, 'Border Patrol Changes Rules at Friendship Park, Upsetting Frequent Visitors'. *San Diego Union-Tribune* (14 February 2018). https://www.sandiegouniontribune.com/news/immigration/sd-me-friendship-park-20180214-story.html.

18 **In 2017, 782 pounds of fentanyl**: Nick Miroff, 'At America's Toughest Border Wall, a Hole Remains'. *Washington Post* (4 June 2018). https://www.

washingtonpost.com/news/national/wp/2018/06/04/feature/trump-touts-san-diego-border-wall-but-theres-a-hole-in-this-success-story/.

18 *spanking new private airport in Tijuana*: Sandra Dibble, 'New Tijuana Airport Bridge Opens'. *San Diego Union-Tribune* (9 December 2015). http://www.sandiegouniontribune.com/news/border-baja-california/sdut-tijuana-airport-bridge-opens-2015dec09-htmlstory.html.

19 *There are around 20,000 Border Patrol agents*: All figures from US Customs and Border Protection. Number of current agents and field offices found in 'August 2018 Snapshot: A Summary of CBP Facts and Figures'. https://www.cbp.gov/sites/default/files/assets/documents/2018-Aug/cbp-snapshot-20180823.pdf. Number of agents in 2000 found in 'United States Border Patrol Agent Nationwide Staffing by Fiscal Year'. https://www.cbp.gov/sites/default/files/assets/documents/2017-Dec/BP%20Staffing%20FY1992-FY2017.pdf. Budget figures found in 'US Border Patrol Fiscal Year Budget Statistics (FY 1990–FY 2017)'. https://www.cbp.gov/sites/default/files/assets/documents/2017-Dec/BP Budget History 1990–2017.pdf.

21 *Muslims fleeing the Middle East*: Office of the United Nations High Commissioner for Refugees, 'Global Trends in Forced Displacement, 2017' (25 June 2018), pp. 39–45. For information on religious affiliation among refugees resettled in the United States: Jie Zong and Jeanne Batalova, 'Refugees and Asylees in the United States'. Migration Information Source (7 June 2017). https://www.migrationpolicy.org/article/refugees-and-asylees-united-states.

22 *In San Diego in summer 2018, in spite of Scott's efforts*: Fiscal year 2018 and fiscal year 2017 data from US Customs and Border Protection, 'US Border Patrol Southwest Border Apprehensions by Sector.' In fiscal year 2018, 38,591: https://www.cbp.gov/newsroom/stats/usbp-sw-border-apprehensions. In fiscal year 2017, 26,086: https://www.cbp.gov/newsroom/stats/usbp-sw-border-apprehensions-fy2017. In October 2018, Customs and Border Protection reported 4,220 total apprehensions at the San Diego Sector, an increase of 77.5 per cent from 2,377 apprehensions in October 2017: https://www.cbp.gov/newsroom/stats/sw-border-migration/usbp-sw-border-apprehensions.

23 *As the US-exported gang violence took hold, the percentage increased*: Nadwa Mossad and Ryan Baugh, 'Refugees and Asylees: 2016'. Office of Immigration Statistics, United States Department of Homeland Security (January 2018). https://www.dhs.gov/sites/default/files/publications/Refugees_Asylees_2016_0.pdf. For percentages of asylum petitions coming from Northern Triangle countries: Office of the United Nations High Commissioner for Refugees, 'Global Trends in Forced

Displacement, 2017' (25 June 2018), p. 40. Further background on the passage of the Refugee Act from Susan Gzesh, 'Central Americans and Asylum Policy in the Reagan Era'. Migration Policy Institute (1 April 2006). https://www.migrationpolicy.org/article/central-americans-and-asylum-policy-reagan-era.

26 Jeff Sessions sought to eliminate domestic violence and gang warfare as reasons: US Attorney General Jeff Sessions, 27 I&N Dec. 316 (A.G. 2018). US Department of Justice, Office of the Attorney General (11 June 2018). https://www.justice.gov/eoir/page/file/1070866/download.

26 human mobility as 'survival migration': Alexander Betts, 'Survival Migration: A New Protection Framework'. *Global Governance: A Review of Multilateralism and International Organizations* 16, no. 3 (July–September 2010), pp. 361–382.

26 But 80 per cent of people who have applied legally for asylum: 'Asylum Denial Rates by Nationality, FY 2011–FY 2016'. Transactional Records Access Clearinghouse, Syracuse University (last accessed 5 December 2018). http://trac.syr.edu/immigration/reports/448/.

27 But that will take three years at least: 'Processing Time for Petition for U Nonimmigrant Status (I-918)'. U.S. Citizenship and Immigration Services (last accessed 5 December 2018). https://egov.uscis.gov/processing-times/.

3. ORDINARY HEROES

29 The migrants are no more likely to be rapists or terrorists: Robert Adelman, Lesley Williams Reid, Gail Markle, Saskia Weiss and Charles Jaret, 'Urban Crime Rates and the Changing Face of Immigration: Evidence across Four Decades'. *Journal of Ethnicity in Criminal Justice* 15, no. 1 (2017). https://www.tandfonline.com/doi/full/10.1080/15377938.2016.1261057.

36 88 per cent of the people are from elsewhere: United Nations Population Division, Trends in Total Migrant Stock: 2015 Revision, 'International Migrant Stock (% of Population)'. World Bank (last accessed 5 December 2018). https://data.worldbank.org/indicator/SM.POP.TOTL.ZS?year_high_desc=true.

37 Dubai, the Emirate next door, has 30,000 prostitutes: William Butler, 'Why Dubai's Islamic Austerity Is a Sham – Sex Is for Sale in Every Bar'. *Guardian* (16 May 2010). https://www.theguardian.com/world/2010/may/16/dubai-sex-tourism-prostitution. Additional context from Brittany Hamzy, 'A Victim's

Crime: Forced Prostitution in the UAE'. Americans for Democracy and Human Rights in Bahrain (12 July 2016). https://www.adhrb.org/2016/07/10379/.

4. TWO SIDES OF A STRAIT

41 *In 2017, Morocco rejoined the African Union*: Ed Cropley, 'In Tilt from Europe, Morocco Rejoins African Union'. Reuters (31 January 2017). https://www.reuters.com/article/us-africa-summit-morocco/in-tilt-from-europe-morocco-rejoins-african-union-idUSKBN15F18Z.

41 *Sub-Saharan migration across the Mediterranean and into Spain jumped tenfold*: Displacement Tracking Matrix, 'Europe – Mixed Migration Flows to Europe, Quarterly Overview (Jul–Sep 2018)'. International Organization for Migration, UN Migration Agency (31 October 2018), pp. 6–7. http://migration.iom.int/reports/europe-%E2%80%94-mixed-migration-flows-europe-quarterly-overview-jul-sep-2018.

41 *Morocco and Spain have negotiated a treaty*: 'Spain/Morocco: Protect Migrants, Asylum Seekers'. Human Rights Watch (24 March 2014). https://www.hrw.org/news/2014/03/24/spain/morocco-protect-migrants-asylum-seekers.

42 *It has between a quarter and half of the world's bauxite reserves*: US Geological Survey, 'Mineral Commodity Summaries, January 2018' (last accessed 5 December 2018). https://minerals.usgs.gov/minerals/pubs/commodity/bauxite/mcs-2018-bauxi.pdf.

42 *Och-Ziff bribed Guinean officials*: US Securities and Exchange Commission, Securities and Exchange Commission v. Michael L. Cohen and Vanja Baros, Civil Action No. 1:17-cv-00430 (filed 26 January 2017, in United States District Court, Eastern District of New York). https://www.sec.gov/litigation/litreleases/2017/lr23728.htm.

42 *The previous year, the firm paid a $213 million criminal penalty*: US Securities and Exchange Commission, 'Och-Ziff Hedge Fund Settles FCPA Charges' (29 September 2016). https://www.sec.gov/news/pressrelease/2016-203.html.

43 *220 Central Park South, the most expensive building in New York*: Ondel Hylton, 'By the Numbers: See Why 220 Central Park South Will Be King of 2018'. CityRealty (6 November 2018). https://www.cityrealty.com/nyc/market-insight/features/future-nyc/by-numbers-see-why-220-central-park-south-will-be-king-2018/15067. More context on 220 Central Park South from Katherine Clarke, 'As Manhattan's Most Secretive Skyscraper Rises, a Super-Elite Clientele Emerges'. *Wall Street Journal* (2 November 2018). https://www.wsj.com/articles/as-manhattans-most-secretive-skyscraper-rises-a-super-elite-clientele-emerges-1541170830.

43 *In 2018, U.S. officials charged him with criminal fraud*: Tom Schoenberg, Katia Porzecanski and Matt Robinson, 'Michael Cohen, Once of Och-Ziff, Charged with Fraud by US'. Bloomberg (3 January 2018). https://www.bloomberg.com/news/articles/2018-01-03/michael-cohen-ex-och-ziff-executive-charged-with-fraud-by-u-s.

43 *The case was later dismissed*: Jonathan Stempel, 'SEC Bribery Lawsuit against Och-Ziff Executives Is Dismissed'. Reuters (13 July 2018). https://www.reuters.com/article/us-sec-ochziff/sec-bribery-lawsuit-against-och-ziff-executives-is-dismissed-idUSKBN1K323D.

43 *Every year, $150 billion leaves Africa for overseas tax havens*: Khadija Sharife, 'The Myth of the Offshore: How Africa Lost $1 Trillion to Tax Havens'. *New African Magazine* (1 June 2017). https://newafricanmagazine.com/current-affairs/investigations/myth-offshore-africa-lost-1-trillion-tax-havens/.

44 *In 2016, for every forty-seven migrants who crossed the Mediterranean*: Office of the United Nations High Commissioner for Refugees, 'Desperate Journeys: Refugees and Migrants Arriving in Europe and at Europe's Borders' (3 September 2018), p. 10. https://www.unhcr.org/desperatejourneys/.

49 *Delta is the richest oil-producing state in Nigeria*: Nigerian National Bureau of Statistics, 'States Nominal Gross Domestic Product (2013–2017)' (last accessed 5 December 2018). https://www.nigerianstat.gov.ng/download/837.

49 *The giant Anglo-Dutch conglomerate has been drilling in the area since 1958*: Ron Bousso, 'In Nigeria, Shell's Onshore Roots Still Run Deep'. Reuters (23 September 2018). https://www.reuters.com/article/us-nigeria-shell-insight/in-nigeria-shells-onshore-roots-still-run-deep-idUSKCN1M3069.

49 *In 2017, Amnesty International uncovered documents*: Amnesty International, 'A Criminal Enterprise? Shell's Involvement in Human Rights Violations in Nigeria in the 1990s' (28 November 2017). https://www.amnesty.org/download/Documents/AFR4473932017ENGLISH.PDF.

53 *According to World Bank estimates*: Dilip Ratha, Supriyo De, Eung Ju Kim, Sonia Plaza, Kirsten Schuettler, Ganesh Seshan and Nadege Desiree Yameogo,

'Migration and Remittances: Recent Developments and Outlook in 2017'. World Bank Group (April 2018), p. 33. https://www.knomad.org/sites/default/files/2018–04/Migration%20and%20Development%20Brief%2029.pdf.

5. COLONIALISM

60 *After the exchange of populations was over*: 'India's Religion by Numbers,' *Hindu* (16 August 2015). https://www.thehindu.com/news/national/religious-communities-census-2011-what-the-numbers-say/article7582284.ece.

60 *Partition was an idea that was hatched in England*: Further general background from Sarah Ansari, 'How the Partition of India Happened – and Why Its Effects Are Still Felt Today'. *Conversation* (10 August 2017). https://theconversation.com/how-the-partition-of-india-happened-and-why-its-effects-are-still-felt-today-81766.

61 *'The main cause was the haste with which we parted with India'*: Dr Kirpal Singh, 'Interview with Lord Patrick Spens, Chief Justice of Federal Court of India and Chairman of Arbitral Tribunal. May 22nd 1963'. *Interviews Relating to Partition of the Punjab – 1947* (Patiala: Punjabi University, 1982; last accessed online 5 December 2018), pp. 222–223. http://www.panjabdigilib.org/webuser/searches/downloadPdf.jsp?file=PL-000839.pdf&docid=48640.

61 *They sent down a barrister named Sir Cyril Radcliffe*: BBC News, 'Cyril Radcliffe: The Man Who Drew the Partition Line' (1 August 2017). https://www.bbc.com/news/av/world-asia-40788079/cyril-radcliffe-the-man-who-drew-the-partition-line.

62 *The two countries also spend an inordinate amount of their GDP*: Information from Stockholm International Peace Research Institute (SIPRI), 'Military Expenditure (% of GDP)'. *SIPRI Yearbook: Armaments, Disarmament and International Security* (last accessed 5 December 2018). https://data.worldbank.org/indicator/MS.MIL.XPND.GD.ZS?end=2017&locations=PK-IN-GB&start=2000&year_high_desc=true. See also from SIPRI, 'Military Expenditure (% of Central Government Expenditure)'. *SIPRI Yearbook: Armaments, Disarmament and International Security* (last accessed 5 December 2018). https://data.worldbank.org/indicator/MS.MIL.XPND.ZS?end=2017&locations=PK-IN-GB&start=1988&year_high_desc=true.

62 *In 2015, Shashi Tharoor*: Shashi Tharoor, 'Viewpoint: Britain Must Pay Reparations to India'. BBC News (22 July 2015). https://www.bbc.com/news/world-asia-india-33618621.

62 *its share of world GDP gradually sank*: Angus Maddison, *Chinese Economic Performance in the Long Run, 960–2030 AD, Second Edition, Revised and Updated*. Development Centre Studies (Paris: OECD Publishing, 2007). Table 2.2a, p. 44. https://read.oecd-ilibrary.org/development/chinese-economic-performance-in-the-long-run-960–2030-ad-second-edition-revised-and-updated/economic-decline-and-external-humiliation-1820–1949_9789264037632-3-en#page4.

62 *ten million people, a third of Bengal, starved to death*: For mortality from Indian famines in this era, Leela Vasaria and Pravin Visaria, 'Population (1757–1947)'. In Dharma Kumar and Meghnad Desai, eds, *The Cambridge Economic History of India: Volume 2, c. 1757–c. 1970* (Cambridge: Cambridge University Press, 1983), Appendix 5.2, pp. 528–531.

63 *'the late Victorian holocaust'*: Mike Davis, *Late Victorian Holocausts: El Niño Famines and the Making of the Third World* (London: Verso, 2001), p. 8.

63 *'No organization in history has done more to promote'*: Niall Ferguson, *Empire: The Rise and Demise of the British World Order and the Lessons for Global Power* (London: Allen Lane, 2002), p. xxi.

63 *'The Case for Colonialism'*: Bruce Gilley, 'The Case for Colonialism'. *Third World Quarterly* (2017). http://www.web.pdx.edu/~gilleyb/2_The%20case%20for%20colonialism_at2Oct2017.pdf.

64 *'balanced reappraisal of the colonial past'*: Nigel Biggar, 'Don't Feel Guilty about Our Colonial History'. *The Times* (30 November 2017). https://www.thetimes.co.uk/article/don-t-feel-guilty-about-our-colonial-history-ghvstdhmj.

64 *59 per cent of Britons surveyed in 2014*: Will Dahlgreen, 'The British Empire Is "Something to Be Proud Of"'. YouGov (poll conducted 24–25 July 2014). https://yougov.co.uk/topics/lifestyle/articles-reports/2014/07/26/britain-proud-its-empire.

64 *'The prime minister believed that Indians were the next worst people'*: Christopher Bayly and Tim Harper, *Forgotten Armies: The Fall of British Asia, 1941–1945* (Cambridge, MA: Harvard University Press, 2005), p. 286.

64 *'I am strongly in favour of using poisoned gas'*: National Churchill Museum, 'Churchill's 1919 War Office Memorandum' (written 12 May 1919). https://www.nationalchurchillmuseum.org/churchills-1919-war-office-memo-randum.html.

65 *'Churchill literally created the kingdom of Jordan'*: Ben Quinn, 'How Churchill Helped to Shape the Middle East We Know Today'. *Guardian* (23 April 2017). https://www.theguardian.com/uk-news/2017/apr/22/winston-churchill-imperial-war-museum-middle-east-legacy.

65 *In all, 40 per cent of the national borders in the entire world today*: For a detailed breakdown of the role colonial powers such as Britain and France played in the creation of arbitrary national borders, refer to Alberto Alesina, William Easterly and Janina Matuszeski, 'Artificial States'. *Journal of the European Economic Association* 9, no. 2 (April 2011), pp. 246–277. http://www.jstor.org/stable/25836066.

65 *The authors of a 2015 study in the* American Economic Review: Stelios Michalopoulos and Elias Papaioannou, 'The Long-Run Effects of the Scramble for Africa'. *American Economic Review* 106, no. 7 (November 2011), pp. 1802–1848.

66 *European countries began importing huge numbers of migrants*: Paul Fogarty, 'Contract Workers in World War One'. British Library (29 January 2014). https://www.bl.uk/world-war-one/articles/contract-workers-in-world-war-one.

66 *In 1951 there were around 157,000 immigrants*: David Coleman, Paul Compton and John Salt, 'Demography of Migrant Populations: The Case of the United Kingdom'. In Werner Haug, Paul Compton, and Youssef Courbage, eds., *The Demographic Characteristics of Immigrant Populations* (Council of Europe Publishing, 2002), p. 504.

67 *Citizens though the north Africans may have been*: For context on the decolonization of Algeria, see Phillip C. Naylor, *France and Algeria: A History of Decolonization and Transformation* (Gainesville: University Press of Florida, 2000).

67 *When France left Algeria in 1962, 85 per cent of the population was illiterate*: UNESCO Institute for Lifelong Learning, 'Literacy, Training and Employment for Women, Algeria' (last updated 24 November 2015). http://uil.unesco.org/case-study/effective-practices-database-litbase-0/literacy-training-and-employment-women-algeria.

68 *A million Haitians have migrated to the United States*: Jennifer Schulz and Jeanne Batalova, 'Haitian Immigrants in the United States'. *Migration Information Source* (2 August 2017). https://www.migrationpolicy.org/article/haitian-immigrants-united-states.

68 *In March 2017, Cuauhtémoc Cárdenas*: Enrique Krauze, 'Will Mexico Get Half of Its Territory Back?' *New York Times* (6 April 2017). https://www.nytimes.com/2017/04/06/opinion/will-mexico-get-half-of-its-territory-back.html.

69 *The film Dunkirk, for example*: John Broich, 'What's Fact and What's Fiction in *Dunkirk*'. *Slate* (20 July 2017). https://slate.com/culture/2017/07/whats-fact-and-whats-fiction-in-dunkirk.html.

69 *Altogether, 2.5 million Indian soldiers*: Yasmin Khan, 'Has India's Contribution to WW2 Been Ignored?' BBC News (17 June 2015). https://www.bbc.com/news/world-asia-india-33105898.

70 *When Columbus arrived in the Americas in 1492*: Numbers for indigenous people living in the Americas at the dawn of the colonial age are the subject of a rich historiography. The numbers of 100 million and 3.5 million are drawn from a combination of Alan Taylor, *American Colonies: The Settling of North America* (New York: Penguin, 2002), pp. 39–40; and David E. Stannard, *American Holocaust: The Conquest of the New World* (New York: Oxford University Press, 1992), p. x.

70 *The London School of Economics anthropologist Jason Hickel observes*: Jason Hickel, 'Enough of Aid – Let's Talk Reparations'. *Guardian* (27 November 2015). https://www.theguardian.com/global-development-professionals-network/2015/nov/27/enough-of-aid-lets-talk-reparations.

70 *'Slave-owning planters, and merchants who dealt in slaves'*: Robin Blackburn, 'Enslavement and Industrialisation'. BBC History (17 February 2011). http://www.bbc.co.uk/history/british/abolition/industrialisation_article_01.shtml. See also Robin Blackburn, *The Overthrow of Colonial Slavery, 1776–1848* (London: Verso, 1988).

71 *Meanwhile, in Congo, Belgium's King Leopold*: Adam Hochschild, *King Leopold's Ghost: A Story of Greed, Terror, and Heroism in Colonial Africa* (London: Pan, 2002), pp. 225–234.

6. THE NEW COLONIALISM

73 *The gas cloud killed more than 20,000 people*: Neeraj Santoshi, 'Bhopal Disaster: So, How Many Died? 32 Years On, No One Sure'. *Hindustan Times* (3 December 2016). https://www.hindustantimes.com/bhopal/bhopal-disaster-so-how-many-died-32-years-on-no-one-sure/story-luLNoQaTxHluo5RTGNHOoI.html.

73 *United States refused to extradite Carbide's president*: Douglas Martin, 'Warren Anderson, 92, Dies; Faced India Plant Disaster'. *New York Times* (30 October 2014). https://www.nytimes.com/2014/10/31/business/w-m-anderson-92-dies-led-union-carbide-in-80s-.html.

74 *Today's multinationals are bigger than entire countries*: Fernando Belinchón, '25 Giant Companies That Are Bigger than Entire Countries'. *Business Insider España* (25 July 2018). https://www.businessinsider.com/25-giant-companies-that-earn-more-than-entire-countries-2018-7.

74 *Over a tenth of all the world's GDP is hidden*: Annette Alstadsæter, Niels Johannesen and Gabriel Zucman, 'Who Owns the Wealth in Tax Havens? Macro Evidence and Implications for Global Inequality'. *National Bureau of Economic Research* (September 2017). https://www.nber.org/papers/w23805.

75 *The City of London effectively operates as the biggest tax haven*: Nicholas Shaxson, 'The Tax Haven in the Heart of Britain'. *New Statesman* (24 February 2011). https://www.newstatesman.com/economy/2011/02/london-corporation-city.

75 *curious voting system, with some 9,000 votes*: Aiden James, 'The Place Where Businesses and Their Office Workers Vote'. BBC News (21 March 2017). https://www.bbc.com/news/uk-politics-39283177.

75 *'When the British empire crumbled'*: Nicholas Shaxson, 'A Tale of Two Londons'. *Vanity Fair* (April 2013). https://www.vanityfair.com/style/society/2013/04/mysterious-residents-one-hyde-park-london.

75 *Developing countries lose three times as much to tax havens*: Max Bearak, 'How Global Tax Evasion Keeps Poor Countries Poor'. *Washington Post* (8 April 2016). https://www.washingtonpost.com/news/worldviews/wp/2016/04/08/how-global-tax-evasion-keeps-poor-countries-poor/.

75 *Money being smuggled out of sub-Saharan Africa*: Dev Kar and Guttorm Schielderup, 'Financial Flows and Tax Havens: Combining to Limit the Lives of Billions of People'. *Global Financial Integrity* (December 2015). https://www.gfintegrity.org/wp-content/uploads/2016/12/Financial_Flows-final.pdf, p. xv.

76 *In 2016, a full 40 per cent of the profits of global multinationals*: Thomas R. Tørsløv, Ludvig S. Wier and Gabriel Zucman. 'The Missing Profits of Nations'. National Bureau of Economic Research Working Paper No. 24701 (issued June 2018, revised August 2018), p. 3. https://gabriel-zucman.eu/files/TWZ2018.pdf.

76 *Of the world's GDP, 11.5 per cent ($8.7 trillion) is being held in overseas tax havens*: Gabriel Zucman, 'How Corporations and the Wealthy Avoid Taxes

(and How to Stop Them)'. *New York Times* (10 November 2017). https://www.nytimes.com/interactive/2017/11/10/opinion/gabriel-zucman-paradise-papers-tax-evasion.html.

77 *Trillions of dollars a year in net resource transfers*: All information in these two paragraphs drawn from Matthew Salomon and Joseph Spanjers, 'Illicit Financial Flows to and from Developing Countries: 2005–2014'. *Global Financial Integrity* (1 May 2017), pp. xi–xv. https://www.gfintegrity.org/report/illicit-financial-flows-to-and-from-developing-countries-2005–2014/.

77 *'If we add theft through trade in services to the mix'*: Jason Hickel, 'Aid in Reverse: How Poor Countries Develop Rich Countries'. *Guardian* (14 January 2017). https://www.theguardian.com/global-development-professionals-network/2017/jan/14/aid-in-reverse-how-poor-countries-develop-rich-countries.

77 *Mexico lost $872 billion in illicit financial outflows*: Dev Kar, 'Mexico: Illicit Financial Flows, Macroeconomic Imbalances, and the Underground Economy'. *Global Financial Integrity* (30 January 2012). https://www.gfintegrity.org/wp-content/uploads/2014/05/gfi_mexico_report_english-web.pdf.

77 *sixteen million Mexicans immigrated to the United States*: Ana Gonzalez-Barrera, 'More Mexicans Leaving than Coming to the US'. Pew Research Center (19 November 2015). http://www.pewhispanic.org/2015/11/19/more-mexicans-leaving-than-coming-to-the-u-s/.

77 *'Citizenship in Western democracies'*: Joseph H. Carens. *The Ethics of Immigration* (New York: Oxford University Press, 2015), p. 226.

78 *'How much money can you ever hope to make in your lifetime?'*: Michael Clemens, 'Why Today's Migration Crisis Is an Issue of Global Economic Inequality'. Ford Foundation (29 July 2016). https://www.fordfoundation.org/ideas/equals-change-blog/posts/why-today-s-migration-crisis-is-an-issue-of-global-economic-inequality/.

78 *According to the economist Angus Maddison*: Jason Hickel, 'Global Inequality May Be Much Worse than We Think'. *Guardian* (8 April 2016). https://www.theguardian.com/global-development-professionals-network/2016/apr/08/global-inequality-may-be-much-worse-than-we-think. Figures taken from Jutta Bolt, Robert Inklaar, Herman de Jong and Jan Luiten van Zanden, 'Rebasing "Maddison": New Income Comparisons and the Shape of Long-Run Economic Development'. Maddison Project Database (2018). https://www.rug.nl/ggdc/historicaldevelopment/maddison/releases/maddison-project-database-2018.

78 *global inequality among the world's individuals has dipped since 2000*: Jutta Bolt, Marcel P. Timmer and Jan Luiten van Zanden, 'GDP per Capita since 1820'. In Jan Luiten van Zanden, Joerg Baten, Marco Mira d'Ercole, Auke Rijpma and Marcel P. Timmer, eds., *How Was Life? Global Well-being since 1820* (Paris: OECD Publishing, 2014), pp. 57–73. https://www.oecd.org/statistics/How-was-life.pdf.

79 *'Most people believe that inequality is rising'*: Hamilton Nolan, 'Global Inequality Explained by Branko Milanovic'. *Gawker* (3 June 2016). https://gawker.com/global-inequality-explained-by-branko-milanovic-1780110436.

79 *Jeremy Corbyn, in a December 2017 speech*: Jeremy Corbyn, 'Speech at United Nation Geneva Headquarters' (8 December 2017). https://labour.org.uk/press/jeremy-corbyn-speech-at-the-united-nations-geneva/.

80 *'he jeopardized foreign relations with former colonial power France'*: Mathieu Bonkoungou, 'Burkina Faso Salutes "Africa's Che"'. Reuters (17 October 2007). https://www.reuters.com/article/us-burkina-sankara-idUSL1757771220071017.

80 *'had become the strongest ally to France and the US in the region'*: Thomas Fessy, 'How Burkina Faso's Blaise Compaore Sparked His Own Downfall'. BBC News (31 October 2014). https://www.bbc.com/news/world-africa-29858965.

80 *in the UN Human Development Index*: United Nations Development Programme, 'Human Development Index and Its Components' (2017). http://hdr.undp.org/en/composite/HDI.

80 *1.5 million Burkinabe have moved to Ivory Coast*: 'Ivory Coast and Burkina Faso: A Measured Reconciliation'. *Stratfor Worldview* (12 August 2016). https://worldview.stratfor.com/article/ivory-coast-and-burkina-faso-measured-reconciliation.

7. WAR

81 *Moro Muslim conflict in the Philippines*: Ralph Jennings, 'Why There's No End in Sight to Violence by Multiple Terrorist Groups in the Philippines'. *Forbes* (30 May 2017). https://www.forbes.com/sites/ralphjennings/2017/05/30/violent-unrest-in-the-philippines/#3fd807ed3605.

81 *Ituri conflict in the Democratic Republic of Congo*: Alex McBride Wilson, 'Violence Returns to DR Congo's Ituri Province'. *Al Jazeera* (11 April 2018).

https://www.aljazeera.com/indepth/inpictures/violence-returns-dr-congo-ituri-province-180410102912520.html.

81 *The Rohingya crisis in Myanmar*: Engy Abdelkader, 'The History of the Persecution of Myanmar's Rohingya'. *Conversation* (20 September 2017). https://theconversation.com/the-history-of-the-persecution-of-myanmars-rohingya-84040.

81 *exacerbated by rumours spread through Facebook*: Paul Mozur, 'A Genocide Incited on Facebook, with Posts from Myanmar's Military'. *New York Times* (15 October 2018). https://www.nytimes.com/2018/10/15/technology/myanmar-facebook-genocide.html.

82 *United Fruit Corporation, which … owned 42 per cent of all the land*: Opoku Agyeman, *Power, Powerlessness, and Globalization: Contemporary Politics in the Global South* (Lanham, MD: Lexington Books, 2014), p. 45.

82 *'Guatemala was chosen as the site'*: Daniel Kurtz-Phelan, 'Big Fruit'. *New York Times* (2 March 2008). https://www.nytimes.com/2008/03/02/books/review/Kurtz-Phelan-t.html.

82 *United Fruit complained to Truman about the reform bill*: More background on the CIA's intervention in Guatemala is drawn from Piero Gleijeses, *Shattered Hope: The Guatemalan Revolution and the United States, 1944–1954* (Princeton, NJ: Princeton University Press, 1991), pp. 223–266.

83 *More than 200,000 Guatemalans died over the next four decades*: Elisabeth Malkin, 'An Apology for a Guatemalan Coup, 57 Years Later'. *New York Times* (20 October 2011). https://www.nytimes.com/2011/10/21/world/americas/an-apology-for-a-guatemalan-coup-57-years-later.html.

83 *The biggest source of Guatemalan foreign income*: Blake Nelson, 'Guatemalans Are Sending a Record Amount of Money Home during Trump's Presidency. Will Their Investment Pay Off?' *PRI's the World* (29 December 2017). https://www.pri.org/stories/2017–12–29/guatemalans-are-sending-record-amount-money-home-during-trump-s-presidency-will.

83 *remittances from the 1.5 million Guatemalans*: James Smith, 'Guatemala: Economic Migrants Replace Political Refugees'. Migration Policy Institute (1 April 2006). https://www.migrationpolicy.org/article/guatemala-economic-migrants-replace-political-refugees.

83 *'Many Americans would prefer to forget that chapter'*: Raymond Bonner, 'America's Role in El Salvador's Deterioration'. *Atlantic* (20 January 2018).

https://www.theatlantic.com/international/archive/2018/01/trump-and-el-salvador/550955/.

84 *Thus was MS-13 born*: Dara Lind, 'MS-13, Explained'. *Vox* (21 May 2018). https://www.vox.com/policy-and-politics/2018/2/26/16955936/ms-13-trump-immigrants-crime.

84 *As late as 2007, Chiquita Brands*: Matt Apuzzo, 'Chiquita to Pay $25m Fine in Terror Case'. Associated Press (15 March 2007). http://www.washingtonpost.com/wp-dyn/content/article/2007/03/15/AR2007031500354.html.

86 *In 2014, Mexican authorities seized 15,397 firearms*: 'Mexico Data Source: Firearms Tracing System Data (January 1, 2012–December 31, 2017)'. Office of Strategic Intelligence and Information, US Bureau of Alcohol, Tobacco, Firearms, and Explosives (as of 9 March 2018). https://www.atf.gov/resource-center/docs/undefined/tracedatamexicocy1217finalpdf/download.

86 *In the Caribbean, 64 per cent of guns coming in are American*: 'Caribbean Data Source: Firearms Tracing System Data (January 1, 2017–December 31, 2017)'. Office of Strategic Intelligence and Information, US Bureau of Alcohol, Tobacco, Firearms, and Explosives (as of 9 March 2018). https://www.atf.gov/resource-center/docs/undefined/tracedatacaribbeancy17finalpdf/download.

86 *All this came out in the open in 2011*: Todd Schwarzschild and Drew Griffin, 'ATF Loses Track of 1,400 Guns in Criticized Probe'. CNN (12 July 2011). http://www.cnn.com/2011/POLITICS/07/12/atf.guns/index.html.

87 *Half of all the civilian guns in the world*: Paul Specht, 'Does America Own 42 percent of the World's Guns?' Politifact (5 March 2018). https://www.politifact.com/north-carolina/statements/2018/mar/05/pricey-harrison/does-america-have-42-percent-worlds-guns/.

87 *Every day, around a thousand migrants are intercepted*: US Customs and Border Protection, 'Southwest Border Migration FY2018 Statistics' (last modified 9 November 2018). https://www.cbp.gov/newsroom/stats/sw-border-migration/fy-2018.

87 *Every day, some 700 guns travel unhindered over the border*: Kate Linthicum, 'There Is Only One Gun Store in All of Mexico. So Why Is Gun Violence Soaring?' *Los Angeles Times* (24 May 2018). https://www.latimes.com/world/la-fg-mexico-guns-20180524-story.html. Further context and statistics on firearms crossing the US–Mexico border from Topher McDougal, David A. Shirk, Robert Muggah and John H. Patterson, 'The Way of the Gun: Estimat-

ing Firearms Traffic Across the US–Mexico Border'. Trans-Border Institute, Joan B. Kroc School of Peace Studies, and the Igarapé Institute (March 2013). https://igarape.org.br/wp-content/uploads/2013/03/Paper_The_Way_of_the_Gun_web2.pdf.

87 *Between 2000 and 2004 alone, the United States dumped 20,000 criminals*: Ana Arana, 'How the Street Gangs Took Central America'. *Foreign Affairs* (May 2005). https://www.foreignaffairs.com/articles/central-america-caribbean/2005-05-01/how-street-gangs-took-central-america.

88 *The vote was 153 countries in favour*: United Nations General Assembly, 67th Plenary Meeting (6 December 2006). http://www.un.org/ga/search/view_doc.asp?symbol=A/61/PV.67.

88 *'The United States was the lone dissenter'*: Rachel Stohl and Doug Tuttle, 'The Small Arms Trade in Latin America'. *NACLA Report on the Americas* 41, no. 2 (2008), pp. 14–20.

89 *One out of ten people born in El Salvador, Honduras and Guatemala*: D'Vera Cohen, Jeffrey S. Passel and Ana Gonzalez-Barrera, 'Rise in US Immigrants from El Salvador, Guatemala and Honduras Outpaces Growth from Elsewhere'. Pew Research Center (7 December 2017). http://www.pewhispanic.org/2017/12/07/rise-in-u-s-immigrants-from-el-salvador-guatemala-and-honduras-outpaces-growth-from-elsewhere/.

89 *'That's almost the combined gross domestic product'*: Roberto Suro, 'We Need to Offer More Than Asylum'. *New York Times* (14 July 2018). https://www.nytimes.com/2018/07/14/opinion/sunday/migration-asylum-trump.html.

89 *The next year, the murder rate in Honduras*: Gustavo Palencia, 'Honduras Murder Rate Fell by More than 25 Percent in 2017: Government'. Reuters (2 January 2018). https://www.reuters.com/article/us-honduras-violence/honduras-murder-rate-fell-by-more-than-25-percent-in-2017-government-idUSKBN1ER1K9.

89 *slashed aid to those countries by over 35 per cent*: Chantal Da Silva, 'How Much Aid Does US Give to Central America? Trump Says He's Cutting Funding to El Salvador, Guatemala and Honduras over Migrant Caravan'. *Newsweek* (22 October 2018). https://www.newsweek.com/how-much-aid-does-us-give-central-america-trump-says-hes-cutting-funding-el-1180732.

89 *To date, 130 countries have signed the 2014 United Nations Arms Trade Treaty*: 'Arms Trade Treaty. New York, 2 April 2013'. United Nations Treaty

Collection (status as of 12 May 2018). https://treaties.un.org/Pages/ViewDetails. aspx?src=TREATY&mtdsg_no=XXVI-8&chapter=26&clang=_en.

90 *According to the Stockholm International Peace Research Institute*: Aude Fleurant, Alexandra Kuimova, Nan Tian, Pieter D. Wezeman and Siemon T. Wezeman, 'The SIPRI Top 100 Arms-Producing and Military Service Companies, 2016' (11 December 2017), pp. 1–2. https://www.sipri.org/sites/default/files/2017–12/fs_arms_industry_2016.pdf.

90 *The UK has sent £4.7 billion in arms to Saudi Arabia*: 'The UK Has Licensed at Least £4.7bn of Arms Exports to Saudi Arabia since the Start of the Yemen War'. Full Fact (7 September 2018). https://fullfact.org/news/uk-has-licensed-least-47bn-arms-exports-saudi-arabia-start-yemen-war/.

90 *$110 billion arms deal*: Bureau of Political-Military Affairs, 'Fact Sheet: US Security Cooperation with Saudi Arabia' (16 October 2018). https://www.state.gov/t/pm/rls/fs/2018/279540.htm.

90 *over 57,000 Yemenis*: Melissa Pavlik, 'Fatalities in the Yemen Conflict'. Armed Conflict Location and Event Data Project (last updated 8 November 2018). https://www.acleddata.com/2018/11/08/fatalities-in-the-yemen-conflict/.

90 *More than two million have been displaced*: Office of the United Nations High Commissioner for Refugees, 'Yemen Update (21st September–12th October 2018)'. https://reliefweb.int/sites/reliefweb.int/files/resources/Yemen%20Update%2021%20Sept-%2012%20October%202018%20FINAL.pdf. For information on famine, see also 'Half the Population of Yemen at Risk of Famine: UN Emergency Relief Chief'. UN News Agency (23 October 2018). https://news.un.org/en/story/2018/10/1023962.

90 *In June 2017, the Senate voted to clear the first part of the deal*: Jeremy Herb, 'Senate Narrowly Votes to Back Saudi Arms Sale'. CNN (13 June 2017). https://www.cnn.com/2017/06/13/politics/senate-saudi-arms-deal-paul/index.html.

91 *death rate is thirty-one times greater than officially acknowledged*: Azmat Khan and Anand Gopal, 'The Uncounted'. *New York Times* (17 November 2017). https://www.nytimes.com/interactive/2017/11/16/magazine/uncounted-civilian-casualties-iraq-airstrikes.html.

91 *in the United States, the vast majority of terror attacks are by white supremacists*: David Neiwert, Darren Ankrom, Esther Kaplan and Scott Pham, 'Homegrown Terror'. Reveal, the Center for Investigative Reporting (22 June 2017). https://apps.revealnews.org/homegrown-terror/.

91 *In Europe, the vast majority of terror attacks are by native-born Europeans*: Amanda Taub, 'Shutting Down Immigration Won't Solve Europe's Terrorism Problem'. *Vox* (22 March 2016). https://www.vox.com/2016/3/22/11285962/brussels-attack-refugees-immigration.

8. CLIMATE CHANGE

93 *'You can drastically reduce your greenhouse gas emissions'*: Michael B. Gerrard, 'America Is the Worst Polluter in the History of the World. We Should Let Climate Change Refugees Resettle Here'. *Washington Post* (25 June 2015). https://www.washingtonpost.com/opinions/america-is-the-worst-polluter-in-the-history-of-the-world-we-should-let-climate-change-refugees-resettle-here/2015/06/25/28a55238-1a9c-11e5-ab92-c75ae6ab94b5_story.html.

93 *a fifth of the world's population will be affected by floods by 2050*: Jonathan Watts, 'Water Shortages Could Affect 5bn People by 2050, UN Report Warns'. *Guardian* (19 March 2018). https://www.theguardian.com/environment/2018/mar/19/water-shortages-could-affect-5bn-people-by-2050-un-report-warns.

93 *at least 200 million people will be displaced by climate change*: International Organization for Migration, 'IOM Outlook on Migration, Environment and Climate Change' (2014), p. 38. http://publications.iom.int/system/files/pdf/mecc_outlook.pdf.

93 *'In some parts of the world, national borders'*: Coral Davenport, 'Major Climate Report Describes a Strong Risk of Crisis as Early as 2040'. *New York Times* (7 October 2018). https://www.nytimes.com/2018/10/07/climate/ipcc-climate-report-2040.html.

93 *'Toward the end of this century'*: Michael B. Gerrard, 'America Is the Worst Polluter in the History of the World. We Should Let Climate Change Refugees Resettle Here'. *Washington Post* (25 June 2015). https://www.washingtonpost.com/opinions/america-is-the-worst-polluter-in-the-history-of-the-world-we-should-let-climate-change-refugees-resettle-here/2015/06/25/28a55238-1a9c-11e5-ab92-c75ae6ab94b5_story.html.

94 *Since 1992, 4.2 billion people*: United Nations World Water Assessment Programme, *Nature-Based Solutions for Water: The United Nations World Water Development Report 2018* (Paris: UNESCO, 2018), p. 17. http://unesdoc.unesco.org/images/0026/002614/261424e.pdf.

94 *three-year drought, the worst in the region's history*: Justin Worland, 'Middle East Drought That May Contribute to Syrian War Is Worst in 900 Years, Study Says'. *Time* (3 March 2016). http://time.com/4246248/middle-east-drought-that-may-contribute-to-syrian-war-is-worst-in-900-years-study-says/.

94 *'strong historical linkages between civil war and temperature'*: Marshall B. Burke, Edward Miguel, Shanker Satyanath, John A. Dykema and David B. Lobell, 'Warming Increases the Risk of Civil War in Africa'. *Proceedings of the National Academy of Sciences* 106, no. 49 (8 December 2009), p. 20670. http://www.pnas.org/content/106/49/20670.

94 *Heatwaves took almost a million people out of the global workforce in 2016*: Nick Watts, Markus Amann, Nigel Arnell, Sonja Ayeb-Karlsson, Kristine Belesova, Helen Berry, Timothy Bouley, Maxwell Boykoff, Peter Byass, Wenjia Cai, Diarmid Campbell-Lendrum, Jonathan Chambers, Meaghan Daly, Niheer Dasandi, Michael Davies, Anneliese Depoux et al., 'The 2018 Report of the *Lancet* Countdown on Health and Climate Change: Shaping the Health of Nations for Centuries to Come'. *Lancet* (28 November 2018). https://www.thelancet.com/journals/lancet/article/PIIS0140-6736(18)32594-7/fulltext.

95 *For every degree Celsius increase in temperature*: Chuang Zhao, Bing Liu, Shilong Piao, Xuhui Wang, David B. Lobell, Yao Huang, Mengtian Huang, Yitong Yao, Simona Bassu, Philippe Ciais, Jean-Louis Durand, Joshua Elliott, Frank Ewert, Ivan A. Janssens, Tao Li, Erda Lin, Qiang Liu, Pierre Martre, Christoph Müller, Shushi Peng, Josep Peñuelas, Alex C. Ruane, Daniel Wallach, Tao Wang, Donghai Wu, Zhuo Liu, Yan Zhu, Zaichun Zhu and Senthold Asseng, 'Temperature Increase Reduces Global Yields'. *Proceedings of the National Academy of Sciences* 114, no. 35 (29 August 2017), p. 9326. http://www.pnas.org/content/pnas/114/35/9326.full.pdf.

95 *At 1.5 degrees, corn yields shrink by 10 per cent*: Jeremy Hodges, 'Food Crops from Corn to Rice Are Seen at Risk from Warmer Change'. *Bloomberg* (8 October 2018). https://www.bloomberg.com/news/articles/2018-10-08/food-crops-from-corn-to-rice-are-seen-at-risk-from-warmer-change.

95 *In 2018, India experienced the worst water crisis*: 'Half of India's Population Does Not Have Access to Safe Water: Niti Aayog'. *Huffington Post* (15 June 2018). https://www.huffingtonpost.in/2018/06/14/half-of-india-s-population-does-not-have-access-to-safe-water-niti-aayog_a_23459543/.

95 *The Indian mortality rate from heat-related deaths*: Mike Ives, 'In India, Slight Rise in Temperatures Is Tied to Heat Wave Deaths'. *New York Times* (8 June 2017). https://www.nytimes.com/2017/06/08/world/asia/india-heat-deaths-climate.html.

95 *Americans are only 4 per cent of the world's population but are responsible for one-third*: Justin Gillis and Nadja Popovich, 'The US Is the Biggest Carbon Polluter in History. It Just Walked Away from the Paris Climate Deal'. *New York Times* (1 June 2017). https://www.nytimes.com/interactive/2017/06/01/climate/us-biggest-carbon-polluter-in-history-will-it-walk-away-from-the-paris-climate-deal.html.

95 *America creates a third of the world's solid waste*: Ann M. Simmons, 'The World's Trash Crisis, and Why Many Americans Are Oblivious'. *Los Angeles Times* (22 April 2016). https://www.latimes.com/world/global-development/la-fg-global-trash-20160422–20160421-snap-htmlstory.html. See also, Abi Bradford, Sylvia Broude and Alexander Truelove, 'Trash in America: Moving from Destructive Consumption to a Zero-Waste System'. Frontier Group, Toxics Action Center and US PIRG Education Fund (12 February 2018). https://frontiergroup.org/reports/fg/trash-america.

95 *consumes a fifth of the world's energy*: US Energy Information Administration, 'US Share of World Energy Consumption, 2016' (last updated 31 October 2018). https://www.eia.gov/tools/faqs/faq.php?id=87&t=1.

95 *The average American uses as much energy as 35 Indians*: Roddy Scheer and Doug Moss, 'Use It and Lose It: The Outsize Effect of US Consumption on the Environment'. *Scientific American* (last accessed 5 December 2018). https://www.scientificamerican.com/article/american-consumption-habits/. See also, World Bank, 'Electric Power Consumption (kWh per Capita)', OECD/IEA Statistics, 2014. https://data.worldbank.org/indicator/EG.USE.ELEC.KH.PC?year_high_desc=true.

96 *Five million Bavarians decided they'd had enough*: Tim McDonnell, 'Did President Trump's Ancestors Migrate to the United States Because of a Changing Climate?' *Washington Post* (21 November 2017). https://www.washingtonpost.com/news/wonk/wp/2017/11/21/did-donald-trumps-ancestors-migrate-to-america-because-of-a-changing-climate.

96 *After Hurricane Maria, half a million Puerto Ricans*: Martín Echenique, 'Exodus: The Post-Hurricane Puerto Rican Diaspora, Mapped'. CityLab (13 March 2018). https://www.citylab.com/equity/2018/03/exodus-the-post-hurricane-puerto-rican-diaspora-mapped/555401/.

96 *land that is currently home to 650 million people may be underwater*: Gregor Aisch, David Leonhardt and Kevin Quealy, 'Flooding Risk from Climate Change, Country by Country'. *New York Times* (23 September 2014). https://www.nytimes.com/2014/09/24/upshot/flooding-risk-from-climate-change-country-by-country.html. Further information in 'New Analysis Shows Global Exposure to Sea Level Rise'. Climate Central Research Report (23 September 2014). http://www.climatecentral.org/news/new-analysis-global-exposure-to-sea-level-rise-flooding-18066.

96 *At the other extreme, by 2050, much of the world*: Josh Gabbatiss, 'More Than Quarter of World's Land Could Become Arid Due to Global Warming, Finds Study'. *Independent* (3 January 2018). https://www.independent.co.uk/environment/global-warming-world-land-arid-desertification-climate-change-study-a8139896.html.

96 *'Twenty million people could be displaced in Bangladesh'*: Harriet Grant, James Randerson and John Vidal, 'UK Should Open Borders to Climate Refugees, Says Bangladeshi Minister'. *Guardian* (4 December 2009). https://www.theguardian.com/environment/2009/nov/30/rich-west-climate-change.

96 *According to the UN high commissioner for refugees, since 2008, 22.5 million people*: Lauren Markham, 'A Warming World Creates Desperate People'. *New York Times* (29 June 2018). https://www.nytimes.com/2018/06/29/opinion/sunday/immigration-climate-change-trump.html. See also Lauren Markham, 'The Caravan Is a Climate Change Story'. *Sierra* (9 November 2018). https://www.sierraclub.org/sierra/root-migration-climate-change-caravan-central-america.

97 *Since the 1950s, the average temperature in the country has risen*: Climate Change Adaptation, Thought Leadership and Assessments (ATLAS), 'Climate Change Risk Profile: El Salvador'. United States Agency for International Development (USAID) (April 2017). https://www.climatelinks.org/sites/default/files/asset/document/2017_USAID%20ATLAS_Climate%20Change%20Risk%20Profile_El%20Salvador.pdf.

97 *Category 3, 4, and 5 hurricanes will increase by 11 per cent in frequency*: Chris Mooney, 'Category 6? Climate Change May Cause More Hurricanes to Rapidly Intensify'. *Washington Post* (11 September 2018). https://www.washingtonpost.com/energy-environment/2018/09/11/category-climate-change-may-cause-more-hurricanes-rapidly-intensify/.

97 *Between 2008 and 2014, 184 million people had to run away from their homes*: Didier Burkhalter, 'Fleeing Floods, Earthquakes, Droughts and Rising

Sea Levels: 12 Lessons Learned about Protecting People Displaced by Disasters and the Effects of Climate Change'. *Nansen Initiative* (November 2015). https://www.nanseninitiative.org/wp-content/uploads/2015/10/12-LESSONS-LEARNED.pdf.

97 *The water in Lake Chad has shrunk by 90 per cent since 1963*: United Nations Security Council, 'Better Governance of Underfunded, Poorly Managed Lake Chad Basin Key to Resolving Conflict, Suffering across Region, Speakers Tell Security Council' (22 March 2018). https://www.un.org/press/en/2018/sc13259.doc.htm.

97 *Twelve million people are at risk of starvation in Kenya, Somalia and Ethiopia*. *Somini Sengupta, 'Hotter, Drier, Hungrier*: How Global Warming Punishes the World's Poorest'. *New York Times* (12 March 2018). https://www.nytimes.com/2018/03/12/climate/kenya-drought.html.

98 *In China, the desert has advanced south and east 21,000 square miles*: Josh Haner, Edward Wong, Derek Watkins and Jeremy White, 'Living in China's Expanding Deserts'. *New York Times* (24 October 2016). https://www.nytimes.com/interactive/2016/10/24/world/asia/living-in-chinas-expanding-deserts.html.

99 *daytime temperatures in the Colombian coastal city of Santa Marta*: Maya Oppenheim, 'Colombians Warned Not to Have Sex as Intense Heatwave Continues'. *Independent* (19 August 2018). https://www.independent.co.uk/news/world/americas/colombians-warned-too-hot-sex-santa-marta-julio-salas-a8498126.html.

99 *'The impacts of climate change may cause instability in other countries'*: United States Department of Defense, *2014 Climate Change Adaptation Roadmap* (2014). https://www.acq.osd.mil/cie/downloads/CCARprint_wForward_e.pdf.

99 *Australia is the world's largest exporter of coal*: Oliver Milman, 'Carbon Emissions: Coal Reliance Puts Australia Second on OECD's Dirt List'. *Guardian* (10 January 2014). https://www.theguardian.com/environment/2014/jan/10/carbon-emissions-australias-growth-puts-it-near-top-of-oecd-rankings.

99 *It will cost $16.5 billion and proposes to extract 2.3 billion tons of coal*: Stephen Long, 'Adani Plans to Export Low Quality, High Ash Coal to India, Court Told'. ABC Australia (2 April 2017). https://www.abc.net.au/news/2017-04-03/adani-plans-to-export-low-quality-coal-to-india-report-says/8409742.

99 *130 million tons of carbon dioxide into the atmosphere*: Michael Slezak, 'Why Adani's Planned Carmichael Coalmine Matters to Australia – and

the World'. *Guardian* (15 August 2017). https://www.theguardian.com/business/2017/aug/16/why-adanis-planned-carmichael-coalmine-matters-to-australia-and-the-world.

100 *'That China, still an emerging economy'*: Qi Ye, 'China's Peaking Emissions and the Future of Global Climate Policy'. Brookings Institution (12 September 2018). https://www.brookings.edu/blog/planetpolicy/2018/09/12/chinas-peaking-emissions-and-the-future-of-global-climate-policy/.

100 *both countries have increased their forest cover in the last few years*: Samuel Osborne, 'India's Forest and Tree Cover Increases by 1% over Two Years, Report Finds'. *Independent* (14 February 2018). https://www.independent.co.uk/news/world/asia/india-forest-tree-cover-increase-climate-change-environment-global-warming-deforestation-a8209371.html.

101 *Environmental pollution kills nine million people a year*: Susan Brink, 'Report: Pollution Kills 3 Times More Than AIDS, TB and Malaria Combined'. NPR (19 October 2017). https://www.npr.org/sections/goatsandsoda/2017/10/19/558821792/report-pollution-kills-3-times-more-than-aids-tb-and-malaria-combined.

9. THE POPULISTS' FALSE NARRATIVE

105 *Take a look at Hungary, where Viktor Orbán has forced out the Central European University*: Marc Santora, 'George Soros-Founded University Is Forced Out of Hungary'. *New York Times* (3 December 2018). https://www.nytimes.com/2018/12/03/world/europe/soros-hungary-central-european-university.html.

105 *Or Poland, whose ruling party purged the judiciary*: Marc Santora, 'Poland's Holocaust Law Weakened after "Storm and Consternation"'. *New York Times* (27 June 2018). https://www.nytimes.com/2018/06/27/world/europe/poland-holocaust-law.html.

105 *stoking voters' fear of migrants, promising to ban new immigrants*: BBC News, 'Europe and Nationalism: A Country-by-Country Guide' (10 September 2018). https://www.bbc.com/news/world-europe-36130006.

106 *'Europe needs to get a handle on migration'*: Patrick Wintour, 'Hillary Clinton: Europe Must Curb Immigration to Stop Right-wing Populists'. *Guardian* (22 November 2018). https://www.theguardian.com/world/2018/nov/22/hillary-clinton-europe-must-curb-immigration-stop-populists-trump-brexit.

106 *In 2015, Israeli soldiers fired on African migrants*: Gili Cohen, 'Migrants Wounded by Israeli Army Fire while Crossing Egypt Border'. *Haaretz* (6 August 2015). https://www.haaretz.com/migrants-wounded-by-idf-fire-while-crossing-egypt-border-1.5383528.

106 *In December 2017, the Knesset passed a law*: Marissa Newman, 'Ahead of Mass Deportations, Knesset Extends Restrictions on Migrants'. *Times of Israel* (11 December 2017). https://www.timesofisrael.com/ahead-of-mass-deportations-knesset-toughens-restrictions-on-migrants/.

106 *It was fear of migrants, principally, that led the British to vote for Brexit*: Washington Post, 'Immigration Worries Drove the Brexit Vote' 16 November 2018. https://www.washingtonpost.com/world/europe/immigration-worries-drove-the-brexit-vote-then-attitudes-changed/2018/11/16/c216b6a2-bcdb-11e8-8243-f3ae9c99658a_story.html?utm_term=.d3846c59438e

107 *In the year after the Brexit vote, hate crimes in England and Wales jumped by 29 per cent*: BBC News, 'Rise in Hate Crime in England and Wales' (17 October 2017). https://www.bbc.com/news/uk-41648865.

108 *Americans think that the foreign-born make up around 37 per cent of the population*: Ana Swanson, 'Here's How Little Americans Really Know about Immigration'. *Washington Post* (1 September 2016). https://www.washingtonpost.com/news/wonk/wp/2016/09/01/heres-how-little-americans-really-know-about-immigration/.

108 *The French think that one out of three people in their country is Muslim*: Pamela Duncan, 'Europeans Greatly Overestimate Muslim Population, Poll Shows'. *Guardian* (13 December 2016). https://www.theguardian.com/society/datablog/2016/dec/13/europeans-massively-overestimate-muslim-population-poll-shows.

108 *A quarter of the French, one in five Swedes, and one in seven Americans*: Eduardo Porter and Karl Russell, 'Migrants Are on the Rise around the World, and Myths about Them Are Shaping Attitudes'. *New York Times* (20 June 2018). https://www.nytimes.com/interactive/2018/06/20/business/economy/immigration-economic-impact.html.

109 *whose economy had the strongest growth in the G7 in 2017*: Eshe Nelson, 'Canada Was the Strongest G7 Economy in 2017'. *Quartz* (2 March 2018). https://qz.com/1220265/canada-was-the-strongest-g7-economy-in-2017/.

109 *Hate crimes against Muslims actually went down in Canada in 2017*: Monique Scotti, 'Hate Crimes against Muslims Are Down as Overall Number of Hate Crimes Increases'. *Global News* (28 November 2017). https://globalnews. ca/news/3884829/hate-crimes-against-muslims-down/.

109 *in its southern neighbour, they jumped by 5 per cent*: Mark Berman, 'Hate Crimes in the United States Increased Last Year, the FBI Says'. *Washington Post* (13 November 2017). https://www.washingtonpost.com/news/ post-nation/wp/2017/11/13/hate-crimes-in-the-united-states-increased-last-year-the-fbi-says/.

10. A BRIEF HISTORY OF FEAR

110 *The legend began with the 'Black Hole'*: Partha Chatterjee and Ayça Çubukçu, 'Empire as a Practice of Power: An Interview'. *Asia-Pacific Journal* 10, issue 41, no. 1 (8 October 2012). https://apjjf.org/2012/10/41/Partha-Chatterjee/3840/article.html.

110 *'What we are ashamed of as if it were a disgrace'*: Claude Lévi-Strauss, *Tristes Tropiques*. Translated by John and Doreen Weightman (New York: Atheneum, 1974), p. 134.

112 *'I have understood the population explosion intellectually'*: Paul R. Ehrlich, *The Population Bomb* (New York: Ballantine Books, 1968), p. 15.

112 *'The United states could take effective unilateral action'*: Paul R. Ehrlich, *The Population Bomb* (New York: Ballantine Books, 1968), pp. 151–152.

113 *'Sometime in the next 15 years'*: Charles C. Mann, 'The Book That Incited a Worldwide Fear of Overpopulation'. *Smithsonian Magazine* (January 2018). https://www.smithsonianmag.com/innovation/book-incited-worldwide-fear-overpopulation-180967499/.

113 *Churchill, in 1945, opined that Hindus*: Mihir Bose, 'Why Did Winston Churchill Hate the Hindus and Prefer the Muslims?' *Quartz* (4 April 2017). https://qz.com/india/948392/why-did-winston-churchill-hate-the-hindus-and-prefer-the-muslims/.

113 *The **Mein Kampf** of the contemporary anti-immigrant movement*: Sarah Jones, 'The Notorious Book That Ties the Right to the Far Right'. *New Republic* (2 February 2018). https://newrepublic.com/article/146925/notorious-book-ties-right-far-right.

114 *'First to land were the monsters'*: Jean Raspail, *Le Camp des Saints* (France: Éditions Robert Laffont, 1973); translated by Norman Shapiro as *The Camp of the Saints* (New York: Scribner, 1975), p. 85.

114 *'Our hypersensitive and totally blind West'*: Matthew Connelly and Paul Kennedy, 'Must It Be the Rest against the West?' *Atlantic* (December 1994). https://www.theatlantic.com/past/docs/politics/immigrat/kennf.htm.

114 *In 1995, Raspail's disease-ridden book crossed over the ocean*: Jason DeParle, 'The Anti-Immigration Crusader'. *New York Times* (17 April 2011). https://www.nytimes.com/2011/04/17/us/17immig.html.

115 *Marine Le Pen, who keeps a signed copy at her desk*: Cécile Alduy, 'What a 1973 French Novel Tells Us about Marine Le Pen, Steve Bannon and the Rise of the Populist Right'. *Politico* (23 April 2017). https://www.politico.com/magazine/story/2017/04/23/what-a-1973-french-novel-tells-us-about-marine-le-pen-steve-bannon-and-the-rise-of-the-populist-right-215064.

115 *Tanton republished* The Camp of the Saints *in 2001*: Paul Blumenthal and J. M. Rieger, 'This Stunningly Racist French Novel Is How Steve Bannon Explains the World'. *Huffington Post* (4 March 2017). https://www.huffingtonpost.com/entry/steve-bannon-camp-of-the-saints-immigration_us_58b75206e4b0284854b3dc03.

11. CULTURE: SHITHOLES VS NORDICS

116 *'Civilization's going to pieces'*: F. Scott Fitzgerald, *The Great Gatsby* (New York: Scribner's Sons, 1925).

117 *'Why should the Palatine Boors be suffered to swarm'*: Catherine Rampell, 'Founding Fathers, Trashing Immigrants'. *Washington Post* (28 August 2015). https://www.washingtonpost.com/news/rampage/wp/2015/08/28/founding-fathers-trashing-immigrants.

117 *In the 1850s, the American Party, or the 'Know-Nothings'*: Lorraine Boissoneault, 'How the 19th-Century Know Nothing Party Reshaped American Politics'. *Smithsonian Magazine* (26 January 2017). https://www.smithsonianmag.com/history/immigrants-conspiracies-and-secret-society-launched-american-nativism-180961915/.

117 *'Californians have properly objected'*: Franklin Delano Roosevelt, 'Editorial in the Macon Telegraph'. *Macon Telegraph* (30 April 1925). https://

georgiainfo.galileo.usg.edu/topics/history/article/the-leo-frank-case/franklin-d.-roosevelts-editorials-for-the-macon-telegraph.

118 *'We favor reducing immigration to nothing'*: Bruce Bartlett, 'Donald Trump Doesn't Need Latino Voters to Win'. *Washington Post* (4 September 2015). https://www.washingtonpost.com/opinions/donald-trump-doesnt-need-latino-voters-to-win-the-nomination/2015/09/04/9fd2e40c-524f-11e5-933e-7d06c647a395_story.html; A. Philip Randolph, 'Immigration and Japan'. *The Messenger* (August 1924), p. 247.

118 *The 'Goddard' in* Gatsby *is a reference to Lothrop Stoddard*: Lewis Turlish, 'The Rising Tide of Color: A Note on the Historicism of *The Great Gatsby'*. *American Literature* 43, no. 3 (November 1971), pp. 442–444. www.jstor.org/stable/2924045.

118 *'Haiti? Why do we want people from Haiti here?'*: Josh Dawsey, 'Trump Derides Protections for Immigrants from "Shithole" Countries'. *Washington Post* (12 January 2018). https://www.washingtonpost.com/politics/trump-attacks-protections-for-immigrants-from-shithole-countries-in-oval-office-meeting/2018/01/11/bfc0725c-f711-11e7-91af-31ac729add94_story.html.

118 *'Today, the West is also confronted by the powers that seek to test our will'*: Donald Trump, 'Remarks by President Trump to the People of Poland' (6 July 2017). https://www.whitehouse.gov/briefings-statements/remarks-president-trump-people-poland/.

119 *'There is only the American dream'*: Samuel Huntingdon, 'The Hispanic Challenge'. *Foreign Policy* (March–April 2004). http://faculty.salisbury.edu/~tjdunn/Immign—Spg%2007/Huntington%2004—edited—07.doc.

120 *'I've never met an illegal Canadian'*: Miriam Valverde, 'Lindsey Graham: "I've Never Met an Illegal Canadian"'. *Politifact* (8 March 2017). https://www.politifact.com/truth-o-meter/article/2017/mar/08/canadians-and-visa-overstay-data/. For more information, see 'Fiscal Year 2017 Entry/Exit Overstay Report'. US Department of Homeland Security (August 2018). https://www.dhs.gov/sites/default/files/publications/18_0807_S1_Entry-Exit-Overstay_Report.pdf.

121 *Periodically, US congressmen of Irish descent fought for legislation*: Celestine Bohlen, 'For Illegal Irish Immigrants, a Time to Test That Luck'. *New York Times* (7 March 1989). https://www.nytimes.com/1989/03/17/nyregion/for-illegal-irish-immigrants-a-time-to-test-that-luck.html?pagewanted=all.

121 *The terms of the diversity program were changed in 1989*: Marvine Howe, 'Irish-Americans Praise New Immigration Bill'. *New York Times* (7 October 1990). https://www.nytimes.com/1990/10/07/nyregion/irish-americans-praise-new-immigration-bill.html.

121 *Again, in 1995, the Irish had priority for visas unclaimed*: Francesca Gaiba, 'I'm a White Immigrant and I Benefited from a Racist Visa Lottery'. *Time* (8 December 2016). http://time.com/4593985/immigration-visa-lotter-racism/.

122 *In 2012, the Massachusetts Republican senator Scott Brown introduced a bill*: Rose Arce, 'Massachusetts Senator Pushes Bill for Irish Work Visas'. CNN (16 March 2012). https://www.cnn.com/2012/03/16/election/2012/brown-irish-immigrant-visas/index.html.

122 *'Ireland estimates as many as 50,000 unauthorized Irish'*: John Burnett, 'Undocumented Irish Caught in Trump's Immigration Dragnet'. NPR (22 January 2018). https://www.npr.org/2018/01/22/578930256/undocumented-irish-unexpectedly-caught-in-trumps-immigration-dragnet.

122 *'Not all cultures are compatible with the culture in this country'*: Thomas Sowell, 'Abstract Immigrants'. Creators Syndicate (4 June 2013). https://www.creators.com/read/thomas-sowell/06/13/abstract-immigrants.

123 *In 2016, the Slovakian parliament*: Gabriel Samuels, 'Slovakia bars Islam from becoming state religion by tightening church laws'. *The Independent* (1 December 2016). https://www.independent.co.uk/news/world/europe/slovakia-bars-islam-state-religion-tightening-church-laws-robert-fico-a7449646.html.

124 *'Earlier, in a 2006 speech'*: http://web.archive.org/web/20080201133647/ http://www.socialaffairsunit.org.uk/blog/archives/000809.php.

12. THE COLOUR OF HATE

125 *2044. That is the year when America is projected to stop being a majority white nation*: Sandra L. Colby and Jennifer M. Ortman. 'Projections of the Size and Composition of the US Population: 2014 to 2060'. United States Census Bureau (3 March 2015). https://www.census.gov/library/publications/2015/demo/p25-1143.html.

125 *'You can shut the door to everyone in the world and that won't change'*: Jeff Stein and Andrew Van Dam, 'Trump Immigration Plan Could Keep Whites in US Majority for up to Five More Years'. *Washington Post* (6 February 2018).

https://www.washingtonpost.com/news/wonk/wp/2018/02/06/trump-immigration-plan-could-keep-whites-in-u-s-majority-for-up-to-five-more-years.

125 *For the first time, half of the babies under the age of one were non-white*: D'Vera Cohn, 'It's Official: Minority Babies Are the Majority among the Nation's Infants, but Only Just'. Pew Research Center (23 June 2016). http://www.pewresearch.org/fact-tank/2016/06/23/its-official-minority-babies-are-the-majority-among-the-nations-infants-but-only-just/.

125 *In 2018, deaths among whites outnumbered births in more than half the states*: Sabrina Tavernise, 'Fewer Births than Deaths among Whites in Majority of US States'. *New York Times* (20 June 2018). https://www.nytimes.com/2018/06/20/us/white-minority-population.html.

126 *Hispanics in the United States have an average age of twenty-eight*: Eileen Patten, 'The Nation's Latino Population Is Defined by Its Youth'. Pew Research Center (20 April 2016). http://www.pewhispanic.org/2016/04/20/the-nations-latino-population-is-defined-by-its-youth/.

126 *The 18 per cent of the population that are Hispanics are the biggest minority group*: Jonathan Vespa, David M. Armstrong and Lauren Medina, 'Demographic Turning Points for the United States: Population Projections for 2020 to 2060'. United States Census Bureau (13 March 2018). https://www.census.gov/content/dam/Census/library/publications/2018/demo/P25_1144.pdf.

126 *The fastest-growing race in the country is now Asian*: Gustavo López, Neil G. Ruiz and Eileen Patten, 'Key Facts about Asian Americans, a Diverse and Growing Population'. Pew Research Center (8 September 2017). http://www.pewresearch.org/fact-tank/2017/09/08/key-facts-about-asian-americans/.

126 *The 2016 median US income for Indian Americans was $110,026*: Valerie Wilson and Zane Mokhiber, '2016 ACS Shows Stubbornly High Native American Poverty and Different Degrees of Economic Well-Being for Asian Ethnic Groups.' Economic Policy Institute (15 September 2017). https://www.epi.org/blog/2016-acs-shows-stubbornly-high-native-american-poverty-and-different-degrees-of-economic-well-being-for-asian-ethnic-groups/.

126 *'White' Americans, as a group, earned $61,349*: Gloria G. Guzman, 'Household Income: 2016. American Community Survey Briefs'. US Department of Commerce, Economics and Statistics Administration (September 2017). https://www.census.gov/content/dam/Census/library/publications/2017/acs/acsbr16-02.pdf.

126 *African immigrants are more accomplished than the average American*: Ann Simmons, 'African Immigrants Are More Educated than Most – Including People Born in US'. *Los Angeles Times* (12 January 2018). https://www.latimes.com/world/africa/la-fg-global-african-immigrants-explainer-20180112-story.html.

127 *Counties that voted for Hillary Clinton account for 64 per cent of US GDP*: Jim Tankersley, 'Donald Trump Lost Most of the American Economy in This Election'. *Washington Post* (22 November 2016). https://www.washingtonpost.com/news/wonk/wp/2016/11/22/donald-trump-lost-most-of-the-american-economy-in-this-election/.

127 *Fifty-eight per cent of Republicans now think that universities are bad for America*: Hannah Fingerhut, 'Republicans Skeptical of Colleges' Impact on US, but Most See Benefits for Workforce Preparation'. Pew Research Center (20 July 2017). http://www.pewresearch.org/fact-tank/2017/07/20/republicans-skeptical-of-colleges-impact-on-u-s-but-most-see-benefits-for-workforce-preparation/.

127 *'One way to think of Trumpism is as an attempt to narrow regional disparities'*: Paul Krugman, 'Know-Nothings for the 21st Century'. *New York Times* (15 January 2018). https://www.nytimes.com/2018/01/15/opinion/trump-american-values.html.

127 *In 2020, whites without a college degree will still be 44 per cent of eligible voters*: Rob Griffin, Ruy Teixeira and William H. Frey, 'America's Electoral Future Demographic Shifts and the Future of the Trump Coalition'. Center for American Progress/Brookings Institution (19 April 2018). https://www.prri.org/wp-content/uploads/2018/04/States-of-Change-2018-Americas-Electoral-Future.pdf.

127 *This is a real sea change'*: Sabrina Tavernise, 'Fewer Births than Deaths among Whites in Majority of US States'. *New York Times* (20 June 2018). https://www.nytimes.com/2018/06/20/us/white-minority-population.html.

127 *Fifty-four per cent of all legal immigrants get naturalized within a decade*: Ana Gonzalez-Barrera, 'Mexican Lawful Immigrants among the Least Likely to Become US Citizens'. Pew Research Center (29 June 2017). http://www.pewhispanic.org/2017/06/29/recent-trends-in-naturalization-1995-2015/.

128 *In the 2018 mid-terms*: CNN, '2018 Midterm Election Exit Polls' (6 November 2018). https://www.cnn.com/election/2018/exit-polls. Historical

numbers from K. K. Rebecca Lai and Allison McCann, 'Exit Polls: How Voting Blocs Have Shifted from the '80s to Now'. *New York Times* (7 November 2018). https://www.nytimes.com/interactive/2018/11/07/us/elections/house-exit-polls-analysis.html.

128 *A total of $4.7 trillion:* Ryan Edwards and Francesc Ortega, 'The Economic Impacts of Removing Unauthorized Immigrant Workers: An Industry and State-Level Analysis'. Center for American Progress (21 September 2016). https://www.americanprogress.org/issues/immigration/reports/2016/09/21/144363/the-economic-impacts-of-removing-unauthorized-immigrant-workers/.

128 *Half of all federal prosecutions already involve immigration:* John Gramlich and Kristen Bialik, 'Immigration Offenses Make Up a Growing Share of Federal Arrests'. Pew Research Center (10 April 2017). http://www.pewresearch.org/fact-tank/2017/04/10/immigration-offenses-make-up-a-growing-share-of-federal-arrests/.

128 *He was called the 'deporter in chief' by immigrant advocates:* Muzaffar Chishti, Sarah Pierce and Jessica Bolter, 'The Obama Record on Deportations: Deporter in Chief or Not?' Migration Policy Institute (26 January 2017). https://www.migrationpolicy.org/article/obama-record-deportations-deporter-chief-or-not.

132 *'In US presidential elections, persons of color whose roots':* Pat Buchanan, 'Trump: In Immigration Debate, Race Matters'. *Townhall* (16 January 2018). https://townhall.com/columnists/patbuchanan/2018/01/16/trump-in-immigration-debate-race-matters-n2434869.

132 *An amateur genealogist named Jennifer Mendelsohn dug up a 1917 court case:* Jennifer Mendelsohn, 'How Would Trump's Immigration Crackdown Have Affected His Own Team?' *Politico* (18 January 2018). https://www.politico.com/magazine/story/2018/01/18/donald-trump-immigration-chain-migration-dan-scavino-tomi-lahren-216332.

132 *'Migrant memoirs and other documents are full of examples of people who lied':* Sewell Chan, 'Immigration in New York City: Taking the Long View'. *New York Times* (14 November 2007). https://cityroom.blogs.nytimes.com/2007/11/14/immigration-in-new-york-city-taking-the-long-view/.

133 *'For Miller to say his family came to America "legally" is simply a ruse':* Rob Eshman, 'Stephen Miller, Meet Your Immigrant Great-Grandfather'. *Jew-*

ish Journal (10 August 2016). https://jewishjournal.com/opinion/rob_eshman/214361/stephen-miller-meet-immigrant-great-grandfather/.

133 *'My nephew and I must both reflect long and hard on one awful truth'*: Aiden Pink, 'Stephen Miller's Family Is Furious over Family Separation Policy'. *Forward* (18 June 2018). https://forward.com/fast-forward/403382/stephen-millers-family-is-furious-over-his-immigrant-family-separation/.

135 *Researchers at the University of Warwick recently studied every anti-refugee attack*: Amanda Taub and Max Fisher, 'Facebook Fueled Anti-Refugee Attacks in Germany, New Research Suggests'. *New York Times* (21 August 2018). https://www.nytimes.com/2018/08/21/world/europe/facebook-refugee-attacks-germany.html.

135 *'If shooting these immigrating feral hogs works'*: Todd Fertig, 'Rep. Apologizes for Remark about Shooting Illegal Immigrants'. *Wichita Eagle* (16 March 2011). https://www.kansas.com/news/politics-government/election/article1060073.html.

135 *'What's so wrong with wanting to put up a fence'*: Andrew Kaczynski, 'Carl Higbie, Who Works at Pro-Trump Group, Says Racist Comments Were "Statistical Observation", 'Out of Context'. CNN (2 May 2018). https://www.cnn.com/2018/05/01/politics/kfile-carl-higbie-says-comments-out-of-context/index.html.

136 *In February 2018, the US Citizenship and Immigration Services (USCIS) removed the phrase 'nation of immigrants' from its mission statement*: Richard Gonzales, 'America No Longer a "Nation of Immigrants", USCIS Says'. *NPR* (22 February 2018). https://www.npr.org/sections/thetwo-way/2018/02/22/588097749/america-no-longer-a-nation-of-immigrants-uscis-says.

138 *Two Indian engineers were having beers on the porch*: John Eligon, Alan Blinder and Nida Najar, 'Hate Crime Is Feared as 2 Indian Engineers Are Shot in Kansas'. *New York Times* (24 February 2017). https://www.nytimes.com/2017/02/24/world/asia/kansas-attack-possible-hate-crime-srinivas-kuchibhotla.html?module=inline.

139 *'A majority of the 2017 murders were committed by right-wing extremists'*: Anti-Defamation League, 'ADL Report: White Supremacist Murders More than Doubled in 2017' (17 January 2018). https://www.adl.org/news/press-releases/adl-report-white-supremacist-murders-more-than-doubled-in-2017.

139 *calculated the ancestries of all 422 people charged with terrorism in America since 2001*: Lyman Stone, 'I Calculated Ethnic Groups' Rates of US Terrorism. Here Are the Results'. *Federalist* (15 November 2017). http://thefederalist.com/2017/11/15/calculated-ethnic-groups-rates-u-s-terrorism-results/.

13. THE ALLIANCE BETWEEN THE MOB AND CAPITAL

140 *The gap between rich and poor in Britain today*: Income inequality, financial crisis and the rise of Europe's far right. France24.com (20 November 2018) https://www.france24.com/en/20181116-income-inequality-financial-crisis-economic-uncertainty-rise-far-right-europe-austerity

140 *In the last three decades, there was zero income growth in the bottom 50 per cent*: Facundo Alvaredo, Lucas Chancel, Thomas Piketty, Emmanuel Saez and Gabriel Zucman, 'World Inequality Report 2018 – Executive Summary'. World Inequality Lab (14 December 2017), p. 12. https://wir2018.wid.world/files/download/wir2018-summary-english.pdf. See also Howard R. Gold, 'Never Mind the 1 Percent. Let's Talk About the 0.01%'. *Chicago Booth Review* (2017). http://review.chicagobooth.edu/economics/2017/article/never-mind-1-percent-lets-talk-about-001-percent.

140 *The bottom 40 per cent of Americans not only don't have any wealth to speak of*: Christopher Ingraham, 'The Richest 1 Percent Now Owns More of the Country's Wealth Than at Any Time in the Past 50 Years'. *Washington Post* (6 December 2017). https://www.washingtonpost.com/news/wonk/wp/2017/12/06/the-richest-1-percent-now-owns-more-of-the-countrys-wealth-than-at-any-time-in-the-past-50-years/.

143 *Warren housed 15,000 souls in 1940, and is now down to 9,478*: All figures on population, poverty and demographics from the United States Census Bureau, 'Community Facts. Warren City, Pennsylvania'. https://factfinder.census.gov/bkmk/cf/1.0/en/place/Warren city, Pennsylvania/POVERTY.

143 *Warren County went for Trump en masse*: Pennsylvania Department of State, '2016 Election Returns by County' (last accessed 5 December 2018). https://www.electionreturns.pa.gov/General/CountyResults?countyName=WARREN&ElectionID=54&ElectionType=G&IsActive=0.

143 *the eight richest individuals on earth, all men, own more than does half the planet*: Deborah Hardoon, 'An Economy for the 99%'. Oxfam (January 2017).

https://www.oxfam.org/sites/www.oxfam.org/files/file_attachments/bp-economy-for-99-percent-160117-en.pdf.

144 *There are 1,542 billionaires today, whose fortunes rose by a fifth in 2017*: Rupert Neate, 'World's Witnessing a New Gilded Age as Billionaires' Wealth Swells to $6tn'. *Guardian* (26 October 2017). https://www.theguardian.com/business/2017/oct/26/worlds-witnessing-a-new-gilded-age-as-billionaires-wealth-swells-to-6tn.

144 *Only 20 to 30 per cent of the children of the poorest 10 per cent go to college*: Gregor Aisch, Larry Buchanan, Amanda Cox and Kevin Quealy, 'Some Colleges Have More Students from the Top 1 Percent than the Bottom 60. Find Yours'. *New York Times* (18 January 2017). https://www.nytimes.com/interactive/2017/01/18/upshot/some-colleges-have-more-students-from-the-top-1-percent-than-the-bottom-60.html.

144 *460 people will bequeath $2.1 trillion to their heirs over the next twenty years*: UBS/PWS, *Are Billionaires Feeling the Pressure? Billionaires Report 2016* (last accessed 5 December 2018). https://www.ubs.com/global/en/wealth-management/uhnw/billionaires-report/new-value/feeling-the-pressure.html.

146 *'alliance between mob and capital'*: Hannah Arendt, *The Origins of Totalitarianism* (Berlin: Schocken Books, 1951), p. 147.

14. THE REFUGEE AS PARIAH

147 *After an epic journey, a Congolese mother and her six-year-old daughter*: Editorial Board, 'Gratuitous Cruelty by Homeland Security: Separating a 7-Year-Old from Her Mother'. *Washington Post* (4 March 2018). https://www.washingtonpost.com/opinions/gratuitous-cruelty-by-homeland-security-separating-a-7-year-old-from-her-mother/2018/03/04/98fae4f0-1bff-11e8-ae5a-16e60e4605f3_story.html.

147 *'screaming and crying, pleading with guards not to take her away'*: Merrit Kennedy, 'ACLU Sues ICE for Allegedly Separating "Hundreds" of Migrant Families'. NPR (9 March 2018). https://www.npr.org/sections/thetwo-way/2018/03/09/592374637/aclu-sues-ice-for-allegedly-separating-hundreds-of-migrant-families.

148 *The refugee ... brings with him the spectre of chaos and lawlessness*: Brad Evans and Zygmunt Bauman, 'The Refugee Crisis Is Humanity's Crisis'. *New*

York Times (2 May 2016). https://www.nytimes.com/2016/05/02/opinion/the-refugee-crisis-is-humanitys-crisis.html.

149 *today, ten million people are officially stateless*: Office of the United Nations High Commissioner for Refugees, 'Ending Statelessness'. UNHCR Refugee Agency (last accessed 5 December 2018). https://www.unhcr.org/en-us/stateless-people.html.

149 *It was only in the early twentieth century that the modern, convoluted superstructure of passports*: Giulia Pines, 'The Contentious History of the Passport'. *National Geographic* (16 May 2017). https://www.nationalgeographic.com/travel/features/a-history-of-the-passport/.

150 *The Orbán government was urging its citizens to vote in a referendum*: Patrick Kingsley, 'Hungary's Refugee Referendum Not Valid after Voters Stay Away'. *Guardian* (2 October 2016). https://www.theguardian.com/world/2016/oct/02/hungarian-vote-on-refugees-will-not-take-place-suggest-first-poll-results.

152 *'All the terrorists are basically migrants'*: Matthew Kaminski, '"All the Terrorists Are Migrants". Viktor Orbán on How to Protect Europe from Terror, Save Schengen, and Get along with Putin's Russia'. *Politico* (23 November 2015). https://www.politico.eu/article/viktor-orban-interview-terrorists-migrants-eu-russia-putin-borders-schengen/.

152 *'Every single migrant poses a public security and terror risk'*: Cynthia Kroet, 'Viktor Orbán: Migrants Are "a Poison"'. *Politico* (27 July 2016). https://www.politico.eu/article/viktor-orban-migrants-are-a-poison-hungarian-prime-minister-europe-refugee-crisis/.

152 *Denmark has gone one step further*: Madeleine Ngo, '"No Ghettos in 2030": Denmark's Controversial Plan to Get Rid of Immigrant Neighborhoods'. *Vox* (3 July 2018). https://www.vox.com/world/2018/7/3/17525960/denmark-children-immigrant-muslim-danish-ghetto.

152 *The initiative includes twenty-two separate measures*: Ellen Barry and Martin Selsoe Sorensen, 'In Denmark, Harsh New Laws for Immigrant "Ghettos"'. *New York Times* (1 July 2018). https://www.nytimes.com/2018/07/01/world/europe/denmark-immigrant-ghettos.html.

153 *what the Danes call a 'meatball war'*: Dan Bilefsky, 'Denmark's New Front in Debate over Immigrants: Children's Lunches'. *New York Times* (20 January 2016). https://www.nytimes.com/2016/01/21/world/europe/randers-denmark-pork.html.

153 *'a danger to all of us'*: Martin Selsoe Sorensen, 'Denmark Minister Calls Fasting Muslims "a Danger" in Ramadan'. *New York Times* (22 May 2018). https://www.nytimes.com/2018/05/22/world/europe/denmark-muslims-ramadan.html.

154 *the Danish parliament passed a law under which newly arrived refugees*: Emma Henderson, 'Refugee Crisis: Denmark Government Defends Plan to Strip Refugees' Valuables "to Pay for Their Stay"'. *Independent* (22 December 2015). https://www.independent.co.uk/news/world/europe/refugee-crisis-denmark-government-defends-plan-to-strip-refugees-valuables-to-pay-for-their-stay-a6782916.html.

154 *In 2006, the Dutch government tried to make itself unattractive*: 'Film Exposes Immigrants to Dutch Liberalism'. Associated Press (16 March 2006). http://www.nbcnews.com/id/11842116/ns/world_news-europe/t/film-exposes-immigrants-dutch-liberalism.

155 *Gatineau, Quebec, published a 'statement of values'*: Ingrid Peritz, 'Gatineau's Values Guide for Immigrants Stirs Controversy'. *Globe and Mail* (4 December 2011). https://www.theglobeandmail.com/news/politics/gatineaus-values-guide-for-immigrants-stirs-controversy/article4236425/.

156 *'We have never believed him [the black man] to be the equal of the white man'*: Bob Herbert, 'The Blight That Is Still with Us'. *New York Times* (22 January 2008). https://www.nytimes.com/2008/01/22/opinion/22herbert.html.

156 *by 2015, the year Sweden took in a record number of asylum seekers*: 'Reality Check: Is Malmo the "Rape Capital" of Europe?' BBC News (24 February 2017). https://www.bbc.com/news/uk-politics-39056786.

156 *'If a rape must be used as the metaphor of the Indo-British connection'*: Salman Rushdie, 'Outside the Whale'. *Granta* (1 March 1984). https://granta.com/outside-the-whale/.

157 *Nobody asked the Aboriginals if Britain could dump its wretched refuse*: Figures in this paragraph drawn from a variety of sources, including Tom Lawson, *The Last Man: A British Genocide in Tasmania* (London: I. B. Tauris, 2014), p. 22; and Lulu Morris, 'The Last Indigenous Tasmanian'. *National Geographic* (8 May 2017). https://www.nationalgeographic.com.au/australia/the-last-indigenous-tasmanian.aspx.

158 *half of Australians are immigrants or their children*: Elle Hunt, 'Barely Half of Population Born in Australia to Australian-Born Parents'. *Guardian*

(27 June 2017). https://www.theguardian.com/australia-news/2017/jun/27/australia-reaches-tipping-point-with-quarter-of-population-born-overseas.

158 *In March 2017, he offered emergency visas to white South African farmers*: Russell Goldman, 'Australian Official Calls for Emergency Visas for White South African Farmers'. *New York Times* (15 March 2018). https://www.nytimes.com/2018/03/15/world/australia/south-africa-white-farmers-peter-dutton.html.

158 *a human version of the famous New York garbage scow*: Alex Pastermack, 'The Most Watched Load of Garbage in the Memory of Man'. *Vice* (13 May 2013). https://motherboard.vice.com/en_us/article/nzzppg/the-mobro-4000.

15. JAIKISAN HEIGHTS

161 *'There is no room in this country for hyphenated Americans'*: 'Roosevelt Bars the Hyphenated', *New York Times* (13 October 1915). https://timesmachine.nytimes.com/timesmachine/1915/10/13/105042745.pdf.

163 *Thirty-eight per cent of New York's population is foreign-born*: Department of City Planning, 'NYC's Foreign Born, 2000–2015' (March 2017). https://www1.nyc.gov/assets/planning/download/pdf/about/dcp-priorities/data-expertise/nyc-foreign-born-info-brief.pdf?r=1.

163 *crime rates have fallen to what they were in the 1950s*: Ray Suarez, 'How Crime Rates in New York City Reached Record Lows'. NPR (30 December 2017). https://www.npr.org/2017/12/30/574800001/how-crime-rates-in-new-york-city-reached-record-lows.

163 *The immigration divide is also an urban–rural divide*: Maria Sachetti and Emily Guskin, 'In Rural America, Fewer Immigrants and Less Tolerance'. *Washington Post* (17 June 2017). https://www.washingtonpost.com/local/in-rural-america-fewer-immigrants-and-less-tolerance/2017/06/16/7b448454-4d1d-11e7-bc1b-fddbd8359dee_story.html.

164 *'It's insensitive and uncaring for the Muslim community to build a mosque'*: Peter Finn, 'Peter King, IRA Supporter and Enthusiastic Counter-Terrorism Advocate'. *Washington Post* (5 March 2011). http://www.washingtonpost.com/wp-dyn/content/article/2011/03/04/AR2011030406635.html.

165 *'We've come here to Governors Island'*: Michael Bloomberg, 'Defending Religious Tolerance: Remarks on the Mosque Near Ground Zero'. *Huffington*

Post (3 August 2010). https://www.huffingtonpost.com/michael-bloomberg/mayor-bloomberg-on-the-ne_b_669338.html.

166 *A few years ago, representatives of the giant warehouse shopping club Costco*: Suketu Mehta, 'The Great Awakening', *New York Times* (19 June 2005). https://www.nytimes.com/2005/06/19/nyregion/thecity/the-great-awakening.html.

16. JOBS, CRIME AND CULTURE: THE THREATS THAT AREN'T

168 *In 2006, Mayor Michael Bloomberg, then a Republican, testified in the Senate*: Michael Bloomberg, 'Mayor Bloomberg Testifies before the US Senate Judiciary Committee Field Hearing on Federal Immigration Legislation'. New York City, Office of the Mayor (5 July 2006). https://www1.nyc.gov/office-of-the-mayor/news/230–06/mayor-bloomberg-testifies-before-u-s-senate-judiciary-committee-field-hearing-federal.

169 *Then there's George Borjas*: Jennifer Rubin, 'What the Anti-Immigrant Movement Really Believes'. *Washington Post* (9 May 2013). https://www.washingtonpost.com/blogs/right-turn/wp/2013/05/09/what-the-anti-immigrant-movement-really-believes/.

169 *In 2015, Borjas published a study claiming that the arrival of the 'Marielitos'*: George J. Borjas, 'The Wage Impact of the Marielitos: A Reappraisal'. *ILR Review* 7, no. 5 (September 2015). https://www.nber.org/papers/w21588.

170 *But later analysis showed that Borjas's study was, at the very least, deeply flawed*: Giovanni Peri and Vasil Yasenov, 'The Labor Market Effects of a Refugee Wave: Applying the Synthetic Control Method to the Mariel Boatlift'. National Bureau of Economic Research Working Paper no. 21801 (December 2015, revised June 2017). https://www.nber.org/papers/w21801.

170 *'In general Özden found that migrants'*: Ruchir Sharma, *The Rise and Fall of Nations: Forces of Change in the Post-Crisis World* (New York: W. W. Norton, 2016), p. 51.

170 *'he [Clemens] and his co-authors, through study of all the available economic literature'*: Shaun Raviv, 'If People Could Immigrate Anywhere, Would Poverty Be Eliminated?' *Atlantic* (26 April 2013). https://www.theatlantic.com/international/archive/2013/04/if-people-could-immigrate-anywhere-would-poverty-be-eliminated/275332/.

171 *Close to half of American farm workers are here illegally*: Tamar Haspel, 'Illegal Immigrants Help Fuel US Farms. Does Affordable Produce Depend on Them?' *Washington Post* (17 March 2017). https://www.washingtonpost.com/lifestyle/food/in-an-immigration-crackdown-who-will-pick-our-produce/2017/03/17/cc1c6df4-0a5d-11e7-93dc-00f9bdd74ed1_story.html.

171 *In 1986, Ronald Reagan signed the Immigration Reform and Control Act*: Rachel Kleinfeld, 'Wanna Cut Crime? Let In More Immigrants, Legal and Illegal'. *Newsweek* (7 September 2017). https://www.newsweek.com/wanna-cut-crime-let-more-immigrants-legal-and-illegal-661183.

172 *four out of eight of Maryland's crab-picking businesses closed in 2018*: Ryan Marshall, 'Shortage of Blue Crab Pickers Forces Maryland Seafood Shops to Shut Down'. *Delmarva Now* (4 May 2018). https://www.delmarvanow.com/story/money/2018/05/04/shortage-maryland-blue-crab-pickers-causes-seafood-shops-shutdown-h-2-b-visa-lottery/577930002/.

172 *'The native-born criminal conviction rate was thus 2.4 times as high'*: Alex Nowrasteh, 'Criminal Conviction Rates in Texas in 2016'. Cato Institute (23 April 2018). https://www.cato.org/blog/criminal-conviction-rates-texas-2016.

172 *A 2018 study in the journal* Criminology: Christopher Ingraham, 'Two Charts Demolish the Notion that Immigrants Here Illegally Commit More Crime'. *Washington Post* (19 June 2018). https://www.washingtonpost.com/news/wonk/wp/2018/06/19/two-charts-demolish-the-notion-that-immigrants-here-illegally-commit-more-crime/.

173 *According to a 2018 Yale survey*: Mohammad M. Fazel-Zarandi, Jonathan S. Feinstein and Edward H. Kaplan, 'The Number of Undocumented Immigrants in the United States: Estimates Based on Demographic Modeling with Data from 1990 to 2016'. *PLOS ONE* (21 September 2018). https://journals.plos.org/plosone/article?id=10.1371/journal.pone.0201193.

174 *'The vast majority of past immigrants changed* their *values'*: Dennis Prager, 'Immigrants Change Cultures – Whether New Yorkers in Florida or Latinos in America'. *Townhall* (17 July 2018). https://townhall.com/columnists/dennisprager/2018/07/17/immigrants-change-cultures—whether-new-yorkers-in-florida-or-latinos-in-america-n2500981.

175 *In 2015, the federal government ... asked*: National Academies of Sciences, Engineering, and Medicine. *The Integration of Immigrants into American Society* (Washington, DC: National Academies Press. 2015), p. 6. https://doi.org/10.17226/21746.

175 *According to a 2013 Gallup poll, 95 per cent of immigrants*: Jeffrey M. Jones, 'Most in US Say It's Essential that Immigrants Learn English'. Gallup (9 August 2013). https://news.gallup.com/poll/163895/say-essential-immigrants-learn-english.aspx.

175 *Only 41 per cent of third-generation Mexican-American children*: Jens Manuel Krogstad and Ana Gonzalez-Barrera, 'A Majority of English-Speaking Hispanics in the US Are Bilingual'. Pew Research Center (24 March 2015). http://www.pewresearch.org/fact-tank/2015/03/24/a-majority-of-english-speaking-hispanics-in-the-u-s-are-bilingual/.

175 *'Cities and neighborhoods with greater concentrations of immigrants'*: Julia Preston, 'Newest Immigrants Assimilating as Fast as Previous Ones, Report Says'. *New York Times* (21 September 2015). https://www.nytimes.com/2015/09/22/us/newest-immigrants-assimilating-as-well-as-past-ones-report-says.html.

175 *86 per cent of first-generation immigrant males participate in the labour force*: 'Report Finds Immigrants Come to Resemble Native-Born Americans over Time, but Integration Not Always Linked to Greater Well-Being for Immigrants'. *National Academies of Sciences, Engineering, and Medicine* (21 September 2015). http://www8.nationalacademies.org/onpinews/newsitem.aspx?RecordID=21746.

176 *The total annual cost to all levels of government is $57 billion*: Julia Preston, 'Immigrants Aren't Taking Americans' Jobs, New Study Finds'. *New York Times* (21 September 2016). https://www.nytimes.com/2016/09/22/us/immigrants-arent-taking-americans-jobs-new-study-finds.html.

177 *'Second generation children of immigrants from Mexico and Central America'*: National Academies of Sciences, Engineering, and Medicine. *The Integration of Immigrants into American Society* (Washington, DC: National Academies Press. 2015), p. 6. https://doi.org/10.17226/21746.

177 *In 1970, only 1 per cent of American babies were descended from parents of different races*: Kim Parker, Juliana Menasce Horowitz, Rich Morin and Mark Hugo Lopez, 'Multiracial in America: Proud, Diverse and Growing in Numbers'. Pew Research Center (11 June 2015). http://www.pewsocialtrends.org/2015/06/11/multiracial-in-america/.

178 *The mayor of Schenectady, New York, realized this in 2002*: Sarah Kershaw, 'For Schenectady, a Guyanese Strategy; Mayor Goes All Out to Encourage a Wave of Hardworking Immigrants'. *New York Times* (26 July 2002). https://www.

nytimes.com/2002/07/26/nyregion/for-schenectady-guyanese-strategy-mayor-goes-all-encourage-wave-hardworking.html.

179 *Now there are 10,000 Guyanese living and working in downtown Schenectady*: Kassie Parisi, 'Guyanese Culture in Spotlight in Annual Schenectady Celebration'. *Daily Gazette* (2 September 2018). https://dailygazette.com/article/2018/09/02/guyanese-culture-in-spotlight-in-annual-schenectady-celebration.

179 *New York State took in 40,000 refugees over the past decade*: Alex Leary, 'In Struggling Upstate New York Cities, Refugees Vital to Rebirth'. *Tampa Bay Times* (17 November 2017). http://www.tampabay.com/news/politics/national/In-struggling-upstate-New-York-cities-refugees-vital-to-rebirth_162688301.

179 *An old Methodist church downtown would have cost the city*: Peter Applebome, 'In This Town, Open Arms for a Mosque'. *New York Times* (18 August 2010). https://www.nytimes.com/2010/08/19/nyregion/19towns.html.

180 *In 2015, Hamtramck became the first American city to elect*: Ryan Felton, 'Michigan Town Said to Have First Majority Muslim City Council in US'. *Guardian* (15 November 2015). https://www.theguardian.com/us-news/2015/nov/15/michigan-muslim-majority-city-council-hamtramck-detroit.

180 *'Back in 2000, you used to see one car in two minutes'*: Susan Shand, 'Study: US Immigration Policies Will Hurt Michigan's Economy'. Voice of America News (10 October 2017). http://m.51voa.com/study-shows-immigration-policies-will-hurt-michigan-economy-76872.

181 *13 per cent of the American population [...] account for 40 per cent of the home-buying market*: Deborah Huso, 'Why Immigrants Are Crucial to the Housing Market'. *Housing Wire* (1 April 2016). https://www.housingwire.com/articles/36630-why-immigrants-are-crucial-to-the-housing-market.

181 *'America is vast, largely empty and often lonely'*: Bret Stephens, 'Our Real Immigration Problem'. *New York Times* (21 June 2018). https://www.nytimes.com/2018/06/21/opinion/trump-immigration-reform.html.

17. WE DO NOT COME EMPTY-HANDED

183 *Immigrants are 13 per cent of the US population, but they have started a quarter of all new businesses*: Figures in this section drawn from Stuart Anderson, '55% of

America's Billion-Dollar Startups Have an Immigrant Founder'. *Forbes* (25 October 2018). https://www.forbes.com/sites/stuartanderson/2018/10/25/55-of-americas-billion-dollar-startups-have-immigrant-founder/#4b1bd8de48ee. Rachel Konrad, 'Immigrants behind 25 Percent of Startups'. Associated Press (3 January 2007). http://www.washingtonpost.com/wp-dyn/content/article/2007/01/03/AR2007010301402.html. Ian Hathaway, 'Almost Half of Fortune 500 Companies Were Founded by American Immigrants or Their Children'. Brookings Institution (4 December 2017). https://www.brookings.edu/blog/the-avenue/2017/12/04/almost-half-of-fortune-500-companies-were-founded-by-american-immigrants-or-their-children/. Stuart Anderson, 'The Contributions of the Children of Immigrants to Science in America'. National Foundation for American Policy (March 2017). http://nfap.com/wp-content/uploads/2017/03/Children-of-Immigrants-in-Science.NFAP-Policy-Brief.March-2017.pdf.

184 *In 2000, Germany realized that it had a shortage of programmers*: 'Germans Debate Technology v Immigration'. BBC News (6 April 2000). http://news.bbc.co.uk/2/hi/europe/704539.stm.

184 *'If you guys cannot figure out your immigration system'*: Ruchir Sharma, *The Rise and Fall of Nations: Forces of Change in the Post-Crisis World* (New York: W. W. Norton, 2016), pp. 49–50.

184 *In 2017, Canada started the Global Talent Stream initiative*: Tracey Lindeman, 'Canada Launches Visa Program for Hiring Specialized Foreign Talent'. *Globe and Mail* (11 June 2017). https://www.theglobeandmail.com/report-on-business/small-business/talent/canada-launches-visa-program-for-specialized-foreign-talent/article35280516/.

185 *by 2020, the booming Canadian economy will have a shortage of 220,000 tech workers*: Jessica Murphy, 'For Hire: American Tech Brains Choosing Canada'. BBC News (3 May 2018). https://www.bbc.com/news/world-us-canada-43930491.

185 *Canada's per capita immigration rate is three times that of the United States*: Jonathan Tepperman, 'Canada's Ruthlessly Smart Immigration Policy'. *New York Times* (28 June 2017). https://www.nytimes.com/2017/06/28/opinion/canada-immigration-policy-trump.html.

185 *'What the findings do tell us – through empirically grounded facts'*: Keith Neuman and Michael Adams, 'Keeping Faith on Immigration'. *Globe and Mail* (7 July 2015). https://www.theglobeandmail.com/opinion/keeping-faith-on-immigration/article25328301/.

185 *As the populations of the developed countries get older*: Ben Cas-selman, 'Immigrants Are Keeping America Young – and the Economy Growing'. FiveThirtyEight (31 October 2016). https://fivethirtyeight.com/features/immigrants-are-keeping-america-young-and-the-economy-growing/. See also Alexia Fernández Campbell, 'Why Baby Boomers Need Immigrants to Fund Their Retirement, in 2 Charts'. *Vox* (1 August 2018). https://www.vox.com/2018/8/1/17561014/immigration-social-security.

186 *In 1960, there were about five workers paying social security*: 'Ratio of Social Security Covered Workers to Beneficiaries Calendar Years 1940–2013'. Social Security Administration (last accessed 5 December 2018). https://www.ssa.gov/history/ratios.html.

186 *In 2016, the US fertility rate fell to an all-time low*: 'Fertility Rate, Total (Births per Woman)'. National Center for Health Statistics (2016). https://data.worldbank.org/indicator/SP.DYN.TFRT.IN?locations=US.

186 *gave out more money in social security than it received in payroll taxes*: 'Summary: Actuarial Status of the Social Security Trust Funds (June 2018)'. Office of Retirement and Disability Policy (2018). https://www.ssa.gov/policy/trust-funds-summary.html.

186 *'The numbers get much larger for longer periods'*: 'A $4.6 Trillion Opportunity'. *Wall Street Journal* (2 June 2013). https://www.wsj.com/articles/SB10001424127887324659404578503172929165846.

186 *undocumented immigrants paid $13 billion in payroll taxes in 2010*: Stephen Goss, Alice Wade, J. Patrick Skirvin, Michael Morris, K. Mark Bye and Danielle Huston, 'Effects of Unauthorized Immigration on the Actuarial Status of the Social Security Trust Funds'. Social Security Administration Office of the Chief Actuary (April 2013). https://www.ssa.gov/oact/NOTES/pdf_notes/note151.pdf.

187 *By the middle of the century, a quarter of the worldwide population*: United Nations, Department of Economic and Social Affairs, Population Division 'World Population Ageing 2017 – Highlights' (2017), p. 1. http://www.un.org/en/development/desa/population/publications/pdf/ageing/WPA2017_Highlights.pdf.

187 *By then, there will be fewer than two workers for every retiree*: Joseph Chamie, 'Number of Workers per Retiree Declines Worldwide'. Yale Global Online (22 December 2015). https://yaleglobal.yale.edu/content/number-workers-retiree-declines-worldwide.

187 *By 2050, the population of Europe and Russia will shrink*: Yomi Kazeem, 'More than Half of the World's Population Growth Will Be in Africa by 2050'. *Quartz* (29 June 2017). https://qz.com/africa/1016790/more-than-half-of-the-worlds-population-growth-will-be-in-africa-by-2050/.

188 *'It is like watching a nation busily engaged in heaping up'*: Sean O'Grady, 'Enoch Powell's "Rivers of Blood" Speech Marked Him Out as the Prototype Trump'. *Independent* (18 April 2018). https://www.independent.co.uk/voices/enoch-powell-rivers-of-blood-speech-50-years-trump-immigration-right-wing-a8299211.html.

188 *The east African Asian refugee community*: Paul Harris, 'They Fled with Nothing But Built a New Empire'. *Observer* (11 August 2002). https://www.theguardian.com/uk/2002/aug/11/race.world.

188 *'Sweden needs immigration to compensate for the decline'*: Swedish Migration Agency, 'Facts about Migration and Crime in Sweden'. Swedish Migration Agency (28 February 2017). http://down.mofa.go.kr/se-ko/brd/m_7987/down.do?brd_id=2550&seq=1285796&data_tp=A&file_seq=1.

189 *Under 2 per cent of Japan's population is foreign-born*: OECD/European Union, 'Socio-Demographic Characteristics of Immigrant Populations'. *Indicators of Immigrant Integration 2015: Settling In* (Paris: OECD Publishing, 2015), pp. 37–51.

189 *By 2050, 40 per cent of Japan will be over the age of sixty-five*: Adam Taylor, 'It's Official: Japan's Population Is Dramatically Shrinking'. *Washington Post* (26 February 2016). https://www.washingtonpost.com/news/worldviews/wp/2016/02/26/its-official-japans-population-is-drastically-shrinking/.

189 *'The lack of manpower here is a real problem'*: Anna Fifield, 'Japanese Towns Struggle to Deal with an Influx of New Arrivals: Wild Boars'. *Washington Post* (9 March 2018). https://www.washingtonpost.com/world/asia_pacific/japanese-towns-struggle-to-deal-with-an-influx-of-new-arrivals-wild-boars/2018/03/05/59af237e-1722-11e8-930c-45838ad0d77a_story.html.

190 *That year, a quarter of new businesses were started by Syrians*: Omer M. Karasapan, 'The Impact of Syrian Businesses in Turkey'. Brookings Institution (16 March 2016). https://www.brookings.edu/blog/future-development/2016/03/16/the-impact-of-syrian-businesses-in-turkey/.

190 *We are the second-largest immigrant group after Mexicans*: Jie Zong and Jeanne Batalova, 'Indian Immigrants in the United States'. Migration Policy

Institute (31 August 2017). https://www.migrationpolicy.org/article/indian-immigrants-united-states. See also Gustavo López, Kristen Bialik and Jynnah Radford, 'Key Findings about US Immigrants'. Pew Research Center (14 September 2018). http://www.pewresearch.org/fact-tank/2018/09/14/key-findings-about-u-s-immigrants/.

191 *We are 8 per cent of America's doctors*: Jason Richwine, 'Indian Americans: The New Model Minority'. *Forbes* (24 February 2009). https://www.forbes.com/2009/02/24/bobby-jindal-indian-americans-opinions-contributors_immigrants_minority.html#2ba5d6fd583b.

191 *Around a fifth of all start-ups in Silicon Valley were founded by Indians*: Paresh Dave, 'Indian Immigrants Are Tech's New Titans'. *Los Angeles Times* (11 August 2015). https://www.latimes.com/business/la-fi-indians-in-tech-20150812-story.html.

18. IMMIGRATION AS REPARATIONS

192 *'Now we have half-stepped away from our long centuries of despoilment'*: Ta-Nehisi Coates, 'The Case for Reparations'. *Atlantic* (June 2014). https://www.theatlantic.com/magazine/archive/2014/06/the-case-for-reparations/361631/.

193 *'America is the worst polluter in the history of the world'*: Michael B. Gerrard, 'America Is the Worst Polluter in the History of the World. We Should Let Climate Change Refugees Resettle Here'. *Washington Post* (25 June 2015). https://www.washingtonpost.com/opinions/america-is-the-worst-polluter-in-the-history-of-the-world-we-should-let-climate-change-refugees-resettle-here/2015/06/25/28a55238-1a9c-11e5-ab92-c75ae6ab94b5_story.html.

194 *'Some say that France was a colonial power'*: Alain Finkielkraut, interviewed by Mathieu von Rohr and Romain Leick, 'French Philosopher Finkielkraut: "There Is a Clash of Civilizations"'. *Der Spiegel* (6 December 2013). http://www.spiegel.de/international/world/interview-french-philosopher-finkielkraut-on-muslims-and-integration-a-937404.html.

194 *'The gains from reducing emigration restrictions'*: Shaun Raviv, 'If People Could Immigrate Anywhere, Would Poverty Be Eliminated?' *Atlantic* (26 April 2013). https://www.theatlantic.com/international/archive/2013/04/if-people-could-immigrate-anywhere-would-poverty-be-eliminated/275332/.

194 *A provocative 2014 article in* The New Republic: Eric A. Posner and Glen Weyl, 'A Radical Solution to Global Income Inequality: Make the US More like Qatar'. *New Republic* (6 November 2014). https://newrepublic.com/article/120179/how-reduce-global-income-inequality-open-immigration-policies.

195 *They send back some $600 billion in remittances every year*: Dilip Ratha, Supriyo De, Eung Ju Kim, Sonia Plaza, Kirsten Schuettler, Ganesh Seshan and Nadege Desiree Yameogo, 'Migration and Remittances: Recent Developments and Outlook in 2017'. World Bank Group (April 2018), p. v. https://www.knomad.org/sites/default/files/2018–04/Migration%20and%20Development%20 Brief%2029.pdf.

195 *Migrants from poor countries alone sent $481 billion in remittances*: 'Migrants Send Home 51 per cent More Money than a Decade Ago Lifting Millions out of Poverty, Says New Report'. International Fund for Agricultural Development (2017). https://www.un.org/sustainabledevelopment/ blog/2017/06/migrants-send-home-51-per-cent-more-money-than-a-decade-ago-lifting-millions-out-of-poverty-says-new-report/.

196 *In the Philippines, its ten million overseas workers are celebrated*: 'OFWs Honored for Their Sacrifices, Awarded with Free Trip Back Home'. *Philippine Star* (6 September 2018). https://www.philstar.com/lifestyle/ on-the-radar/2018/08/02/1832899/12-ofw-heroes-honored-second-edition-moneygram-idol-awards.

196 *reduce the fees on money transfers, which exceed $30 billion*: Stephen Cecchetti and Kim Schoenholtz, 'The Stubbornly High Cost of Remittances'. VOX CEPR Policy Portal (27 March 2018). https://voxeu.org/article/stubbornly-high-cost-remittances.

197 *'The state's right to control immigration'*: Michael Walzer, *Spheres of Justice: A Defense of Pluralism and Equality* (New York: Basic Books, 1984), pp. 61–63.

197 *Miller has a theory of 'weak cosmopolitanism'*: James Ryerson, 'Deep Thinking about Immigration'. *New York Times* (26 July 2016). https://www.nytimes.com/2016/07/31/books/review/immigration-strangers-in-our-midst-david-miller.html.

198 *Migrants are 3 per cent of the world's population but contribute 9 per cent of its GDP*: Global Migration Data Analysis Centre, International Organization for Migration, *Global Migration Indicators, 2018* (Germany:

12 October 2018), p. 19. https://publications.iom.int/system/files/pdf/global_ migration_indicators_2018.pdf.

199 *Today, there are nine million Americans living abroad*: Philip Bump, 'Millions of Americans Have Moved Overseas – and It's Not Because the US Is a "Shithole"'. *Washington Post* (12 January 2018). https://www.washington-post.com/news/politics/wp/2018/01/12/millions-of-americans-have-moved-overseas-and-its-not-because-the-u-s-is-a-shithole/.

200 *In 1990, fewer than seven million Indians lived overseas*: United Nations, 'Origins and Destinations of the World's Migrants, 1990–2017'. Pew Research Center visualization using data from the United Nations Population Division (28 February 2018). http://www.pewglobal.org/2018/02/28/global-migrant-stocks/?country=IN&date=2017.

200 *A little over a third of Americans own a passport*: Niall McCarthy, 'The Share of Americans Holding a Passport Has Increased Dramatically in Recent Years'. *Forbes* (11 January 2018). https://www.forbes.com/sites/niallmcca-rthy/2018/01/11/the-share-of-americans-holding-a-passport-has-increased-dramatically-in-recent-years-infographic/#7b8cdeba3c16.

201 *American pilots working in Chinese airlines*: Jethro Mullen, 'Want to Earn $300,000 Tax Free? Try Flying a Plane in China'. CNN (15 November 2016). https:// money.cnn.com/2016/11/15/news/economy/china-airlines-foreign-pilots-pay/index.html.

202 *immigrants are more willing to move to fast-growing, high-income, dense cities*: Giovanni Peri, 'The Economic Benefits of Immigration'. *Berkeley Review of Latin American Studies* (Fall 2013). https://clas.berkeley.edu/research/immi-gration-economic-benefits-immigration.

EPILOGUE: FAMILY, REUNIFIED – AND EXPANDED

204 *'Lo, soul, seest thou not God's purpose'*: Walt Whitman, 'Passage to India' (1868). From *Walt Whitman: Selected Poems* (New York: Dover, 1991), p. 104.

204 *New York City today has 270 magazines and newspapers in 36 languages*: Devjyot Ghoshal, 'Newspapers That Aren't Dying'. *Atlantic* (26 June 2014). https://www.theatlantic.com/business/archive/2014/06/newspapers-that-arent-dying/373492/.

205 *The first foreign group that came in large numbers to Silicon Valley*: Vivek Wadwha, 'The Face of Success, Part I: How the Indians Conquered Silicon Valley'. *Inc.* (13 January 2012). https://www.inc.com/vivek-wadhwa/how-the-indians-succeeded-in-silicon-valley.html.

209 *A 1911 committee set up by Congress studied 246,000 immigrants*: Jennifer Mendelsohn, 'Missing from the Immigration Debate: Receipts'. *Los Angeles Times* (9 February 2018). https://www.latimes.com/opinion/op-ed/la-oe-mendelsohn-resistance-genealogy-20180209-story.html.

210 *Latinos are 18 per cent of the population – fifty-seven million Americans*: Antonio Flores, 'How the US Hispanic Population Is Changing'. Pew Research Center (18 September 2017). http://www.pewresearch.org/fact-tank/2017/09/18/how-the-u-s-hispanic-population-is-changing/.

214 *In 2017, two-thirds of the 1.1 million green cards*: Jie Zong, Jeanne Batalova and Jeffrey Hallock, 'Frequently Requested Statistics on Immigrants and Immigration in the United States'. Migration Policy Institute (8 February 2018). https://www.migrationpolicy.org/article/frequently-requested-statistics-immi-grants-and-immigration-united-states. See also Miriam Jordan and Sabrina Tavernise, 'One Face of Immigration in America Is a Family Tree Rooted in Asia'. *New York Times* (16 September 2018). https://www.nytimes.com/2018/09/16/us/immigration-family-chain-migration-foreign-born.html.

216 *His mother, Mary Anne MacLeod, moved from a village in Scotland*: Jason Horowitz, 'For Donald Trump's Family, an Immigrant's Tale with 2 Beginnings'. *New York Times* (21 August 2016). https://www.nytimes.com/2016/08/22/us/politics/for-donald-trumps-family-an-immigrants-tale-with-2-beginnings.html.

219 *According to a 2018 Ipsos poll of 20,000 people in twenty-seven countries*: 'Canada and the US Have the Most Inclusive Views of Nationality'. Ipsos Global Advisor Survey (25 June 2018). https://www.ipsos.com/en-us/news-polls/Canada-US-have-most-inclusive-views-of-nationality.

220 *first Indian-American state senator in North Carolina history*: Henry Gargan, 'NC's First Indian-American Legislator Sworn in at Morrisville Town Hall'. *News and Observer* (12 January 2017). https://www.newsobserver.com/news/local/community/cary-news/article126109539.html.

ACKNOWLEDGEMENTS

Grateful acknowledgments to my wonderful agent, Suzanne Gluck, who first suggested I do this book, and to my editor, Alex Star, whose intelligence and dedication has shaped every page. To everyone at FSG, including Jonathan Galassi, Dominique Lear, Sarita Varma, M. P. Klier and Henry Kaufman. To Bea Hemming at Jonathan Cape.

To Amy Finnerty for commissioning the article that led to the book.

To Rajae El Mouhandiz in Tangier and Tarifa, Enrique Morones of the Border Angels, Maria Teresa Fernandez and Dan Waterman at Friendship Park.

To Sadia and Cassim Shepard, and Jennifer Acker and Nishi Shah, for the gift of their beautiful homes.

To Alistair Mackay for fact-checking, and Laura Sofia Diaz for transcribing.

To my colleagues at the Arthur Carter Journalism Institute at New York University, for their faith in my work. To the memory of James Alan McPherson and U. R. Ananthamurthy, my gurus.

And to my family: Ramesh and Usha Mehta; Gautama and Akash Mehta; Sejal, Jay, Leeya and Neel Chaudhuri; Monica, Anand, Anokhi and Alisha Mehta. This book is your book.

INDEX

Bearak, Max, 76
Belgium, 193
Benali, Abdelkader, 30
Berlusconi press (Italy), 134
Betts, Alexander, 26
Bhopal, 73
Biggar, Nigel, 64
Blackburn, Robin, 70–1
Blair Company Museum, War-
    ren, Pa, 141–2
Bloomberg, Michael, 164,
    164–5
Boko Haram, 97
Bonner, Raymond, 83–4
Border Angels (USA), 14
Borjas, George, 169–70, 172,
    175
Bosnians: in Utica, NY, 179
Bowles, Paul, 47
Boyle, Frankie, 71
Bracero 'guest worker' pro-
    gramme (USA), 171
Brands, Chiquita, 84
Break of Dawn (garbage ship),
    158
Breitbart News, 122
Breivik, Anders Behring, 152
Brexit, 106–7, 163, 187–8
Brin, Sergey, 183
Britain (United Kingdom)
    arms exports to Saudi Ara-
        bia, 90
    attitude to immigrants, 219
    Caribbean immigrants, 134

colonial empire, 62, 187
East African Asian refugees
    in, 188
expats, 199
fear of migrants leads to
    Brexit, 106, 188
gap between rich and poor,
    140
immigrant quotas, 193, 215
Industrial Revolution,
    70–1
Muslim numbers in, 108
oil imports, 91–2
and slave trade, 70–1
Broich, John, 69
Brookings Institution, 100
Buchanan, Pat, 132
Burkina Faso, 79–80
Burroughs, William, 47
Bush, George W., 129

Calcutta: image, 110–11
Camus, Renaud, 114
Canada
    citizens welcomed in USA,
        120–1
    Global Talent Scheme initia-
        tive, 184
    Provincial Nominee Pro-
        gram, 180
    welcomes immigrants, 108,
        180, 184–5, 219
Cardenas, Cuauhtémoc, 68
Carens, Joseph, 77